Shattering the Illusion

D1320117

Shattering the Illusion

Child Sexual Abuse and Canadian Religious Institutions

Tracy J. Trothen

WILFRID LAURIER
UNIVERSITY PRESS

This book has been published with the help of a grant from the Canadian Federation for the Humanities and Social Sciences, through the Aid to Scholarly Publications Program, using funds provided by the Social Sciences and Humanities Research Council of Canada. Wilfrid Laurier University Press acknowledges the financial support of the Government of Canada through the Canada Book Fund for its publishing activities.

Library and Archives Canada Cataloguing in Publication

Trothen, Tracy J. (Tracy Joan), 1963–
    Shattering the illusion : child sexual abuse and Canadian religious institutions / Tracy J. Trothen.

Includes bibliographical references and index.
Issued also in electronic formats.
ISBN 978-1-55458-356-0

    1. Child sexual abuse by clergy—Canada. 2. Child sexual abuse—Religious aspects—Christianity—History of doctrines. 3. Child sexual abuse—Canada—Prevention. I. Title.

BX1912.9.T76 2012   261.8'3272088282   C2012-903300-6

———

Electronic monograph.
Issued also in print format.
ISBN 978-1-55458-407-9 (PDF).—ISBN 978-1-55458-408-6 (EPUB)

    1. Child sexual abuse by clergy—Canada. 2. Child sexual abuse—Religious aspects—Christianity—History of doctrines. 3. Child sexual abuse—Canada—Prevention. I. Title.

BX1912.9.T76 2012   261.8'327208828   C2012-903301-4

Cover design by David Drummond using image from Shutterstock. Text design by Angela Booth Malleau.

This book is printed on FSC recycled paper and is certified Ecologo. It is made from 100% post-consumer fibre, processed chlorine free, and manufactured using biogas energy.

Printed in Canada

Every reasonable effort has been made to acquire permission for copyright material used in this text, and to acknowledge all such indebtedness accurately. Any errors and omissions called to the publisher's attention will be corrected in future printings.

RECYCLED
Paper made from
recycled material
FSC
www.fsc.org   FSC® C103567

Contents

Acknowledgements

THERE ARE MANY PEOPLE to whom I owe a debt of gratitude in seeing this book through to fruition. First, this book would have been many more years in the making without the expertise and dedication of my research assistants. Tim Crouch and Ryan McNally were involved in this project for close to three years intermittently. Barb Adle helped out at a time when she was much needed. We were all inspired to investigate these policies and their attendant evolutions out of a commitment to the work of justice and the protection of the vulnerable.

Religious communities have a particular responsibility to safeguard the children in their midst and to nurture their spirits. Yet widespread child sexual abuse continues. This book is born of the outrage that must stoke any crucible of justice. To all of you who have suffered such abuse, I am truly and deeply sorry. No child should ever be abused.

I am both heartened by the work done at a policy level and overwhelmed by the need for more healing and prevention. Numerous individuals in the religious institutions examined in this book have invested much courage, soul, and wisdom in the crafting of policies and procedures addressing child sexual abuse within their faith communities. To them I extend heartfelt gratitude; this is not easy work.

The research and the preparation of this book was supported financially by the following organizations and institutions: Queen's University, where I am employed, and, indirectly, by the Cornwall Public Inquiry, with whom I had a contract to produce the paper "A Survey of Policies and Practices in Respect to Responses by Religious Institutions to Complaints of Child Sexual Abuse and Complaints by Adults of Historical Child Sexual Abuse, 1960–2006." This paper was one of four tabled as exhibits in Phase 1 of the inquiry. I did not influence or discuss evidence with the commissioner or anyone else associated with the inquiry in respect to Phase 1 factual determinations. This report for the inquiry formed the base for this book. Additional research and writing was done to complete this book in the years following the submission of the research paper to the inquiry.

Heartfelt appreciation goes to my outstanding research assistants, the anonymous peer reviewers who provided invaluable critique, and always to the wonderful people at Wilfrid Laurier University Press, in particular Leslie Macredie, Lisa Quinn, and Rob Kohlmeier, for their encouragement and assistance. Any mistakes remaining in these pages are mine alone.

Introduction

THE WRITING OF THIS BOOK was inspired by the Cornwall Public Inquiry into institutional responses to complaints of organized historic child sexual abuse in Cornwall, Ontario, purported to have occurred between the 1950s and the early 2000s.

This was one of the most costly and thorough public commissions ever undertaken. Lasting over more than three years, testimony from approximately 175 people was heard, and more than 3,400 exhibits were entered into evidence. Estimates of the cost of the Inquiry range from $40 million to $50 million. Regarding the scope of the Inquiry, reporter Trevor Pritchard pointed out that other commissions "pale in comparison. The recently completed Goudge Inquiry into the forensics work of Dr. Charles Smith, for example, heard from a mere forty-seven witnesses over fifty-two days. The O'Connor Inquiry into *E. coli*-related deaths in Walkerton lasted ninety-five days and heard from 114 witnesses."[1]

For those interested in the Inquiry's precipitating events, the following is a summary of that story. Prior to the launch of the Cornwall Public Inquiry, Cornwall had been the site of "on-again, off-again police inquiries" and allegations of child sexual abuse. Further, there were accusations that institutional actors, including some police and Roman Catholic priests, had either ignored victims or actively engaged in a cover-up.[2] The first known allegations were made by an adult victim of historic child sexual abuse in early 1992, with other allegations following. The now adult complainant, David Silmser, said he was first abused in the 1970s.[3] In 1992 he summoned the courage to tell "police that [as a boy] he had been sexually assaulted by a Cornwall priest."[4] Subsequently Silmser was given $32,000 by the Roman Catholic Church to drop his allegations. This settlement became public when Const. Perry Dunlop, who was to become a pivotal agent in the Cornwall saga, discovered the complaint and passed it on to child welfare authorities. This revelation generated an Ontario Provincial Police (OPP) investigation that concluded in 1994 with no criminal charges. (Later, Dunlop would refuse to testify at the Cornwall Inquiry because he was convinced that justice would not result. Consequently, in 2008 he was convicted of contempt and spent seven months in jail.)[5]

The case was reopened in 1995 after the lawyer, Malcolm MacDonald, employed by the Church to settle the Silmser complaint, was found guilty of obstructing justice. This led to criminal charges against Father Charles MacDonald—seven counts of indecent assault on three boys.

After this turn of events and several more complaints from other alleged victims, the OPP initiated Project Truth in 1997. The media and possibly some individuals associated with the OPP misinterpreted the purpose of Project Truth as an investigation into the existence of a purported Cornwall pedophile ring believed to have been comprised of prominent men, including Roman Catholic priests, doctors, police officers, and probation officers. Rather, it was an investigation into a series of particular complaints of child sexual abuse that resulted in fifteen area men being charged with 115 sex crimes committed between 1997 and 2001. These charges culminated in only one conviction—Father Paul Lapierre, who "was convicted in Quebec after being exonerated in Ontario."[6] Of those charged, four died of natural causes and two committed suicide. The court proceedings closed in 2004. Further, according to media reports, the investigation found "no evidence to back claims that a ... pedophile ring, complete with bizarre ritualistic orgies, operated clandestinely out of the eastern Ontario town of Cornwall,"[7] but again it was not made clear that Project Truth's mandate did not include an investigation into the existence of a "ring."

In the thirteen years between the first allegations and the initiation of the Public Inquiry in 2005, citizens' groups agitated for action on these allegations of child sexual abuse committed by a "pedophile-ring."[8] Notably, community member and MPP Garry Guzzo, who had long agitated on behalf of victims, continued to believe in the existence of an organized pedophile ring.[9]

Only weeks after the conclusion of Project Truth, Lapierre, who was charged as a result of the investigation, "took the witness stand in his own defence and told a stunned courtroom that, while he himself was innocent of the three counts of indecent assault and two counts of gross indecency laid against him, a ring of sorts did exist in the Cornwall area and that Catholic authorities knew about it."[10] Further, Lapierre claimed that "other priests told him of indecent acts against several boys," and that one priest "kept pictures of naked boys."[11] To the shock of victims, residents, and supporters, Lapierre was acquitted on all charges "on the grounds of reasonable doubt."[12]

The Cornwall Public Inquiry was created, by Order in Council 558/2005, on April 14, 2005, with the Honourable Justice G. Normand Glaude as commissioner.[13] In explaining the rationale behind the Public Inquiry, Order 558/2005 states that "allegations of abuse of young people have surrounded the City of Cornwall and its citizens for many years," and since criminal investigations and prosecutions had concluded, and as "[c]ommunity members have indicated that a public inquiry will encourage individual and community healing," an inquiry was judged worthy and appropriate.[14]

Specifically, the commission's mandate was to

> inquire into and report on the institutional response of the justice system and other public institutions, including the interaction of that response with other public and community sectors, in relation to:
>
> (a) allegations of historical abuse of young people in the Cornwall area, including the policies and practices then in place to respond to such allegations, and
>
> (b) the creation and development of policies and practices that were designed to improve the response to allegations of abuse in order to make recommendations directed to the further improvement of the response in similar circumstances.[15]

In addition, the commission was to examine and report upon "processes, services or programs that would encourage community healing and reconciliation in Cornwall."[16] The final report, "containing findings, conclusions and recommendations," would be submitted to the attorney general and made available for public release in both official languages.[17] The Inquiry was directed not to find civil or criminal liability but attempt to discover what happened in two phases.[18]

Phase 2 of the Inquiry involved working with the residents of Cornwall for healing and reconciliation. Various models and approaches to systemic healing after a community has been mired in deep conflict were of interest in this phase, but most important were approaches to healing from child sexual abuse.

In Phase 1, the Inquiry held public hearings into allegations of abuse; examined the response of the justice system and other public institutions, including religious institutions, to abuse complaints; and made recommendations accordingly. This investigative phase focused on the possibility of a cover-up (but not the investigation of a ring) and recommendations for avoiding similar dynamics in the future. In addition to obtaining factual evidence and testimony from parties to the hearings, the commission was empowered to seek "medical, professional, social science and similar evidence and background information related to the causes, consequences, and responses to the abuse of young people" (O.C. 558/2005: S.5.d). To this end, in Phase 1 the commission charged a number of researchers to undertake background studies. These four studies concerned, respectively, the practices and policies of Canadian police, government agencies involved in child sexual abuse complaints, child welfare agencies, and religious institutions.[19] I, together with research assistants Tim Crouch, Ryan McNally, and Barb Adle, compiled the latter report, entitled: "A Survey of Policies and Practices in Respect to Responses by Religious Institutions to Complaints of Child Sexual Abuse and Complaints by Adults of Historical Child Sexual Abuse, 1960–2006." This book builds on that report with some significant additions and changes.

The final report of Inquiry Commissioner Justice Normand Glaude, twice delayed, was released December 15, 2009. In his statement accompanying the four-volume report, Glaude reiterated that the Inquiry was not a civil or criminal trial. He addressed the issue of a pedophile ring in Cornwall and is clear that neither this Inquiry nor Project Truth were mandated to investigate or draw conclusions regarding the existence of such a ring; Glaude states that the mandate of Project Truth was not to discover if there "was an endemic problem of sexual abuse in the Cornwall area and whether prominent people were acting together to perpetrate or cover up this abuse."[20] However, he continues on to indicate that there may well have been such a ring, but he was not asked to make a decision on that: "The Ontario Provincial Police concluded Project Truth by saying there was no paedophile ring in Cornwall. Since they did not investigate this, they could not have reasonably come to this conclusion. This does not mean that I find there was a ring of paedophiles. It is not my role to make such a finding. But I do find that no investigation provided conclusive evidence on this point."[21]

Glaude's report includes numerous recommendations for the improvement of several agencies related to child sexual abuse complaints. At the outset he assigns culpability to those in positions of trust and their respective institutions: "institutions that became aware of misconduct by their employees were often less concerned about victims than about public embarrassment, or about the perceived difficulty of disciplining or reporting employees."[22] And, again, later in his statement he names this prioritizing of image over children's well-being, specifically castigating the Church:

> the response of senior diocese officials was preoccupied with avoidance of scandal—desiring to keep issues "within the church." This meant that they did not contact the Children's Aid Society or police when they should have ... and did not turn their concern and resources to the support of those reporting or their families. In some cases, those with a confirmed history of sexual abuse were permitted to stay in roles where they were a risk to young people.... When police investigations did occur, cooperation from the diocese was grudging and guarded....[23]

He makes a number of recommendations specifically to the Roman Catholic Diocese of Alexandria-Cornwall, including the following: that they "revis[e] their guidelines to ensure that they immediately report allegations of abuse to the Children's Aid Society, and not wait until the Diocese conducts a preliminary inquiry ... [; that] information-sharing between dioceses ... be open and detailed in respect to abuse by clergy. Record keeping and note taking should be improved and relevant training provided to clergy, employees and all volunteers. The Diocese should institute rigorous procedures to evaluate the suitability of priests it supports for ministry."[24]

Glaude ultimately was optimistic regarding the Diocese. Owing to evidence of change both in response to and preceding the Inquiry, he found cause to "believe that the page has been turned."[25] Certainly one constructive outcome has been the furthering of knowledge regarding child sexual abuse in Canadian institutions. This book, hopefully, will stand as one valuable moment in this emergent dialogue.

Chapter 1

Child Sexual Abuse in Religious Institutions

CHILD SEXUAL ABUSE HAPPENS in faith communities. The appalling stories are found under headlines such as these far too often: "Children Beaten, Raped at Irish Schools: Report,"[1] "Southern Baptists Face Sexual Abuse Crisis,"[2] "Canadian Churches Accept Ruling on Indian Sex-Abuse Claims,"[3] and "Lahey Laptop Had Many Porn Files."[4]

Yet the denial persists at some level. There is still a wish that it can't happen in *my* church/synagogue/mosque; the possibility of child sexual abuse by trusted religious leaders can be shattering. The deconstruction of the illusion of religious leaders and religious institutions as moral exemplars, incapable of evil, has been necessary to the generation of effective accountability mechanisms. This book focuses on one such mechanism: the development of policy.

This book is the first published comparative analysis of policies addressing child sexual abuse complaints in a selection of religious institutions in Canada. Although there is a substantial body of literature regarding Christianity and sexual abuse, there is very little regarding religious institutions in Canada and their respective policies. This comparative study is the first of its kind in the Canadian context.

Whenever there is sexual activity involving a child, there is abuse. Religious institutions condemn this abuse in principal, and have begun to respond concretely through the creation of policies. Policy is a significant and necessary component of a just response to child sexual abuse.

This book focuses exclusively on one particular moment of sexual abuse ethical discourse: the historical review of sexual abuse policies of some major religious institutions in Canada. This book does *not* provide a literature review of material addressing the dynamics of sexual abuse. It also does *not* investigate the efficacy of these policies as experienced by those who use them. These latter two dimensions are equally necessary moments of this discourse, but not the topic of this particular book.

This book focuses on policies and procedures in Canadian religious institutions that address child sexual abuse complaints directed at paid and voluntary faith community representatives and/or leaders. It is not possible to examine

1

adequately the approach of a faith group to complaints without also examining preventative dimensions, in addition to the responsive dimension, such as screening measures and the production of educational resources. Further, some institutionalized religions have emphasized the educational piece more than the development of policy and procedure.

The emergence of policies to address child sexual abuse complaints has required that particular illusions be dismantled and shattered. The causal factors underlying the shattering of these illusions have been necessary to the emergence of policies, hence, the title of this book: *Shattering the Illusion: Child Sexual Abuse and Canadian Religious Institutions*. These illusions include: the illusion that religious institutions are pure or moral; the illusion that religious communities always respond justly and effectively to abuse; and the illusion that religious leaders are pure and moral and therefore beyond any need for accountability mechanisms. These illusions are connected to a conviction that because religions centre on the numinous—that is, a divine, transcendent god figure or spirit that can be found internally or in the world—the religious institution itself is somehow closer to this divinity than is the rest of the world. This conviction has contributed to the avoidance of needed accountability mechanisms, including policy development.[5]

Behind the development of policy are several causal factors precipitated by particular agents. At minimum, beginning with the most important, those doing the shattering have included: sexual abuse survivors, the media, advocates for change in the religious institutions—particularly from those within the institutions—and people who have confessed to abusing children. These agents gain some visibility, sometimes between the lines, through the historical review of sexual abuse policies in each chapter.

Child sexual abuse is not new.[6] But the emergence of policies to address such complaints within religious institutions is. All of the religious institutions examined in this book concur that child abuse is wrong.

Research Method

The first task in the writing of this book was to select the religious institutions to examine. While recognizing its limitations,[7] Canadian census data was used as a guide in selecting some of these institutions. The most recent relevant Canadian census data (2001) indicates that the most populous religious institutions in Canada were, at the time of writing this book, three Christian Churches: the Roman Catholic Church, comprising 43.2 percent of the population; the United Church of Canada, which, at 9.6 percent of the population, was the most prevalent Protestant Christian Church; and the Anglican Church at 6.9 percent.[8] Canadians self-identifying as belonging to world religions other than Christianity, beginning with the largest percentage, were: Muslim (2.0 percent), Judaism (1.1 percent), Hinduism (1.0 percent), and Buddhism (1.0

percent).[9] Because Christianity is overwhelmingly the largest religion adhered to by Canadians as of the last census, this study, which extends from 1960 until 2009, focuses on Christian religious institutions: the Roman Catholic Church (as the largest religion in Canada), the United Church of Canada (as the largest Canadian Protestant Church and the second largest following of any institutional religion in Canada), the Anglican Church, and the Mennonite Church (in this case, not because of their numbers but because they have produced some of the earliest and most progressive policies regarding child abuse among religious institutions in Canada). The Muslim faith tradition in Canada was selected as the largest religious institution in Canada that is not Christian. Finally, the Canadian Unitarian Council/the Unitarian Universalist Association was also selected as an example of one of the very small religious institutions in Canada that are not Christian, of which there are several.[10]

Not surprisingly, there was significantly more relevant material found regarding the first three religious institutions: the Roman Catholic Church, the United Church of Canada, and the Anglican Church, in relation to child sexual abuse complaints and policies. Not only are these religious institutions much larger than the others studied, they also, for the most part, have much longer histories of work related to children, sexuality, and abuse. Further, in part because of their much larger memberships, these institutions have been confronted by significant numbers of allegations of sexual abuse. Undoubtedly, the increasing volume of lawsuits functioned as a significant motivator for the creation of legally appropriate and constructive faith-informed policies for responding to such allegations in conjunction with legal protocols.

After the first task in the writing of this book was accomplished—the identification of the religious institutions—the next steps were to investigate any official policies and procedures of these institutions, as well as relevant background material regarding sexuality and abuse in these institutions from 1960 to 2009. This historical investigation required archival research; the collection of official statements, policies, and procedures from the identified institutions; the gathering of other directly relevant primary and secondary sources; and electronic and oral interviews as necessary and possible.

The last area of research—electronic and verbal interviews—was the least important and yielded, in most cases, the most limited amount of information. This particular research was used, largely to get a sense of the pervasiveness of a policy when it was not a binding one but a recommended one, or to see what individual faith communities were doing if their larger institution did not recommend a policy, and sometimes to help uncover additional documents. The most common response indicated compliance with insurance company requirements and the secular law, at minimum; most religious communities that received our emails or voice mail messages did not respond. For the most part, responses from faith group representatives were very helpful and forthcoming;

understandably, to some degree, a few reacted defensively and/or were not interested in discussing child sexual abuse policy.

Interestingly, it was challenging in many cases to even *find* relevant policies, procedures, and statements, and, secondly, to contextualize these in the faith group's history. This challenge was, in some part, due to the complicated and usually decentralized structure of the religious institution. Perhaps it is easier for members of the respective religions to locate and understand these policies, or perhaps this poses difficulties for members as well as external researchers.

Various stumbling blocks had to be navigated throughout the research process. For example, although archives were easily located for the United, Anglican, and Roman Catholic Churches, access to them was not always possible; in order to access Roman Catholic archives, which are usually located in each diocese or archdiocese, one must get the permission of the bishop or archbishop. Although access was not given to the two requested archives, in one case, diocesan representatives met with research assistant Crouch and provided him with some very helpful material and responded graciously to his many questions.

The national offices of each of the religious institutions were important sources of information, as were their official websites. Archives, when accessible, provided numerous important historical documents and records. Very little was available regarding relevant policies through secondary published material; there were no secondary sources that considered even parts of this policy history in a comparative manner.

Overview of the Chapters

Where possible, the same format was used for each chapter so as to best facilitate comparisons, contrasts, and the identification of any overarching patterns among the identified religious institutions. The first three institutions examined are the largest: the Roman Catholic Church in Canada, the United Church of Canada, and the Anglican Church in Canada. The next three chapters address the Mennonite Church in Canada, Islam in Canada, and the Canadian Unitarian Council/Unitarian Universalist Association, respectively; these are in random order.

Each chapter begins with an introduction in which the governing structure of the religious institution is described and some general comments made regarding the historical context of the institution in terms of sexuality, children, and abuse.

The second part of each chapter provides a brief exploration of the particular institution's approach to child sexual abuse and closely related issues between 1960 and 1980. Material—including statements, policies, and practices addressing issues concerning sexuality, children, and/or abuse—are included and described in this section.

By the late 1970s and early 1980s, the second wave of feminism and its accompanying women's movements had generated awareness across Canada and elsewhere of "women's concerns." With groundwork laid by the 1960s' rise of some marginalized voices through civil rights movements, and no war to subsume collective energy, many women in Canada asserted their voices, particularly regarding abortion and pornography and, in the United States, abortion.[11]

These feminist movements were often mirrored by the rise of gender or women's groups and task forces *within* religious institutions, and particularly in the Roman Catholic, United, and Anglican Churches. Moreover, the 1970s, and particularly the 1980s, saw the development of feminist theologies informed by women's experiences of systemic marginalization, including woman and child abuse.

Much of the research prior to the emergence of policy statements involved the examination of material related to the wider topics of sexuality and/or children. For example, before the emergence of a concrete policy regarding child sexual abuse complaints, woman abuse has tended to have emerged as an issue in the religious institution. In addition, the identification of sexism as a systemic socio-cultural issue, occurring within society and religion, has arisen before the naming of child sexual abuse; it seems probable that women's voices assisted in getting abuse issues on the agenda. This is one example of the importance of establishing this context for each institution; common factors can be located and causal connections posited as a result of these commonalities.

These developments in the 1960s through the 1970s fostered a transition time in which some religious institutions not only became aware of child sexual abuse but gradually became less able to deny that it occurred internally. Adults who had been victimized as children began to name their abusers more frequently against the backdrop of second wave feminism and social justice agitation. These contextual factors paralleled the increasing identification of issues related to child sexual abuse in official documents of religious institutions.

This section of each chapter concludes in 1980 to reflect the first of two significant transition times that emerged through the research for this book. Religious institutions did not begin to name or address child sexual abuse in any comprehensive way until the 1980s, and policies generally did not emerge until the early 1990s.

The third part of each chapter addresses the period from 1981 to 1991. As in the previous section, the institutions' respective approaches to child sexual abuse as expressed through official documents, including statements, policies, and procedures, are examined. The year 1991 is identified as the end point for this period because 1992 marked the emergence of nationally recommended or binding—in the case of the United Church of Canada—policies to respond to complaints of child sexual abuse.

A number of events occurred in the 1980s that generated widespread awareness of the occurrence of child sexual abuse in society, particularly in the Christian Churches. The first such event was the release of the Badgely Report in 1984. This national study found that one in two girls and one in three boys (defined as those under the age of eighteen) were victims of unwanted sexual advances. The Badgely Commission's findings, as well as some concerns regarding their recommendations, generated shock, awareness, and dialogue. For example, the "Church Council on Justice and Corrections (CCJC) began to wrestle with the problem of violence against women and children in response to the ... report."[12]

Also in 1984, the case of the sexual abuses by Roman Catholic priest Father Gilbert Gauthe in Lafayette, Louisiana, made headlines in the United States and Canada.[13]

The early 1980s saw the first notable scholarly published works regarding religion and abuse. In particular, theological ethicist Marie Fortune published *Sexual Violence—the Unmentionable Sin: An Ethical and Pastoral Perspective* in 1983.[14] Further, liberation and feminist theologies flourished in the 1980s.

By the late 1980s, some religious organizations in Canada were producing resources regarding child sexual abuse under the rubrick of family violence. For example, Roberta Morris wrote *Ending Violence in Families: A Training Program for Pastoral Care Workers*, an inter-church project funded by the Family Violence Prevention Division of the Department of National Health and Welfare.[15] (Later it became better understood that framing child sexual abuse as part of family violence was misleading since such abuse occurs both inside and outside of families. Further, this definition of the issue fails to recognize the systemic tendency for the significant majority of perpetrators to be heterosexual men.)[16]

One of the most striking findings to emerge from this book is the convergence of much policy creation in 1992. The first policies for responding to child sexual abuse complaints emerged in 1987 in some individual Roman Catholic dioceses, but it was not until 1992 that nationally recommended policies emerged in the Roman Catholic and Anglican Churches, and a nationally binding policy in the United Church. The fourth part of each chapter concerns the years extending from 1992 until 2009.

Undoubtedly the precipitating factors behind the emergence of policies include the sexual abuses at Mount Cashel orphanage, which exploded across the media in 1989. The Congregation of Christian Brothers, who ran the Newfoundland orphanage, had been sexually abusing children for years. Mount Cashel was closed in 1990 as a result of a Royal Commission, the Hughes Inquiry, and well-publicized lawsuits that continued through the 1990s. Concurrently, revelations of systemic sexual abuses at Church- and government-run residential schools of Aboriginal children and youth became widely known by the late 1980s. By this time, it was clear to most Canadians that religious leaders were not necessarily above child sexual abuse; such presumptions of moral goodness had been soundly challenged.

Lawsuits, subsequent insurance requirements, and media exposure have been important factors in shattering the silence regarding child sexual abuse and motivating religious institutions to establish policies.[17] Lawsuits have had not only the obvious function of reminding an institution of its financial culpability, they have also forced constructive change. Similarly, the media has assisted in forcing religious institutions into greater ownership of culpability and responsibility by refusing to accept backroom deals and the silencing of victims. The survivors of abuse, the law, and the media have contributed to policy development by shattering the illusions that have denied truth-telling and justice.

In conjunction with the publicized sexual abuse cases, there was a growing recognition in both Church and society of the personhood of children. In churches it was not uncommon during the 1980s for children's involvement in worship to be debated with much interest in increasing their participation and developing more age-appropriate ways to involve them. In society, on December 13, 1991, the Government of Canada ratified the *United Nations Convention on the Rights of the Child*. This event generated more attention to the rights of children and their vulnerability to abuse.

In the legal realm, of interest are the reforms made to provincial mandatory reporting laws following the United Nations statement. Although "child protection" laws were established in Ontario in 1883—with the other provinces following so that "by the early years of the twentieth century, every province had similar child protection legislation"[18]—legislation specific to child sexual abuse did not emerge until much later. In Ontario, for example, it was not until the *Child Welfare Act* of 1978 that "sexual molestation" was included as a form of abuse; "sexual molestation," it should be noted, was not defined in this legislation.[19] Further, legislation committing to a duty to report did not emerge until the 1960s and, at least in Ontario, did not use the term "abuse" until the *Child and Welfare Act* of 1978.[20] Complicating the mandatory reporting laws was ambiguity regarding the meaning of abuse and the degree of certainty required to have the "reasonable grounds to believe," as stated in the 1984 Ontario legislation.

Adding to the complexity is that legislation concerning child sexual abuse and mandatory reporting has been uneven across the provinces and territories; this unevenness is not unlike the unevenness characterizing several of the religious institutions examined in these pages. A few examples of this unevenness are the following: the definition of a child varies from jurisdiction to jurisdiction (in British Columbia a child is anyone under age nineteen, while in Ontario a child is anyone under age sixteen); the definition or lack thereof of abuse; the penalties for failure to report vary; and the role of the child in terms of participation in the proceedings also vary.[21]

With the recognition explicit in the *United Nations Convention on the Rights of the Child* of children as people with fundamental rights of their own, mandatory reporting legislation arguably took an overall turn toward favouring children's rights over the right of the family unit to preservation. (Importantly, the reason cited by Alberta as the lone province not to endorse the 1991 United Nations statement immediately [Alberta endorsed it in 1999] was their prioritization of the "privacy of the family.")[22] For example, in Ontario, the *Child and Family Services Act* of 1984 was amended, in 1999, to "state that professionals have a duty to report if they have reasonable grounds to *suspect* that a child has been sexually molested or sexually exploited or is at risk to be harmed in these ways. The previous legislation had said that professionals required reasonable grounds to believe that a child had been abused."[23] As R. Brian Howe concludes regarding the 1999 legislation, "The new *Child and Family Services Act* made it clear that the paramount purpose of the child protection system is to promote the best interests and well-being of the child, not to ensure family preservation."[24]

Canadian jurisdictions have struggled with an inclination to protect the family over protecting children. This commitment to a belief in the moral purity of the family parallels in some sense the commitment of religious institutions to a belief in their moral purity as faith communities or families; faith communities were not the only institutions in need of self-critique and confession. As the territories and provinces enacted legislation prioritizing the right of children not to be abused, "child maltreatment investigations" in Ontario have skyrocketed in number: there were about 45,000 investigations in 1993 and almost 130,000 in 2003.[25]

While government legislation regarding mandatory reporting shifted in favour of children's rights, earlier in the same decade but also following the 1991 *United Nations Convention on the Rights of the Child*, the larger Canadian religious institutions established policies for receiving complaints of child sexual abuse.

As the first policies emerged in the Roman Catholic, Anglican, and United Churches, they addressed particular issues, including the following questions:

- Who could file such a complaint under the respective policy's terms?
- Did the complainant have to be a member?
- Was there a time limitation on the filing of a complaint after the abuse had occurred?
- Against whom could complaints be made?

Accordingly, these and other questions are examined in the policy description and analysis section of each chapter. Later, the issue of third-party complaints is considered. In addition to these issues, sections are included regarding the policy's procedures for responding to complaints once these complaints are established to fall within the purview of the respective policy. If the policy includes investigative procedures, this step is described. Also identified are responses to the involved people. These responses are described as they pertain to procedures, consequences, and spiritual care.

The remaining section of this part of each chapter addresses the more proactive measures being implemented by the religious institutions. In particular, a section on screening policies and mandatory education for people in positions of responsibility is included. Lastly, the chapters are completed with summaries of significant developments and issues.

In the concluding chapter, overarching themes and historical shifts in the religious institutions are identified. Differences between the institutions are also named and considered. Future directions for the researched religious institutions and for research more generally are discussed.[26]

There are several limitations to this book. First, most policies and statements will have been updated and/or revised since this research concluded in 2009. This book represents a particular period in history regarding a subject area that is evolving and, thankfully, in flux with emerging new information and awareness. Also, due to the decentralized structure of most of the religious institutions researched, it was not possible to represent fully the approaches of each identified religious institution to child sexual abuse complaints. Only one of the studied religious institutions—the United Church of Canada—has a single binding policy that covers all complaints. In many cases, the development of institutional policy depends on religious leaders such as bishops and boards, and often varies from region to region or from jurisdiction to jurisdiction; in many religious institutions, the national body can suggest policies, but the particular faith communities can choose whether or not to follow the suggested approach or policy, to develop a similar one, to develop a different one, or not to use one at all. Consequently, the only way to get a complete picture of the state of such policies would be to consult with every individual diocese, mosque, pastoral charge, or other particular faith community. Further, each such community would need to choose whether or not to respond to this inquiry. As evidenced by the research for this book, not every individual faith community chose to respond and disclose their respective policies to outsiders. As a result of these constraints, this study does not claim to represent all of the communities that together form these particular religious institutions in Canada.

With the exception of the Roman Catholic Church in Canada, all of the existing policies examined are designed to address *all* complaints of sexual abuse; in other words, child sexual abuse complaints are one type of sexual abuse complaint covered by the policies. As a result, some parts of the policies do not attend to the particularities of *child* sexual abuse, but this distinction is not always clearly identified in the policies. Further, because of this generalized nature of most policies, sometimes a distinction between complaints of historic child sexual abuse and current child sexual abuse is not identified explicitly.

This study examines a limited number of faith traditions and therefore can make claims regarding only these particular religious institutions in Canada. It will be important for future studies to examine additional religious institutions, including, but not limited to, Judaism, Buddhism, Hinduism, Jainism, Daoism, Paganism, Wicca, and several Christian institutions such as Baptists, Presbyterians, and Methodists. Again, there are many more religious institutions not mentioned here that are equally important. This book is one way of talking about the development of child sexual abuse policies in religious institutions; it is not the only way. This book is a starting point for further study of all of these significant institutions.

A further limitation pertains to information regarding policy implementation. Information related to particular cases is often confidential and, further, statistics regarding the number of cases and their outcomes either have not been collected or are not made publicly available. A few very brief case sketches are provided as windows into how policies have been applied or experienced, but they cannot be presumed normative.

Also, the scope of this research is necessarily limited by time and resource constraints; books could be written regarding each individual faith group and child sexual abuse policy, procedure, and implementation. Additionally, while brief background remarks are made regarding historical context, the focus of this book is on the official policies of these individual faith groups.

Since the focus is on official policy, no claims are made regarding the perceptions or awareness of grassroots religious community members of these policies or approaches to child sexual abuse. It may be that in some religious institutions, the majority of followers are not aware that a policy exists or may perceive the policy as unhelpful or helpful. Also, only the years from 1960 to 2009 are considered, and with a degree of brevity. A broader historical contextual study would be helpful.

This book's focus on policy in Canadian religious institutions makes it an original, albeit limited, contribution to the discourse on child sexual abuse.

Chapter 2

The Roman Catholic Church in Canada

THE ROMAN CATHOLIC CHURCH (RCC) led the way among institutional religions in addressing child sexual abuse complaints.[1] Policies for responding to complaints emerged in some dioceses in 1987. Further, the RCC is the only religious institution examined in this book to create policies exclusively addressing complaints of child sexual abuse; other institutions have developed policies that respond to complaints of sexual abuse against both children and adults.

In 1992 a central policy document, entitled *From Pain to Hope*, was created and recommended for use in the Church's dioceses and archdioceses. Many have chosen to follow the guidelines in this document while others have developed their own or do not indicate what, if any, policy they choose to follow. In the course of the research for this book, all seventy-one dioceses were contacted via email and asked if they had a policy and, if so, for any information about that policy. Of the seventy-one, seventeen responded. However, although it is not clear if all dioceses have implemented a policy, during the Cornwall Inquiry, Father Thomas Doyle, expert in canon law and child sexual abuse, testified that he did not know of any diocese in Canada that did not have a binding diocesan protocol and, in "many cases, these protocols were based on the provisions in the CCCB document [e.g., *From Pain to Hope*]."[2]

Church Structure and Description of the Context

The Roman Catholic Church in Canada is the largest religious institution in the country, 2001 census data from Statistics Canada indicates that Roman Catholics are "the largest religious group, drawing the faith of just under 12.8 million people, or 43% of the population."[3]

Geographically, the RCC is divided into ecclesiastical provinces, with each archdiocese headed by an archbishop, and each diocese headed by a bishop. In each ecclesiastical province there is one diocese that is recognized as the first diocese, or the archdiocese. The bishop of that diocese is thus an archbishop. The archbishop has no structural power over other bishops within the same ecclesiastical province; rather, the role is considered honorific. Each diocese and archdiocese consists of a number of deaneries that are comprised of parishes, which are served by priests.

The Catholic Church in Canada consists of seventy-one dioceses, including sixty-two in the Latin rite, eight eparchies (of the eastern rite), and one military ordinariate.[4] A diocese and an eparchy are areas of jurisdiction in the Roman Catholic Church.

The RCC, as with other religious institutions, includes those who have been baptized into the faith, including lay members, adherents, volunteers, leaders, and specially mandated leaders (religious, e.g., those who are in a specific order in the Catholic community), and priests. At its head is the successor of St. Peter, the pope (also known as the pontiff or the bishop of Rome), who is elected by the College of Cardinals. The other role of the College of Cardinals is to advise the pope.[5] The pontiff selects cardinals.[6] The pope exercises full authority over the Church.[7] He is assisted by the Roman Curia, whose members perform a variety of roles in governance in the name of the pontiff.[8] The Church is divided into nine administrative departments called congregations, each of which is headed by a cardinal. For example, the Congregation for the Doctrine of the Faith exists within the Curia to promote Church doctrine and morality. Since 2001 it is this congregation to which all cases of alleged sexual abuse involving priests must be sent.[9]

The Church is administered out of the autonomous state of Vatican City by the Roman Curia, which acts under the Vatican's Secretary of State.[10] Also leading the Church is the Episcopal College, of which the pope is head. The Episcopal College consists of the bishops of the Roman Catholic Church. They are considered the successors of the Apostles. They have authority over the Church only when they act in union with the pope.[11] Individually, (arch)bishops exercise authority over their particular (arch)dioceses.[12]

The role of the laity in the Church significantly changed in the twentieth century. The Council of Trent (1546) solidified a hierarchical "pyramidal structure," with the laity at the bottom. Vatican II, in the 1960s, challenged this with a new understanding of the Church that put more of an emphasis on the whole "People of God."[13] Notably, lay people were identified as participants in ministry in the *Dogmatic Constitution on the Church*, one of the documents that emerged from Vatican II. In 1972, Pope Paul VI wrote the apostolic letter, *Ministeria Quaedum*.[14] In this letter he establishes non-ordained designated ministries and affirms that all ministries are valuable in their own right. No longer were non-ordained ministries steps below the priesthood.[15]

The Canadian Conference of Catholic Bishops (CCCB) is the National Assembly of the Bishops in Canada, created in 1943 and officially recognized by Rome in 1948. The CCCB is a collegial group, exercising little authority over individual dioceses, and "respecting the autonomy of each Bishop in the service of his particular Church."[16] The role of the CCCB is to provide "ways for assisting the Canadian bishops in their pastoral responsibilities and in different areas such as ecumenism, theology, liturgy, social affairs, Christian education and communications…. [It] provides the bishops a forum where they can share their experience and insight on the life of the Church."[17] The CCCB can offer advice or guidance or even "general decrees for the whole Church in Canada."[18] However, structurally each bishop is accountable *only* to the Vatican. According to its statutes and an apostolic letter written by John Paul II, the CCCB can vote to petition the Apostolic See for doctrinal declarations in Canada,[19] including, theoretically, a mandatory national sexual abuse policy, but this does not seem to have been attempted. Possible reasons for this include the fear that such a vote, if successful, would create division within the CCCB by instigating a move that would effectively usurp part of the bishops' authority. Further, there may be concern that such a move, if successful (although it could be quite difficult to achieve the required two-thirds of the bishops to vote in favour), could set a precedent for CCCB control over individual dioceses. An additional and likely most significant possible reason is fear of litigious consequences. Having a centralized sexual abuse policy would make the whole Roman Catholic Church in Canada or the CCCB more vulnerable to lawsuits from complainants whereas, currently, only the particular diocese is vulnerable; as Commissioner G. Normand Glaude summarizes in his *Report of the Cornwall Inquiry*, "The federal, provincial, and territorial governments of Canada do not recognize the Catholic Church as a legal entity. They recognize only the corporations under which Catholic dioceses operate. Diocesan corporations are autonomous, private corporate entities."[20]

There are four regional assemblies of the CCCB, which are the Western Catholic Conference (WCC), the Ontario Conference of Catholic Bishops (OCCB), the Assembly of Quebec Catholic Bishops (AQCB), and the Atlantic Episcopal Assembly (AEA). "These regional assemblies enable the bishops to deal directly with pastoral questions related to regional matters."[21]

The laws of the Catholic Church were first codified in 1917 and ratified as the *Code of Canon Law*. In this first code, there are two canons that are clearly applicable to cases of sexual abuse. *Canon 2354*

> states that if a cleric is convicted of raping a youth of the opposite sex, he will be: "… punished by an ecclesiastical tribunal, according to the varying degree of the fault, with penances, censures, privation of office and dignity and, if it seems necessary, also with deposition." Canon 2359 … states that if a cleric engages with a minor under sixteen years old in a number of sexual acts, including sodomy, he will be "suspended, declared infamous," and "deprived of any office, benefice, dignity" and responsibility within the Church.

It seems that these canons were used rarely: as Father Morrisey testified at the Cornwall Inquiry, "few dioceses conducted canonical penal processes.[22]

The year 1922 saw the emergence of a document entitled *Instructio de modo precedendi in causis sollicitationis*. This document contains instructions, not laws, on how to address what were identified as the "worst crimes" committed by clerics. Named among these crimes, significantly, was sex with minors. A minor was defined as prepubescent, which meant the age of twelve for girls and fourteen for boys. There were no diocesan tribunals, however, set up to respond to these worst crimes until the 1940s. Further, these instructions were shrouded in secrecy; they were not taught in seminaries and kept only in the secret archives. Over time, it seems likely that knowledge of their existence gradually faded. The strictures around secrecy also bound anyone involved in an ecclesial investigation from disclosing any information to civil authorities; if this secrecy was breached, excommunication was the result. These instructions were amended, with minor changes, in 1962.[23]

Approach to Child Sexual Abuse, Including Relevant Statements, Policies, and Practices: 1960–80

The initial response of the Catholic Church to reports of clergy's sexual abuse of minors was reluctant at best. As with other religious institutions, awareness of women's issues, human sexuality, and the Church's complicity in systemic oppression was needed before complaints of child sexual abuse against priests could be acknowledged and addressed. Acknowledgement of clergy's sexual abuse of minors hinged largely on the acceptance of the fallibility of priests and the Church. Until this foundational work was deepened and widespread public awareness generated, it was not possible for the RCC to begin addressing internal child sexual abuse complaints in a publicly accountable manner: "At first, accusations were generally met with denial."[24] There was little guidance for the Church and "although some canons, such as c. 1395, alluded to sexual acts committed by clerics against minors, they did little to address long-term issues."[25]

In the global context, liberation theology was generated primarily by Roman Catholic theologians in the 1960s and 1970s. In the 1980s much was written, at least partially in response to feminist challenges, by the Roman Catholic Church concerning women and their changing roles. Of note is Pope John Paul II's Apostolic Letter *On the Dignity and Vocation of Women*. Issued in 1988, this papal statement indicated respect and appreciation for women, but unequivocally reinforced the normative nature of women's roles as mother and wife.[26] Several feminist, womanist, mujerista, and other theologians committed to writing from a conscious standpoint of women emerged and gained increasing voice during this time period. A sustained and impassioned conversation had emerged as women claimed their voices and named their experiences of marginalization and abuse in Church and society.

The Canadian Roman Catholic Church also began producing literature on both woman abuse and child abuse, including its first policies, in the late 1980s.

For example, the Quebec Assembly of Bishops produced a resource entitled *A Heritage of Violence—a Pastoral Reflection on Conjugal Violence* in 1989.[27] The authors credited their work to "the feminist movement and to certain individual women to have first drawn attention to this reality [of conjugal violence]...."[28] Work toward producing this resource began in March 1986 at the Assembly of Quebec Bishops' study session addressing the "women's movement and the Church." The topic of violence against women emerged along with a commitment to study it further via the formation of a task force on violence against women.[29] This "consciousness-raising document" was written mainly for "clergy and pastoral staff ... [to] help them to support those who speak out against conjugal violence, to facilitate the detection of violent situations and to encourage the creation of more adequate services to both victims and aggressors."[30] In addition to examining the experiences of abused women, the resource also discussed the effects of "conjugal violence" on children.[31] Grounding the topic in faith claims, the authors clearly named the issue, took a strong stand against such violence, and understood work to end this violence as part of the Church's biblical and theological mandates.

To further contextualize this resource, it is helpful to identify some of the resources used in its writing. The task force drew on resources produced in the wider Church community, including John Paul II's *On the Dignity and Vocation of Women*, Roberta Morris's *Ending Violence in Families, a Training Program for Pastoral Care Workers* (published by the United Church of Canada), and *Family Violence in a Patriarchal Culture, a Challenge to Our Way of Living* (by the Church Council on Justice and Corrections and the Canadian Council on Social Development); theological works by scholars, including Monique Dumais, Marie Fortune, Elizabeth Möltmann, Jurgen Möltmann, and Mary Pellauer; as well as other contemporary secular and government resources.

The 1970s and particularly the 1980s saw wider Canadian society become increasingly aware of women's and children's systemic marginalization. As painful as it has been for faith communities to confess their complicity in these patterns of violence, this growing awareness was necessary to the establishment of concrete abuse policies. Generating this awareness was largely the result of increased women's voices, together with the widespread media and legal attention on child sexual abuse cases in the Roman Catholic Church.

Case Examples

There are a number of child sexual abuse cases that emerged during this time period and contributed significantly to the creation of the first diocesan policies in 1987. The two high-profile cases summarized in the following pages furthered discussion in the Church regarding not only child sexual abuse but the underlying issues of what it means to be a priest, and the Church's theological approaches to sexuality. The need to recognize and respond to child sexual abuse committed by priests and religious was underscored and pushed to the forefront by these cases. Although only a very few Church leaders commit such abuse, it does happen and the harm is lasting and multi-layered.

Charles Sylvestre, a former priest with the Diocese of London (DoL), charged with crimes related to the sexual abuse of minors, pleaded guilty to cases that dated as far back as 1954. The Diocese announced that in the course of a court-mandated search of diocesan documents, "staff discovered copies of three police witness statements from 1962 alleging abuse by Charles Sylvestre."[32] As reported by the Canadian Broadcasting Corporation (CBC), this contradicts earlier claims that the Diocese had "believed reports of his abuse were first made in 1989."[33] According to this article, in "the documents were transcribed interviews with three girls who told police how Sylvestre had touched them and exposed himself." In their statement announcing the existence of the documents, the Diocese stated that there "is no indication how or when the documents were first received by the Diocese but it is certainly possible that they were given to diocesan officials in 1962."[34]

The discovery of these documents validates a statement made by former Bishop John Michael Sherlock, whose tenure as bishop ran from 1978 until his retirement in 2002. In an article entitled "Our Former Bishop Reflects on Personal Experience of Church's Journey from Pain to Hope Regarding Sexual Abuse Scandals," the author wrote:

> an early response ... was to protect the priesthood and the church. He [Sherlock] ventured that "the culture of silence" around sexual abuse cases may have resulted from priests being "victims of their own theology." There was a belief that "a priest is a priest forever ..." and should not be removed from ministry. "It took time for the protection of children to become foremost," he said.[35]

The CBC article quoted the present bishop, Ronald Fabbro, as stating that "his counterpart in 1962 would have been told about the police reports."[36] And the *Windsor Star* described a "culture of secrecy that allowed Sylvestre to continue preying on young girls after victims complained to nuns, priests, police, parents, and the Bishop over the decades."[37] In the CBC article a woman who claimed to be a victim of Sylvestre from the mid-1970s is quoted as saying "I would imagine that there are many more. Certainly, I myself had gone to the diocese and reported abuse and ... I also reported it to police, and it was buried by both [the police and the diocese]."[38]

In Newfoundland in the 1970s, a number of cases arose that were removed quietly from the public eye and public accountability. Father James Hickey, a Roman Catholic priest, served in a variety of positions in the Archdiocese of St. John's before the Mount Cashel scandals broke open in the late 1980s. As early as 1975, complaints against him were made to the archdiocese, "but the church never did anything about these complaints, partly to avoid a scandal and partly because Hickey managed to convince his superiors that the allegations against him were false."[39]

At the same time in Newfoundland, claims of abuse in the Christian Brothers' Mount Cashel Orphanage began to surface. In the 1970s the Newfoundland constabulary began to uncover the sexual abuse, but members of the "justice system terminated an ongoing criminal investigation ... [and] the same authorities tried to get the police report of the Mount Cashel investigation altered to remove all references to sexual abuse."[40]

In the 1950s the Department of Social Services began using the Mount Cashel orphanage for wards of the province, with the Christian Brothers continuing to run the institution.[41] When a group of boys brought an early case of sexual abuse in the orphanage to the attention of the superintendent, Brother John Barron dealt with the offending brother by transferring him to a monastery at which he continued to have access to young boys. Two years later he was back at Mount Cashel.[42] Reports of abuse were later given to public officials in the mid-1970s, but generated little response.[43] The investigation was handed over to the superintendent of the orphanage, Brother Douglas Kenny, along with numerous additional reports by public officials and complainants. When the case hit the public's attention in the 1980s, he was one of those charged with physical and sexual abuse.

Although the Christian Brothers funded counselling for their own, there was no similar provision of care for the victims of the abuse.[44] By 1977, the two brothers who had confessed were finished with treatment and teaching again. Other brothers who had been involved were reassigned to different positions around Canada.

Approach to Child Sexual Abuse, Including Relevant Statements, Policies, and Practices: 1981–91

In 1983, a new *Code of Canon Law* was promulgated that abrogated the laws of the 1917 *Code*. The new *Code of Canon Law* "is to be regarded as an indispensable instrument to ensure order both in individual and social life, and also in the Church's own activity."[45] However, it is unclear as to whether the instructions of 1962 were abrogated since the instruction was not law and the 1983 *Code* only abolished previous *legislation*.[46]

The 1983 new procedure for addressing complaints of sexual abuse by clergy is outlined in *Canon 1395*. This canon, together with *Canon 1336*, suggest a graduated penalty system, leaving dismissal from the priesthood as a consequence only after repeated offences with less severe penalties.[47]

The issue of child sexual abuse by clergy and religious made headlines in 1988–89. In Newfoundland and the rest of Canada, the case of Father James Hickey, of the Archdiocese of St. John's, was splashed across the media, concurrent with disclosures of the Mount Cashel abuses. In 1987, a priest who had been victimized as a child by Father Hickey wrote a letter to the provincial Department of Social Services in St. John's and approached the archbishop with a formal complaint against Hickey, who had abused him as his guidance counsellor. Because of action initiated by the Department of Social Services, Father Hickey was charged formally two months later on January 11, 1988, "with thirty-two counts of criminal sexual behaviour."[48] Hickey pleaded guilty to twenty counts and was sentenced to five years. A handful of other priests in Newfoundland faced similar charges.[49]

The questions that arose out of the Newfoundland cases resulted in Archbishop Alphonsus Penney establishing the Winter Commission in May 1989. This Inquiry, headed by Gordon A. Winter, a former lieutenant governor of Newfoundland and an Anglican, investigated how this widespread child sexual abuse by priests had continued for so many years, and made recommendations to the archbishop regarding preventative and healing measures.[50] Similar to the Cornwall Inquiry, the commission was generated in part by accusations of a systemic cover-up and the failure to provide adequate pastoral care.[51] Accordingly, during one of these sessions, Winter explained to those in attendance that the commission was not "under the thumb of the Archbishop."[52]

In the fall of 1989, the commission sent out letters to the involved dioceses to "become as fully informed as possible of protocols and administrative procedures that may be in place in the light of canon law, or civil law, or both."[53] Subsequently, the commission indicated serious concern for what they saw as inadequate attention in many policies to pastoral care provisions for the complainant(s). One of the commission's recommendations in 1990 was "a revision of the diocesan protocols, trying to give them a more pastoral tone," and pointedly stated that the Church's pastoral response must not be "overshadowed by concerns for legal liabilities."[54] In conclusion, the commission found that the archdiocesan leadership did cover up complaints of abuse, including child sexual abuse by priests, since the mid-1970s.[55] The abuse did not go undetected; rather, the archdiocese was aware of the allegations since 1975, but chose to ignore them.[56] Similarly, psychotherapist and former priest Richard Sipe, a long-standing expert on child sexual abuse in the US Roman Catholic Church, concluded that:

> In the period from 1985 to 1992, there was a growing sensitivity to the realization that Catholic bishops and religious superiors could be involved in concealing knowledge of criminal activities by Catholic priests and religious. A growing mass of people who had been violated began to share some of their experiences with psychologists, psychiatrists, spouses, parents, friends, and attorneys. Sharing created a body of hundreds of thousands of people who knew a reality that hitherto had not been publicly discussed.[57]

Covering up child sexual abuse was no longer as viable; by the late 1980s aware-ness had grown, and the marginalized began to seize their collective voice.

Contributing significantly to the growing popular awareness of Roman Catholic priests' sexual abuse of children were the high-profile cases emerging in the 1980s in the United States. The first such case was that of the Reverend Gilbert Gauthe from the Diocese of Lafayette in Louisiana, who had sexually abused several children in his parish. The lawsuits that were generated in 1983 were settled for over $10 million.[58]

Church authorities began to struggle with how to relate cases of sexual abuse to canon law. In response to the Gauthe case, Doyle, along with Ray Mouton and Reverend Michael Peterson, began to work as advisory counsel to the American bishops. Together, they produced a lengthy report entitled the *1985 Doyle-Mouton-Peterson Manual*, which included proposals to address the issue of child sexual abuse by clergy.[59] Although the US bishops did not immediately embrace all of the proposals, years later many dioceses made use of the recom-mendations in their protocols.[60]

This document, commonly referred to as *The Manual*, provided the founda-tion for the subsequent *1987 Guidelines*.[61] However, primary author Doyle later criticized *The Manual* as "biased in favor of the bishops' concerns for image, money, and control."[62] Many of the thus biased recommendations concern con-fidentiality, litigation, and other legal responsibilities.

The Manual also addresses a number of spiritual issues related to the victims/survivors. For example, the authors identify the "damage done to the child's faith in the sacraments as sources of grace and communications with Christ." Guilt that the victims/survivors and their families might feel regarding the abuse is also raised as a concern. Offenders are mentioned in the spiritual concerns section of *The Manual*: "[h]elp must be given to priest-offenders to discern the nature of their commitment to the priesthood, the reasons for their choice of this voca-tion, their hopes and plans for the future, and the real possibility that they are almost totally unfit to be priests."[63] *The Manual* leaves open the possibility of offenders returning to ministry in some form.

Partly reflective of the preoccupation of some bishops with protecting the Church's image, there is concern expressed in *The Manual* for the effect that offending priests may have on non-offending priests in the wider Church. First, non-offending priests may be afraid "of even touching children such as blessing them, making normal signs of affection." Second, there is concern that the public perception of the Church and of priests will be tarnished. The authors of *The Manual* worry that the Church may be perceived as a haven for sexual perverts, and that the wider community may believe that Church authorities mishandle cases of sexual abuse.[64]

Structurally, the authors of *The Manual* recommended the establishment of two national committees: the Crisis Control Team and the Policy and Planning

Group. The Crisis Control Team's function was to advise the bishop regarding responses to allegations of priest–child sexual abuse.[65] Members of the team were to include secular and canonical legal representation and a psychiatrist. The Policy and Planning Group was to be comprised of psychiatrists and psychologists "with expertise in evaluation and treatment of offenders as well as victims and their families [... and] in screening, testing, and evaluating emotional stability and vocational suitability."[66]

Shortly after the 1985 release of *The Manual*, in both the US and Canada, individual dioceses began to implement protocols. In Canada, 1987 saw the release of an initial protocol by the CCCB, building on Doyle's work.[67] The protocols were established to ensure that dioceses had a resource available for use at a bishop's discretion that fulfilled legal (civil and canonical) and pastoral obligations.

The first section of these 1987 CCCB guidelines outlined appropriate response procedures immediately upon receiving a complaint. Of the eleven points put forward, only one refers to care for the victims and their families: "*suitable persons* should be designated to meet with the parents, and eventually the children involved, provided the parents so consent."[68] There is no definition provided for "suitable persons." Regarding the accused, the need for care from a psychological treatment facility that would "offer complete medical and neurological facilities" is identified.[69]

The other articles concern legalities, finances, and the establishment of diocesan policies. The document calls for a team consisting of, "at minimum a canonist, a specialist in civil and criminal law, [and] a medical doctor who is experienced in the treatment of persons who suffer from disorders related to pedophilia and similar illnesses." The mandate of this team is to "establish a *basic policy* or contingency plan which would take into account existing Church and civil laws applicable to the territory."[70] The rest of the guidelines addressed proper insurance coverage and procedures, financial contingencies, media relations, and the education of diocesan priests and religious on the policy.

The second section outlined a process for responding to allegations of child sexual abuse. First, a clergy delegate should "meet with the parents on behalf of the diocese." Following this meeting the victim should, "with the parents' consent, be interviewed by a mental health professional familiar with the problems of children in this age group. If the parents do not consent, advice should be offered to them as to where to obtain appropriate professional counseling for themselves and the children."[71] There were numerous recommendations concerning legal counsel for the accused and the importance of legal presence at all times during the Inquiry. An immediate leave of absence from duties, presumably with pay though this is unstated, was recommended. These guidelines were intended primarily for complaints of current child sexual abuse, but did not exclude complaints of historic abuse.

Notably, the diocesan bishop and any other involved priests were prohibited from hearing the "sacramental confession of the accused cleric."[72] In an article written a couple of years later, Morrisey confirmed that the purpose of this prohibition was legal; it was to ensure "that the persons directly involved in the process … are not in conflict with obligation arising from applicable secular laws and from the inviolable law pertaining to the sacramental seal."[73] This Roman Catholic requirement to maintain the confidentiality of the confessional continues to pose a potential ethical dilemma for many priests: the potential harm done by breaking confidentiality must be weighed against the potential harm done by allowing someone to continue to abuse.

Next, an Inquiry was to be directed by the designate with lawyers in attendance. Following the Inquiry, the designate would report to the bishop as to whether or not there was "substance to the accusations." This preliminary Inquiry consisted of the designated priest "hearing those who are bringing the complaint … [as well as hearing] the accused priest." If the decision was to proceed, then the priest would be "referred immediately (no later than the next day) to the selected treatment center for medical and psychological evaluation." After the cleric had been evaluated, the aforementioned team was to determine whether or not to proceed to a canonical trial, where possible canonical penalties could be deliberated.[74] Further, as per an understanding of the mandatory reporting laws, the practice was not to report any allegations to secular authorities until after a preliminary Inquiry found that there was substance. (This practice was strongly criticized in the commissioner's report regarding the Cornwall Inquiry.)

The third section addressed responses to the involved parties if sexual abuse was verified through a canonical trial. The document underscores the importance of ongoing care for children and their families: "special care should be taken to show the Church's concern for the victims of such actions, even though the matter is painful. The spiritual well-being of the children and of the parents is of primary concern."[75]

Regarding responses to an offending priest, if he is permitted to remain a priest, he must be assessed carefully before any return to active ministry is considered by the advisory team. The document's primary concern is with offending priests, but complaints against others in positions of trust are not excluded. Should the cleric return to ministry, he would be required, minimally, to continue receiving psychological therapy.

The fourth section details the keeping of written records of proceedings for "the benefit of the legal counsel of the diocese."[76]

There are some notable omissions within this early set of guidelines and recommendations. First, there is little discussion of Church interaction with secular authorities. Legal reporting standards may have been presupposed, but they are not stated in this document. Further, mandatory reporting laws, as discussed in Chapter 1 of this book, tended to be interpreted such that complaints would be reported to secular authorities *only* if the preliminary investigation found that there is substance to the complaint. Nor does the document address the question of potential overlap between a secular investigation and a Church investigation. Another omission concerns financial responsibility for the counselling suggested to both the victim and family. Further, the policy addresses allegations against clerics; it is not stated if there were any differences in protocol when the accused is not a cleric. Also, complaints of historic child sexual abuse are not addressed explicitly.

Because of the bishops' autonomy, each diocese or archdiocese made its own decision regarding how or if to implement this 1987 set of CCCB-issued guidelines. For this reason, two examples of such early diocesan policies will be summarized.

The Archdiocese of Toronto created a policy in 1989.[77] This protocol builds on the 1987 guidelines and includes an in-depth investigative step and focuses more on the care of the victims than does the CCCB guidelines, requiring "appropriate professional counseling services for the child, the parents and siblings, to begin immediately."[78] Further, the protocol explicitly applies to allegations of sexual misconduct against anyone, not only clerics, under the employ of the archdiocese.

A diocesan investigation was required by this policy following any secular investigation, and was required to proceed even if secular investigations result in no charges.[79] Further, for the diocesan process to continue, the investigator need not "be satisfied beyond a reasonable doubt that the allegation is true, or even that the allegation is probably true. The investigator should find that there is substance to the allegations unless he or she has been persuaded that there is a substantial probability that the allegations are not true."[80] This preliminary investigation is to occur quickly, "within one hour if possible and should be completed as quickly as possible."[81] The investigator was required to meet with the complainant(s) as well as the accused to first gather the different stories.[82] The judicial vicar followed with canonical proceedings and immediate treatment for the accused following this preliminary investigation if the complaint was found to have substance.

If the preliminary investigation finds the complaint to have substance, the 1991 procedures direct the investigator to request that the judicial vicar arrange for any investigatory hearing.[83] The investigatory hearing was to be closed; only invited parties could attend. At this hearing a "party may ... (a) be represented by counsel; (b) call and examine witnesses and present arguments and submissions, (c) conduct cross-examinations of witnesses at the hearing reasonably required for a full and fair disclosure of the facts in relation to which they have given evidence."[84] This hearing involved submission of evidence, including testimonies and other documents, "whether or not given or proven under oath or affirmation or admissible as evidence in canonical proceedings or a court of law."[85] The regulations delineated the conduct of hearings, the order of proceedings, and issues concerning the questioning of parties. Based on this hearing, the investigator was to make a report to the archbishop and advise how to proceed within the Roman Catholic Church system.

The archdiocese, under the discretion of the chancellor, was to "pay the legal and other expenses of the complainant incurred in respect of an investigatory hearing."[86] Similarly, the respondent's fees were to be paid. In both situations, such payment was at the discretion of the chancellor, who may "terminate the obligation of the Archdiocese to pay under this paragraph from and after the date fixed in the notice."[87]

The original policy neither prescribed nor recommended preventative measures.[88] The policy was updated in 1991 with minor revisions. These revisions included a change to the age when reporting is required. Previous mandatory reporting was required for those eighteen and under. The updated policy changed this age to sixteen and under, consistent with secular law in the jurisdiction of Ontario. Complaints of historic abuse are received and investigated, although it can be more difficult to investigate such complaints.

Under the 1991 revised policy, the archdiocese receives complaints directly from the complainant and also from third parties. However, there are difficulties regarding how best to deal with the alleged victim when a third-party complaint is filed, including the challenge of approaching the alleged victim; the provision of appropriate pastoral care; and the risk of additional harm to the alleged victim through interviews that may be unwanted. The archdiocese does not accept anonymous complaints. Also, if a complaint is withdrawn but a respondent has been identified, the archdiocese will continue with an investigation.[89]

The Diocese of London (DoL) in Ontario implemented a protocol in 1989 and, in so doing, joined the Archdiocese of Toronto in becoming "one of the first in Canada to do so."[90] The DoL process is quite consistent with the *Morrisey Guidelines*. According to Father John Sharpe, the present chair of the Diocesan Sexual Abuse Committee, it is "probable" that the *Morrisey Guidelines* greatly influenced the development of the protocol.[91] This diocese has been very transparent regarding its policies, and the history of these policies. This information is easily accessed on the diocesan website.

Decisions regarding complaints were to be made by a sexual abuse committee and the chair. The committee was to "consist of a civil lawyer, a licensed psychologist, a canon lawyer and a director of education."[92] Although the document does not clarify her role, "[a]t the suggestion of the Diocesan Women's Commission, a woman was added to the group."[93]

The Diocese of London's protocol required that any allegation made to a cleric, "whether it involves themselves or another priest or person who may be considered under the direction or control of the Roman Catholic Church," to be reported immediately to the chair of the Committee on Sexual Abuse.[94] To be very clear regarding the mandatory nature of reporting complaints, the protocol states that members "of the priesthood are not to exercise any discretion in fulfilling this reporting obligation."[95] Once the complaint has been reported to the committee, what amounted to a preliminary investigation was to begin. If the chair determined that there was substance to the complaint, the investigation would continue. Regardless, the chair was to inform the committee lawyer.[96]

Next, the chair of the committee was to meet with the accused. (The policy did not say what would be done if the accused was deceased.) Following that meeting, "two persons would do the investigation and certainly one thing we would be looking for would be the involvement of minors or vulnerable persons."[97] If a decision is made not to proceed, the lawyer on the committee must first be consulted. It was the responsibility of the chair of the committee to make the necessary reports to the diocesan authorities, child welfare authorities, and insurers.[98] If the investigation proceeded, meetings with the alleged victim or legal guardian(s) and the alleged offender would follow.[99] Following the investigation, the protocol outlined steps to be taken, including the provision of legal counsel and possible canonical proceedings, such as a trial.[100]

The alleged offender was to be granted, or to have imposed, a leave of absence, as well as the "removal of a priest's faculties to preach or right to hear confession."[101] Perhaps surprisingly, other diocesan policies and all of the existing policies of other religious institutions—during this time period—examined in this book did not necessarily automatically *require* a suspension during an investigation, which would help to safeguard the complainant and other vulnerable people. The argument often is made that a mandatory leave is not fair to the accused as it could prejudice the community against the accused. However, usually word gets out regardless. Further, if a paid leave is not automatic, the cases in which such leave is imposed are far more likely to generate prejudiced speculation. Certainly, in the cases in which someone is unjustly accused, the damage will take intentional work and time to heal.

Under this 1989 London policy, professional counselling for both the alleged victim and the offender was to be provided.[102] Provision of care continues to be recommended following the adjournment of proceedings, including any penal hearings and/or public prosecution: "the Committee should consider the continued provision of assistance to the victim or family, and therapy or other assistance to a priest or other person."[103]

The DoL protocol was reviewed in 1994, following the publication of *From Pain to Hope* (*FPtH*), with the conclusion that no revisions were necessary to make the protocol consistent with *FPtH*.[104]

Approach to Child Sexual Abuse, Including Relevant Statements, Policies, and Practices: 1992–2009

In October 1989, the CCCB created an "Ad Hoc Committee on child sexual abuse by priests or male religious."[105] This arose out of a need for national guidelines that respected diocesan autonomy and discretion.[106] In November, a bishop, the Most Reverend Roger Ebacher, was named chairperson and the work began.

The initial mandate given to the Ad Hoc Committee consisted of five parts, with particular attention given to pastoral care of involved people and proactive measures:

1 Completion/expansion of the 1987 suggested guidelines, in the light of their use in dioceses, other recent experiences, etc.
2 Additional guidelines/policies for the extended pastoral care of victims and their families.
3 Guidelines/policies for the extended pastoral care and future of priest offenders.
4 Guidelines (models) for diocesan community self-awareness ("auto-critique") and prevention strategies and mechanisms, which foster and facilitate a fuller human support system for all priests and indeed for all parishioners.
5 Guidelines for affirmative activities at the local level, to help Church members join other people of good will to help break the cycle of sexual abuse.[107]

The committee slightly revised this mandate in August 1990. "We decided to combine points 4 and 5 into a single project. In addition we identified 'the selection and training of candidates for the priesthood' as a specific question that needed to be addressed."[108] The committee met over the course of two years, from April 1990 to April 1992. Their work culminated in the publication of *From Pain to Hope: Report from the CCCB Ad Hoc Committee on Child Sexual Abuse* in June 1992. The group also produced a study guide "to raise consciousness at the most basic levels of the Church to the reality of child sexual abuse."[109] This guide was entitled *Breach of Trust—Breach of Faith* and was released at the same time.

Complaints of Child Sexual Abuse and Complaints by Adults of Historical Childhood Sexual Abuse

FPtH defines "direct victims of sexual abuse against children" as "the child who has been abused by an adult; or the adult survivor of child abuse."[110] The RCC has an obligation to provide pastoral care to "children who are victims of sexual abuse and to adults who were sexually abused in their childhood."[111] The RCC is to seek justice and care for all who claim to have experienced childhood sexual abuse, according to *FPtH*.

The authors of *FPtH* wrote the document with a commitment to breaking the silence regarding child sexual abuse and working for justice. Accordingly, they outlined four "truths" for the Church to confess and resolve. The first truth is that "child sexual abuse occurs and will continue to occur [so long as we accept] … a climate of deception, hypocrisy, and lies." To this is tied the second truth: there is virtue in humility, an admission that there are problems, and a commitment to addressing the abuse rather than justifying or hiding it. The third is conversion. When it is resolved that "something is lacking within the Church," the Church is called to change or convert. Forgiveness is the final truth and can neither come easily, nor be demanded at the cost of "concealing an unhealed wound."[112]

The recommendations made in this 1992 *FPtH* document are directed toward five groups: (1) the Catholics of Canada, (2) the bishops, (3) those who direct priestly formation, (4) those responsible for priests, and (5) the CCCB. The first set of recommendations is directed to all in the RCC and is very general. All Catholics are implored to "break the silence and become actively involved in addressing and eradicating this social affliction." The recommendations promote support for the victims and for all priests as they often bear the brunt of the fallout from allegations. Education is also encouraged regarding the legalities relevant to sexual abuse.[113]

The second set of recommendations is directed toward the bishops. These recommendations address structural matters regarding diocesan policy and procedure beginning with the directive to establish a committee and then create an appropriate diocesan protocol. All priests and religious personnel then must be made aware of that protocol and educated accordingly.[114]

The uniqueness of each diocese is the reason given within the report for not recommending one universally binding protocol. Specifically, the authors cite the differences between "various provincial laws on reporting …; the [differences involved in] coordination of interventions between child protection agencies and the office of the local Provincial Crown Attorney …; [and the differences between] the basic diocesan organizational structures."[115] Although it is recommended that each diocese establish its own protocol, "dioceses can inform one another of their experiences in this regards;" collegiality between dioceses is encouraged.[116] These do not seem to be insurmountable obstacles to a national policy; the national policy of the United Church provides for provincial legal variations.

Recommendation 13 calls for the bishop to "designate, if this has not already been done, one competent person who will be responsible for dealing with the media and who will answer all questions concerning sexual abuse or allegations of abuse in the diocese."[117] Somewhat paradoxically, this recommendation is intended to assist the Church in being "open" while "protecting the right of the accused to a fair trial; safeguarding the right of the victims to maximum privacy; [and] safeguarding the right of the state to initiate legal proceedings."[118] Further recommendations directed toward the bishops can be found in the "Responses" section of this chapter. Recommendations to those in charge of priestly formation can be found in the "Screening" section.

The final set of recommendations is directed to the CCCB. These outline proactive initiatives on a national level. Such actions include creating distressed youth telephone services and "working towards healing ... with the Native peoples following revelations concerning the former Indian residential schools."[119] Also called for is "immediate and continuing research in the social sciences regarding the complex reality of human sexuality (both heterosexual and homosexual orientations), the sexuality of celibates, and the issues linked to the deviant expression of sexuality."[120]

Following the publication of *FPtH*, more dioceses began to create protocols for sexual abuse complaints. For example, the Archdiocese of Edmonton published *Guidelines for Dealing with Cases of Sexual Abuse* in June 2000.[121] This protocol is divided into three sections. The first deals with adult complaints of abuse against adults. The second concerns complaints involving youth and children. The third specifically addresses complaints against priests, religious, and members of the pastoral team. The first two sections outline how to respond to any complaint, and the third section provides an addendum of additional guidelines when a complaint is made against Church employees. For example, if a priest is informed of child abuse by someone not involved with the Church, the priest would follow the guidelines for reporting and care found in section two. If a priest is informed of child abuse perpetrated by Church personnel, the priest would follow the guidelines for reporting and care given in sections two and three.

The first section identifies contexts in which sexual abuse can occur between adults. It makes specific note of contact that "is apparently consensual, but which involves a breach of the boundaries that exist in a relationship of trust," including the relationship that exists between a priest and parishioner.[122] There is no legal obligation on the part of the priest or other person who hears this complaint to report; however, this person may "wish to discuss the option of reporting the matter with the survivor, or the party making the complaint." The protocol provides for third-party complaints: "in some cases the person receiving the report will feel morally obliged to report the matter, especially if that seems to be the only way of preventing the re-occurrence."[123]

If the reported abuse involves a child, the Edmonton *Guidelines*, in accordance with the law, directs the person receiving the complaint to "report the allegations and the information on which it is based to a director of Child Welfare immediately, that is, on the same day as the determination that there are reasonable and probable grounds."[124] Again, although timeliness is stressed, it is only after a preliminary investigation that the complaint—if found to have substance—is reported to child welfare services. After this report has been made to a child welfare agency, a report is then to be made to archdiocesan authorities (or within the religious order if the allegation involves a religious). The *Guidelines* are clear that something more substantial than "suspicion or rumour" is required before a report becomes necessary.[125] Other such circumstances include cases where the abuse occurred in the past and there is "no prospect of it reoccurring in the future."[126] A risk assessment tool is included.

Other dioceses and archdioceses have procedures that also address many of the additional issues (to those identified in *FPtH*) raised in the Edmonton *Guidelines*. For example, the Archdiocese of Regina also makes distinctions between abuses against different age groups, and provides basic procedures for dealing with different reports, cases involving adults or children, and cases involving priests, parish ministers, or religious.[127]

In 1993, the Archdiocese of Ottawa produced a policy and protocol using *FPtH* as a guide.[128] For more detail on this 1993 protocol, see the "Investigative Procedures" and "Responses" sections of this chapter. The archbishop's delegate, in forming a response to a complaint, is to take "the recommendation of the Committee and, as directed by the Archbishop, do what is needed to remedy the situation."[129] This protocol was reviewed in 2001, with minimal updates.[130] In 2007 further revisions were underway.

In April 2002, the OCCB released a statement declaring that "all Ontario dioceses have policies and protocols in place for processing these cases of abuse in an open, fair and firm manner and in cooperation with civil authorities."[131] Across Canada, policies began to be revised and released publicly.

In May of that same year, the Bishop of Calgary discussed a policy similar to that in *FPtH* in his "Message."[132] In July 2002 Antigonish released a revised policy "regarding complaints of sexual misconduct made against clergy or anyone employed by the Diocese."[133] Again, this document follows the recommendations in *FPtH*. It does go into particular detail regarding expenses incurred during the process (see the "Responses" section of this chapter).

Changes in policy have begun to extend beyond responses to sexual misconduct complaints. In particular, screening policies have developed together with policies that are designed to proactively safeguard youth and children under the care of Church personnel (see the "Screening Policies" section in this chapter).

During this time there were relevant changes at the Vatican. In 2001, the Vatican released *Litterae motu proprio datae*, a document containing revised and new norms for addressing clerics' sexual abuse of minors. For example, a minor was defined as anyone under eighteen years old; the age had been increased from under sixteen. The limitation on reporting was also increased from five to ten years, with the ten years beginning only once the minor turned eighteen. (Further, in 2002 adaptations made to the 2001 norms allowed the bishop to waive this limitation.) Also, as of 2001 it was stated that only the Congregation for the Doctrine of the Faith can prosecute these cases.[134] The diocesan bishop is to conduct a preliminary investigation and then, if he decides the complaint has substance, he must forward the complaint and his analysis to the congregation.

The congregation can "(1) direct the diocese that sent the complaint to prosecute the case in its own or another diocese; (2) prosecute the complaint in its own tribunal; or (3) recommend an administrative dismissal from the clerical state."[135] If the first option is chosen, the diocesan policy is to be followed.

Secrecy is required once the ecclesial process of sending the complaint to the Congregation for the Doctrine of the Faith has begun; no one involved, including the complainant, can break this silence without the threat of excommunication by the bishop.[136]

From Pain to Hope: 2005 Review. Ten years after its initial release, the CCCB established a task force to review, assess, and propose revisions of *From Pain to Hope*, as necessary. The mandate of this task force was:

1. To review the document *From Pain to Hope* in the light of the experience of Canadian dioceses since its publication and in view of related worldwide developments,
2. To examine specific elements:
3. Creation of safe environments for pastoral work, especially with regard to the protection of children
4. Improvement of transparency at all levels
5. Establishment of accountability at all levels without reducing diocesan autonomy
6. To recommend changes to general policies and the development of resources, including measures needed for follow-up by the Conference.[137]

The primary resources for the review came from information gathered from experts in the field after ten years of experience with *FPtH*, as well as interviews and discussions with both complainants and those accused. In September 2005, the task force released its report.

The responses given by the complainants contacted were mixed; individuals were "pleased with the review process undertaken by the CCCB ... [however] their comments were generally critical of the management and orientation of the institutional Church in cases of sexual abuse by clergy, as well as with the way the Catholic Bishops of Canada had implemented the recommendations in *From Pain to Hope*."[138]

The complainants often indicated that they experienced little sensitivity. The review states that though "*From Pain to Hope* contains recommendations on care and attention for victims, their perception is that the Church's actions and the measures it implements are aimed more at preserving the financial and pastoral integrity of the institution, protecting priests, even known abusers, and the systematic challenging of victims, rather than their protection."[139]

Further, many complainants experienced isolation from the wider Church. It "was suggested that victims would be less mistrustful of the institutional Church if effective, publicly known measures for the prevention of sexual abuse of minors were fully implemented in the dioceses."[140] Such preventative measures, as articulated by complainants, included a commitment to never, under any circumstances, allow those who are found guilty to minister among children again.

Feedback included comments that "focused on the reliability of the implementation of its recommendations."[141] Further, there was a call for "the bishop to be responsible for his acts before the community and, when sexual abuse occurs by a member of his clergy, to acknowledge his responsibility as well as to express his remorse and his willingness to settle the situation in a pastoral manner." Overall, previous victims wanted more transparency and accountability:

> Victims were critical of the lack of information and the reluctance of the bishop to communicate, even regarding the general procedures or policies implemented to address cases of sexual abuse.... This lack of communication taints the credibility of the bishop and supports the perception that the Church has something to hide. Victims expressed the wish that information on existing sexual abuse concerns be made available: case statistics, implementation or preventive measures, and the corrective measures in place, as well as an evaluation of the effectiveness of these measures.[142]

The task force subsequently proposed "a mechanism to strengthen the application of the recommendations in the 1992 report and to ensure that all Catholic dioceses in Canada adopt measures and implement them effectively." Also it encouraged greater transparency on the part of the dioceses "so that bishops are accountable for their management of this issue."[143] It was recommended that "each bishop ... oblige himself not only to implement the mechanisms for the prevention and treatment of cases of sexual abuse in his diocese as described in the protocol, but also be accountable for his management by producing an annual report to his regional Episcopal assembly."[144] This report ideally would be made public through the regional assembly and the national body. Further, the task force boldly recommended that a record of the dioceses' compliance with the protocol be kept and made available publicly. Possibly it was surmised that this strategy would serve as a less overt and therefore less controversial means of ensuring bishops' compliance without actually dictating the policy.

The task force also declared a strong commitment to the protection of children as the first priority regardless of potential harm to the Church's image and finances, stating that "protecting clergy and diocesan employees, preserving the integrity of the institutional Church, economic and legal issues related to sexual abuse cases, and the shame and general discomfort surrounding these acts must not relegate the protection and safety of children to a position of secondary importance."[145] It is indeed telling that this statement needed to be made.

The report carries with it a draft series of protocols that reiterate and supplement many of the recommendations put forward in *FPtH*.[146] Structurally, the bishop is advised to appoint a delegate and create an advisory committee to receive all reports of sexual abuse. The committee is also to be responsible for developing and/or updating diocesan protocols. These recommendations stipulate that the diocesan protocol be communicated widely and made "available to the faithful of the diocese and the general public, whether by brochure or on the diocesan website if one exists."[147] The protocols prioritize care of the vulnerable. For example, it is suggested strongly that each diocese designate a particular person responsible for the care of victims. This person would offer support and resources, including access to pastoral counselling and therapy.

Although most of the procedures for responding to complaints have remained the same, the document makes a few significant additions and changes to *FPtH*, which are described in the "Responses" and "Screening" sections in this chapter.

This review also recommends that this protocol be updated at least once every four years, by consulting feedback submitted in bi-annual reports by the bishops to their respective regional assemblies (such as the OCCB), which would also make reports to the CCCB every four years.[148]

Orientations: 2007. The CCCB produced *Orientations* in response to the task force's recommendations. While few, the differences between the two documents are significant. First, *Orientations* emphasizes and protects the autonomy and authority of the diocesan bishops. Further, *Orientations* does not include a recommendation that any respondent found culpable to be prohibited from ever returning to ministry. *Orientations* underlines a commitment to openness and care for affected communities.[149]

Released in October 2007, *Orientations* includes a number of the task force's recommendations and mostly adheres to *FPtH*. Transparency and public accountability are priorities. For example, policies are to be available to the public through websites, brochures, and other media. Information on specific cases is to be released to the relevant communities and parishes, withholding only personal information in accordance with legal requirements.[150] This effort toward greater transparency is understood as part of appropriate care extended to parishes in which a complaint of child sexual abuse by a priest has been made. Accountability to the parish community is promoted. In an open and honest environment, the parish may find the healing it needs, and it may be better equipped to support the healing of victims/survivors.

This effort toward accountability, however, falls short of the *Report*'s proposed measures. Specifically, *Orientations* did not include the task force's proposal that the bishops report to the CCCB regarding the diocesan's relationship to *FPtH*. As a result, bishops can choose to report or not. Those bishops who choose not to implement a diocesan protocol do not need to report this or explain it to the CCCB.

The *Report* makes one further recommendation concerning accountability not included in *Orientations*. It proposed the compilation and publication of statistics regarding child sexual abuse complaints and findings.[151] Without such information, it is more difficult to establish transparency, accountability, and more effective policy responses to broader trends and themes.

Orientations does not embrace the conviction expressed in the *Report* that offenders must be prohibited from returning to ministry. The reviewers who authored the *Report* had recommended that the bishop prohibit "a priest who has been convicted of sexual abuse of a minor, and who has been either sentenced or received a suspended sentence, from exercising any public ministry, that is any pastoral charge or activity which is exercised in the presence of the members of the community."[152] The authors of *Orientations* delineate a range of consequences if one is found culpable of abuse that allow for the possibility of a return to ministry; in the section on "Canonical Procedures," it states that "a temporary or permanent suspension of the exercise of ministry, or even a request for laicization" may be consequences imposed on the offender.[153]

Orientations addresses the themes of systemic justice, mission, forgiveness, and public accountability in ways that earlier policies did not. Of particular importance is the introduction of more preventative measures. This is at least partially a response to feedback gathered from victims/survivors as part of the writing of the *Report*.[154] Consistent with the task force's recommendations, *Orientations* puts a strong emphasis on establishing a program of prevention of sexual abuse, including training on sexual abuse and screening all those who work with children.[155]

Investigative Procedures Regarding Complaints

FPtH includes an investigative step and urges all dioceses and archdioceses to follow accordingly. The Archdiocese of Ottawa's policy begins the investigative process with the archbishop appointing a delegate to "secure as much information about the matter as possible" within the first twenty-four hours.[156] The delegate is to follow secular law and report any complaints found to have substance, and keep the archbishop informed regarding all complaints. If an active religious is accused, the delegate is to seek the assistance of the superior, or hand the matter over to the superior. If the religious works under the archdiocese, the archbishop is to be involved. If not, the complaint is to be referred to the religious's superior. Secular proceedings are not to be interfered with: "a canonical inquiry, if desired by the Archbishop, will begin only after criminal proceedings, and if any, civil proceedings, have been concluded."[157]

The Edmonton *Guidelines* are similar to that of the above protocol in that investigations are to be conducted by a delegate of the archbishop, who is generally the chancellor.[158] Meetings are held with the complainant and with the alleged perpetrator. The protocol stipulates that during this initial meeting, the alleged perpetrator "should not be permitted to resign or make other final decisions about his ministry."[159]

Throughout this investigation those involved are encouraged to "cooperate with civil authorities carrying our statutory responsibilities."[160] The delegate is to make an assessment based on several factors, including interviews "with the person or persons making the allegation, and with any other person as may seem appropriate."[161] After conducting the interviews and assessing all the relevant material, the delegate is to write the assessment and arrive at a recommendation to the Advisory Committee, which will make the final decision regarding the guilt or innocence of the accused.[162]

Should the alleged perpetrator be a member of a religious community, "the Archbishop's Delegate will refer it immediately to the competent Superior." The superior is then given three options: "(a) consent to the application of the Procedure in respect of the allegation; (b) taking the place of the Archbishop's Delegate, utilize the Procedure; or (c) with the approval of the Archbishop, invoke the Religious community's own procedure for dealing with such matters."[163]

Complaints Regarding People Who Are Not Church Personnel and Complaints Regarding People Who Are Church Officials and/or Employees

Policy has been developed specific to complaints of sexual abuse committed by priests, deacons, lay personnel, and religious. In the Archdiocese of Edmonton, for example, the special procedures in the third portion of the *Guidelines* address "offence[s] alleged to have been committed by a person over whom the Archbishop has jurisdiction."[164] The Edmonton protocol is similar to that proposed in *FPtH*.

A complaint can be made by anyone who experiences sexual abuse by Church officials, employees, or lay members in positions of trust, such as Sunday school teachers and youth leaders; complaints can pertain to current or historical sexual abuse, particularly if the alleged perpetrator continues to be in a position of trust with children and/or youth.

Should a religious be accused of abuse, responsibility to investigate falls to the superior of that order, not to the diocesan bishop. Subsequent to the investigative step, when the accused is a priest or religious, canonical procedures must be followed. If the alleged perpetrator is deemed to be even partly responsible, then one of the following courses must be requested by the respondent: "to submit the allegation to an Arbitral Tribunal appointed by the Archbishop for adjudication; to resign; to retire; or to petition for a rescript from the Apostolic See returning him to the lay state."[165] Should the request of the respondent be considered inappropriate, a judicial vicar may be brought in from outside the archdiocese "to determine whether it is appropriate to recommend that a canonical penal trial be commenced."[166]

Third-Party Complaints

Third-party complaints are received in the RCC, although responding to them can be very problematic.[167] The Archdiocese of Edmonton writes in its *Guidelines* that should the report be made by someone other than the survivor, "the person receiving the report can discreetly invite the alleged survivor to discuss the matter."[168] In all protocols reviewed for this study, contacting the alleged victim is permitted and encouraged as part of the investigation. Presumably, the victim may choose to participate or not. Of course, without the victim's direct story, it is more difficult for the investigator and advisory committee to reach an informed conclusion.

In the Archdiocese of Toronto, while third-party complaints are addressed, anonymous complaints are not, and measures are taken to encourage those who make complaints to do so formally in person. There was no specific mention of anonymous complaints in any of the other diocesan policies reviewed at the time of this research.

A serious issue regarding third-party complaints concerns priests who may learn of sexual abuse via the confessional. The confidentiality (seal) of the confessional is understood as unbreakable; "it is absolutely forbidden for a confessor to betray in any way a penitent in words or in any manner and for any reason."[169] As stated in the Edmonton *Guidelines*, "the confessional seal is inviolable despite the requirements of the civil law … although the penitent should be encouraged to make disclosure outside the confessional."[170]

For this reason neither the bishop nor any other priest involved in an investigation is to hear the confession of the accused. For example, the Regina *Guidelines* state that "care must be taken not to give unqualified undertakings of confidentiality to persons who want to discuss undefined 'problems'" in the confessional.[171]

The punishment for breaking the sacramental seal is excommunication.[172] The reason for this harsh consequence is twofold. The first concerns the potential consequences to confessors. Regarding perpetrators, the argument, firstly, is that if one is penitent, then presumably one is aware of the moral implications of one's actions, and may be more open to seeking accountability and stopping the abusive behaviour. In the case of an abuser's confession, often the confessor is seeking help and can be encouraged to seek additional assistance beyond the confessional. Furthermore, if the confidentiality of the sacrament is broken, then people may choose to no longer use the confessional to admit to their abusive behaviour without this guarantee. Secondly, the Gruenky case set the legal precedent that disclosure of what was said in the confessional is not required.[173]

If a perpetrator of child sexual abuse tells someone about his or her abusive behaviour, that person is compelled legally and morally to lodge a third-party complaint to the appropriate authorities if the offender will not do so. The Archdiocese of Edmonton states in its *Guidelines*:

If no child is in immediate danger, it is permissible to give the offender a chance to turn himself or herself in to the civil authorities. The person receiving the information should advise the offender of the recipient's obligation to report, and should give the offender reasonable time (usually three business days) to consult a lawyer and report to the authorities. At the expiration of the time given, the person who received the report from the offender must make an independent report to the civil authorities; unless the information was received in a sacramental forum.[174]

Responses to Involved People

Responses incorporated in diocesan policies include care as well as disciplinary actions when appropriate. The provision of appropriate pastoral care is included in the bishop's responsibilities in *FPtH*. The bishop is encouraged to "provide a sympathetic hearing within the church to each victim of sexual abuse committed by a priest or a religious." Further, the formation of a multidisciplinary committee to provide care for the complainant is recommended before the allegations are investigated and assessed.[175] The document states that victims/survivors should receive "the services of qualified resource persons who can provide the pastoral support wanted, counseling and if necessary, therapy" following the pronouncement of sentence against a priest for sexual abuse.[176] The Edmonton *Guidelines* (2000) addresses the provision of pastoral care by encouraging the person receiving the complaint: "(a) to counsel the survivor and/or affected parties; (b) where appropriate, to counsel the offender; (c) to assist the survivor in withdrawing from a situation that leaves him or her vulnerable to further abuse; [and] (d) to refer the survivor to the Sexual Abuse Survivors Assistance Committee, Catholic Social Services or another professional or social agency."[177]

Any pastoral assistance offered through the Church, however, must receive "proper authorization … from police or judicial authorities, in order to avoid unwarranted interference"; secular proceedings are to be respected and not hindered. The provision of pastoral care may also be limited by the terms of insurance company contracts.[178] Moreover, dioceses encourage their priests to be aware of their own limitations when providing care for those who have been abused. The Archdiocese of Toronto advises that "if it is going to take more than three sessions, then you are not competent," as long-term therapy requires more skills than possessed by most priests.[179]

Recommendation 19 in *FPtH* names the parish community as one of the victims of child sexual abuse, and encourages pastoral support for the community as well as fellow priests of the accused. However, no concrete plan or directives are presented. Pastoral care is provided for the accused throughout the process and afterwards.[180]

In all dioceses and archdioceses, an accused priest or other paid personnel may be placed on leave with full salary and benefits, in accordance with the law, during the proceedings because of possible risk to involved parties. Some dioceses and archdiocese require this leave, giving priority to possible safety concerns; the Archdiocese of Ottawa, for example, states that administrative leave "will be granted immediately to anyone who stands accused of sexual abuse."[181]

In addition to mandatory or permitted leave, an accused priest or religious may face other consequences for the duration of the proceedings. The Edmonton *Guidelines*, for example, provide recommendations that the advisory committee could make to the archbishop in section III.36. These include providing an immediate leave of absence, restricting contact with vulnerable parties, and assigning residence.

For priests or religious, a legal finding of guilt could result in: voluntary laicization, retirement, canonical penal proceedings, or formal prohibition of exercising any pastoral ministry while earning their living.[182] In addition, any convicted priest "should be asked to contribute as much as possible … towards paying the expenses incurred because of his conduct," and may be required to repay the diocese for legal counsel following a guilty verdict.[183] Other consequences could occur following a guilty verdict or an out-of-court settlement. For example, in the Diocese of London in March 2004, "Bishop Fabbro agree[d] to dispense with the 'confidentiality clause' in legal settlements for all persons who request it,"[184] to aid in the victims' healing. This order allowed anyone who had been bound by such a clause in cases settled out of court to speak publicly. The first person to gain this release stated that "the gag order prevented her from achieving closure and healing, keeping her a victim of abuse."[185]

Regarding the possibility of an offending priest being "reintegrated" into the ministry, the dioceses were encouraged to enter into a contract with a clinic that allows for the sharing of "professional information" acquired during treatment so that professional therapeutic assessments can be part of the decision-making process.[186] The Archdiocese of Edmonton, for example, in the *Guidelines* (III.38), identifies relevant factors when assessing "the re-employment of lay personnel or the return of a priest or Religious to the ministry, either conditionally or unconditionally":

- the nature of the offence;
- the outcome of any program of therapy, and the recommendations of theprofessional therapists;
- the risk of re-offending, and the protection of the public;
- the wishes of the survivor, the parish, the priest or employee, the Senate of Priests, and the Catholic Community;
- the effect of re-employment or return of the priest on the Church, and on Catholic institutions; [and]
- all other relevant considerations.

The original *FPtH* encourages dioceses to avoid "extreme positions for or against re-entry."[187] Of greatest concern is the safety of children.[188] Thus, if reintegration is recommended, ongoing monitoring is required. Further, "before appointing a priest who has been reintegrated into the pastoral ministry, ... the receiving parish community [must be told of the priest's history and must agree to] ... support the initiative of this appointment."[189]

The possible reappointment of an offending priest to public ministry has been very contentious. The authors of the 2005 Review were clear than an offending priest should never be reappointed. The authors of *Orientations* (2007) disagreed. However, possible legal consequences have often discouraged reappointment.

Legally, not only is the convicted abuser responsible for his or her actions, so too is the diocese. For example, the Diocese of St. George's was forced to seek bankruptcy protection following abuse lawsuits after the Supreme Court of Canada "assigned blame to the Episcopal Corporation of St. George's [not the Roman Catholic Church] ... ruling that it is legally liable."[190] The successful argument made by the Roman Catholic Church was that "there is no foreign or corporate entity known as the 'Roman Catholic Church.'"[191] Rather, there are only individual dioceses and archdioceses. The Roman Catholic Church in Canada, as a whole, thus officially became an entity that cannot be sued; only individual dioceses or archdioceses can be sued.

Screening Policies and/or Mandatory Education for Church Volunteers, Employees, and/or Officials

Regarding the preparation of its clergy, the RCC has been very intentional. *FPtH* includes recommendations regarding "some of the conditions needed for the psycho-affective development of the candidate to the priesthood in order to foster the interiorization of his vocation, the strengthening of his commitment, and the integration of his vocation as priest."[192] Priests must have a well-developed self-awareness and the ability to seek help when needed, particularly in times of stress:

> In times of personal crisis, certain priests may feel overwhelmed by the urge to act out their sexual fantasies. Church authorities must be able to listen to their problems *before* abuse actually occurs, and provide a pastoral and clinical response.[193]

Accordingly, it is recommended that both a suitable mentor and an appropriate counsellor be found for each candidate.[194] Further, this formation process should involve additional people with a variety of expertise and experience, and must include women.[195] Early in the process, a psychological assessment of each candidate is strongly advised to provide part of the foundation necessary for such work.[196]

Many of the initial recommendations made in this section address the development and support of a candidate's strengths, including Recommendation 26, which encourages those responsible for priestly formation to "implement a selection process for candidates which focuses more on the candidate's personal fundamental strengths, rather than on factors of vulnerability, without however disregarding the latter."[197] Further, it is suggested that many of these recommendations can be addressed through a clinical pastoral education unit, which most bishops require of their priests and seminarians.

Mandatory education regarding family and sexual violence is also strongly recommended. The importance of familiarity with provincial legislation regarding the reporting of child abuse is underscored. More generally, education is needed to communicate and explain the reality of child sexual abuse in the Church and to examine possible ways to eradicate such violence.

The next recommendations are directed at those responsible for priests in each diocese and are concerned with such matters as the integration of newly ordained priests, the importance of continuing education, and the preparation of "policies regarding the need for periodic up-dating, renewal and specialized training."[198]

In addition to priestly formation, the task force for reviewing *FPtH* attended to proactive diocesan measures, advising preventative education, screening programs, and risk-management steps for anyone working with children. Further, acknowledging children's agency, the authors suggested that "an information program on sexual abuse [be] given to all children receiving pastoral services."[199]

In 1999, a pivotal document entitled *Screening in Faith* was published as the outcome of work funded by the Ontario Minister of Citizenship, Culture, and Recreation, and undertaken by Volunteer Canada, under the auspices of the Ontario Screening Initiative (OSI).[200] The initiative was carried out "by a consortium of provincial umbrella organisations," including "faith, community support sport, rural, and recreations sectors ... to increase the well-being of children and other vulnerable people through the introduction of screening practices."[201] Funded by the Ontario government and managed by Volunteer Canada, a consortium of faith partners—including the Ontario Conference of Catholic Bishops, the Anglican Synod of the Ecclesiastical Province of Ontario, the United Church of Canada, and the Canadian Unitarian Council—each sent one member to the consortium gathering, where "screening experience" was shared.[202] The Catholic contingent came out of the OSI meeting committed to "introducing the concept of screening to dioceses and parishes."[203]

Dioceses in Ontario began to respond and early screening policies were established in some dioceses, including Hearst. The Diocese of Hearst created a protocol, approved in December 2000, based on *Screening in Faith*. A risk assessment is the first step and is based on relevant factors, including the "vulnerability of the person or persons being served—children, teens, mentally or physically challenged, and the elderly—all these being the most vulnerable."[204] Other factors included the "'perceived authority' of the person delivering the service," the setting in which the services are to take place, the intimacy and "intensity of the relationship," and the need for supervision.[205]

Interviews are to be given to all applicants for such positions, with the discussion attending to the assessed level of risk. For high-risk positions, multiple interviewers are to be involved.[206] References cannot include an applicant's family members, and must "confirm the background, gifts, talents and skill of the applicant and ... provide an outside opinion as to the suitability of the person for the ministry."[207] The policy recommends reference checks for people applying for any position, including volunteer positions. For high-risk positions, the policy mandates a police record check.[208]

Once the position has been filled, the next step is for "orientation to the ministry ... [to be] provided along with guidelines for working within the volunteer ministry or paid position."[209] Appropriate supervision and feedback are required.[210] The final recommendation of the policy is for supervisors to follow up, ensuring satisfaction on the part of the volunteer or paid employee, as well as making random spot checks.

If a position is assessed as high risk, the diocese is advised to question the position and related activity; for example, a "parish may decide an overnight camping trip with altar services is an activity with unacceptable risks."[211] The level of risk should be minimized.

In February 2001, the OCCB released its *Provincial Guidelines for Development of Diocesan Policies on Screening*, pursuant to the *Screening in Faith* protocol. The OCCB outlines the same ten steps provided by *Screening in Faith* in its recommendations.[212] Dioceses across Ontario developed their own policies, usually building on *Screening in Faith*. For example, the Diocese of Thunder Bay created a policy and added case illustrations of how to lessen risk in different situations: in Sunday School "the rooms must have doors with windows so that anyone at any given time may be able to look from outside without being noticed."[213]

The Archdiocese of Toronto created a manual entitled *Strengthening the Caring Community: Parish Volunteer Screening Program*. Within this manual there are guidelines for volunteers that "are intended to provide a general overview of how ministry interaction should incur."[214] Furthermore, it includes a detailed section specific to children. These guidelines include such rules as "adults who form a relationship with children through our faith community's activities should not seek out opportunities to spend time with the child 'off site.' ... If help with toileting is required permission must be given by the parent or guardian before toileting or changing help is given."[215]

The manual provides a protocol for reporting abuse and misconduct by or toward a volunteer. Concerning suspected abuse of children under sixteen, the first step is to contact the Children's Aid Society (CAS). The person who suspects abuse is "not to pass the information to the Pastor with the expectation that he will report it." Rather, once CAS has been informed, the pastor is to be contacted.

The pastor will then "notify the volunteer that she/he is to immediately withdraw from her/his ministry until further notice."[216] It is then the pastor's responsibility to notify authorities within the Church, in this case the manager of human resources at the Catholic Pastoral Centre. For people above the age of sixteen, the pastor is to be informed first. Subsequently, he will notify the manager.[217]

The Diocese of Hamilton requires that the pastor of each parish form a screening committee that comprises at least two members. The responsibilities of this committee include: "reviewing position descriptions, updating volunteer lists from the ministry leaders, and updating the Offence Declarations. The screening committees are also responsible to help ministry leaders implement the ongoing screening measures."[218]

The Diocese of Prince Albert has created a policy for working with young people. This includes a set of guidelines addressing intimacy, drugs and alcohol, and driving standards. The policy sets out number ratios for supervision and age, including a requirement that at "least two qualified adults ... be present on all trips and outings. If both male and female youth are present, both male and female adult leadership is required."[219] Further, standards for training and orientation for both youth ministry and catechetics are outlined.

Similarly, the Diocese of Calgary has created a code of conduct that addresses issues such as confidentiality and conflicts of interest, as well as sexual conduct and conduct with youth.[220] This code requires that "Priests, Deacons and Religious Brothers and Sisters ... review and know the contents of the child abuse regulations and reporting requirements for the Province of Alberta."[221] When working alone with youth, it encourages those involved to "be aware of their own and others' vulnerability."[222]

The 1999 *Screening in Faith* document served as a much needed starting point for the faith communities represented in its planning consortium. Since the release and endorsement of this document, many dioceses have either adopted it or built upon it to serve the particularities of their context.

Chapter Summary

In the late 1980s Father Hickey and his abuses became well publicized; child sexual abuse by priests had made the headlines. In 1987, based largely on Father Doyle's work, a protocol was designed by the CCCB and recommended for use by the dioceses. At the time of the writing of this book, *From Pain to Hope* remains the most significant policy document regarding child sexual abuse in the Roman Catholic Church in Canada. Created in 1992 and significantly updated since, this has been the guiding document for the Church. Transparency and accountability have been governing principles for both the task force and the authors of *Orientations*, released in 2007. In addition to *From Pain to Hope*, the 1983 *Code of Canon Law*, the 2001 (and adaptations of 2002) norms, and other laws as implemented by the respective bishops for their dioceses, are applicable in terms of protocols and legislation for complaints of child sexual abuse in the Roman Catholic Church in Canada.

The structure of the Roman Catholic Church is such that individual dioceses and archdioceses are governed by their own policies. Respective bishops and archbishops make autonomous decisions regarding these policies. Many dioceses and archdioceses have chosen to follow the CCCB's recommendation and use *From Pain to Hope* as their base.

Not surprisingly, the focus of the Roman Catholic Church's sexual abuse policies has been on children as potential victims and priests as potential perpetrators. This is not so for other religious institutions in Canada that established policies at about the same time; the focus of the Anglican and United Churches, for example, has been on adults, particularly adult women, as potential victims and clergy as potential perpetrators. Nonetheless, there is more direct attention given to people besides clergy who are in positions of authority and trust in Anglican and United Church policies than there is in most Roman Catholic policies. Although the focus is undeniably on priests, complaints against anyone in a position of trust in the Roman Catholic Church can be lodged within the purview of all (arch)diocesan policies examined for this study.

A few significant issues have emerged from the Roman Catholic Church's experiences with its sexual abuse policies. First, moral and legal conflicts are potential consequences of breaking the seal (i.e., confidentiality) of the confessional. A report of child sexual abuse made in the confessional cannot be disclosed against the confessor's will. Excommunication is the consequence for any priest breaking the seal.

Second, although third-party complaints are received, they are problematic if they cannot be corroborated by the victim; usually the victim's story is essential to an investigation and potential finding of guilt.

Third, proactive measures, including training candidates for the priesthood, are of significant concern in many screening policies and other relevant documents. One of the issues generating concern or sometimes fascination is priestly celibacy. Although, as the Winter Commission found, there is no clear "direct correlation ... [and] the incidence of sexual abuse of children among celibate clergy is no different from that among other groups within the general population," it is an issue that directs attention to the importance of addressing human sexuality openly within the Church and among the Church's leadership.[223]

Fourth, much rests on the effectiveness of a particular bishop or archbishop. The RCC has opted to place a priority on the autonomy and power of the bishop or archbishop and his wisdom regarding the value of following *FPtH* and its revisions approved by the CCCB. This decision has meant that complainants and those accused cannot expect uniform treatment among the (arch)dioceses.

Lastly, effective after care of parishes that have been subject to child sexual abuse by a person in authority remains a concern. Some (arch)dioceses are more attentive to this than others. Certainly most of these issues are also relevant to other religious institutions examined in this study; these issues are not peculiar to the Roman Catholic Church. Much work has been done and, of course, more remains.

Chapter 3

The United Church of Canada

THE UNITED CHURCH OF CANADA, unlike the other institutions examined in this report, has developed a binding policy across the Church. Similar to the Roman Catholic and Anglican Churches, it was not until the early 1990s that the United Church of Canada developed a policy for addressing internal complaints of child sexual abuse.[1]

Church Structure and Description of the Context

The United Church of Canada (UCC) has a conciliar structure. Individual churches are grouped into pastoral charges. A pastoral charge may have one or more churches in it. Most urban charges have one church, whereas rural pastoral charges are often "multi-point," meaning that they contain more than one church. Pastoral charges are grouped into presbyteries. There are ninety-one presbyteries in the UCC. Presbyteries are organized into conferences of which there are thirteen. General Council is the church's highest court. The official United Church web page, at the time of the writing of this book, describes General Council as follows:

> The church's highest legislative court. Ordained, commissioned, and lay commissioners are elected by the Conferences and meet every three years to set church policy. An Executive and Sub-Executive govern between meetings of the council. Policy is implemented through four permanent committees of the General Council and a staff group organized into ten working units. There are also about 100 committees and task groups, composed of voting members from across the country and General Council staff as corresponding members.[2]

The moderator of the UCC is the elected (by General Council) head of the Church in a figurative sense. He or she has no voting or policy-making power (except in the case of a tie), but can hold a great deal of influential power. There are close to 3 million members and adherents worshiping in approximately 3,362 congregations. Care is provided to some 443,372 Canadian households.[3]

It was not until the 1960s that the United Church turned critical attention to its own identity as a fallible "family" that not only tried to be the nation's conscience but also stood inside the nation and, as such, was vulnerable to the same flaws and abuses of power as was the rest of Canada. Before the 1960s, on an official level, there was no indication that the UCC recognized that some of its members, volunteers, or ordered ministers might abuse children. However, the UCC took a more progressive stance on some issues related to human sexuality than did other mainline religious institutions.

Perhaps most notably, in 1932 and 1936 the UCC advocated for the legalization and availability of birth control. Although the primary purpose of marriage at that time continued to be seen as procreation, the UCC argued that there were some conditions that warranted the use of birth control, including the possibility that a child would not be cared for adequately.[4] Accordingly, although the 1932 report entitled *The Meaning and Responsibilities of Christian Marriage* contended that the "primary function of marriage ... was the rearing of children and the protection of the mother during the period of infancy," in the context of a persistent economic Depression, in 1936 the UCC argued for the availability and use of contraception in 1936, contending that contraception could strengthen what was often a severely stressed family life.[5] Thus, the strengthening and maintenance of intact nuclear families was valued over moral concerns about contraception.

Underlying this moral weighing was the theological conviction that the nuclear family was necessary to survival and salvation; as the Board of Evangelism and Social Service later noted, "As fares the family so fares the nation and her citizens overseas and at home."[6] The Christian family, as defined by the 1932 report, consisted of two parents—a woman and a man—and their children. The wife was expected to be the domestic caregiver, while the husband was to provide economically for his family. This normative definition placed the traditional family beyond scrutiny so long as these prescribed gender roles were reasonably well followed. The preservation of this traditional nuclear family, during these early years of the UCC, took precedence over the well-being of individual members largely due to a glorification of the assumed goodness of this so-called private realm: "It was not so much that the maintenance of the nuclear family unit was valued above the well-being of individual family members, but that the very question of the well-being of individual family members, within an intact nuclear family, was posed rarely."[7]

Another window into the UCC's early approach to children and abuse is its participation in the work and leadership of "redemptive homes." The Methodist Church began this work in 1910 with the purpose of rescuing young women and girls who had "gone astray."[8] These wayward young females were defined as such usually because they were unmarried, pregnant, and thus in need of not only shelter and food but, it was judged, a moral education. Until 1935 there were eight redemptive homes. The "inmates," as they were called, were "considered to be 'fallen' by virtue of the fact that they were in a Rescue Home.[9] The practices of rescue work continued to treat all women in rescue homes as requiring conversion and reform, regardless of their guilt or innocence."[10] Clearly, pregnancy when unmarried was perceived as a sexual and therefore moral sin regardless of age or consent; the act of sex outside of marriage was sinful by definition for both people involved, even if one was very young and/ or was forced. Although the work of these rescue homes was informed by the assumptions and understandings of fallen-ness and sexual sin, care was provided to young women who were often socially outcast and without resources. The work of rescue homes continued into the 1960s.

Approach to Child Sexual Abuse, Including Relevant Statements, Policies, and Practices: 1960–80

During these years, the UCC developed a greater critical awareness regarding both the nuclear family and the UCC family. The deepening of this awareness was necessary to the subsequent recognition of child sexual abuse within the Church. Part of this shift included the insistence that mutual consent was a necessary moral condition of "sexual union" within marriage and could not be assumed simply because the sex occurred within a marital relationship.[11]

Questions regarding human sexuality continued to gain volume within the UCC. In response, the 25th General Council (1972) affirmed the need for further study and education regarding human sexuality and mandated the Executive of General Council to appoint a committee to explore this issue.[12] Indicative of an increasing shift away from a primarily act-centred sexual ethic toward a primarily relational sexual ethic, this committee approached human sexuality as "interpersonal rather than merely technological or physiological."[13]

The 28th General Council (1980) approved the report on *Contraception and Abortion*, which included a similar understanding of sexuality and linked this to a need to educate children accordingly: "We call on all persons to appreciate their own sexuality primarily in terms of personal relationships and only secondarily in terms of physiology, programs, techniques and services; and charge parents, educators and churches to represent adequately sexuality as intimate, awesome and holy.... We call on all parents to accept the responsibility to discuss sexual attitudes and information with their children as frankly and as fully as necessary, from the time children begin to ask such questions or need such enlightenment."[14] This position was a significant move away from a primarily act-centred sexual ethic that focused on the moral rightness or wrongness of particular sexual acts toward a primarily relational sexual ethic that considered the whole person. This committee was the first in a series of UCC committees and task groups on human sexuality in the 1980s.

This increased attention to sexuality reflected a growing willingness to address sexuality in the Church. Increasingly, the UCC raised concerns regarding the quality of the relationship within which sexual expressions occur. This slow breaking of silence, combined with a new questioning of the nuclear and

Church families as holding the potential for both harm and good, eventually contributed to the naming of child sexual abuse within both the family and the Church.

By the late 1970s, at an official level the UCC began to recognize some forms of sexual abuse, including pornography and sexual harassment. By the late 1970s the UCC was moving to condemn pornography not primarily because it exerted an unhealthy influence but because much of it was abusive and hateful toward women and children.[15] Earlier, in keeping with a primarily act-centred sexual ethic, the Board of Evangelism and Social Services expressed concern regarding the moral "challenge" to the family and nation posed by "printed and photographic material and movies of the baser sort."[16] At that point in time there was little recognition of pornography's systemic roots and, therefore, no explicit connection drawn between child pornography and child sexual abuse. However, the meaning of sin as related to sexuality was shifting; reports to General Councils in the late 1970s and 1980s defined pornography as sinful on the basis that it is "degrading, abusive and/or violent" to the human person and to women and children in particular.[17] This was a change from earlier reports that understood sexual sin as sexual acts outside of marriage and/or not directed toward the deepening of a marriage union, instead of focusing on the harm done to sexually violated people. This shift helped pave the way to a clearer recognition of child sexual abuse both outside and within the Church as the 1980s unfolded.

Approach to Child Sexual Abuse, Including Relevant Statements, Policies, and Practices: 1981–92

In the UCC, the 1980s began with attention to children and also to sexuality and abuse, although at the beginning of the 1980s the topics were not linked explicitly. By the end of the 1980s child sexual abuse had been named at an official level, but policy and procedures regarding complaints within the Church were not implemented until 1992.

Two significant reports on human sexuality were received by General Council in the first half of the 1980s: *In God's Image … Male & Female* (1980) and *Gift, Dilemma, and Promise* (1984), with the latter's "affirmations" officially endorsed by the Church. Although both reports critiqued the "enshrinement of the nuclear family,"[18] there was very little examination of sexual abuse aside from a general condemnation: "We affirm the church's call to proclaim the worth of human sexuality and to speak out concerning the abuses of human sexuality … [and] We affirm that the church is called to initiate and support research and educational programs to increase our understanding of the causes of exploitative sexual behaviour and other destructive expressions of sexuality."[19] There was no specific reference to the sexual abuse of children.

Pornography continued to gain the most attention in the early 1980s of any form of abuse. The 1980 General Council, in response to a petition from Alberta

Conference, recommended that "in any further work on the issue of human sexuality, ... sexploitation (sex and violence) be a matter of serious concern for both the Division of Mission in Canada, and the Division of Communication."[20]

In 1983, in response to grassroots concerns such as these, the Division of Mission in Canada established the Task Force on Pornography. The task force produced a report and an educational kit on pornography in 1984.[21] General Council received and supported the report, endorsed the recommendations, and requested the widespread distribution of the kit. The report is important to this book for two reasons: it defined pornography in relation to systemic marginalization and as violence, not sex. The authors were clear that pornography "is about injustice toward women and children" and it is connected to the systemic oppression of women and children.[22] The main criteria that the task force relied on to inform this ethical analysis were their interpretations of the teachings of Jesus and of human experience, particularly experiences of suffering.

Further, the authors claimed that the perpetrator of sexual violence that was linked to pornography was almost without exception male, and the victim was almost always a woman or a child.[23] Building on these claims, the authors suggested that the central ethical question was this: "Is the right of male gratification more important than the rights of women and children?"[24] The *Pornography Kit* became one of the first resources available that examined pornography in a theological context. The task force disbanded after the kit was produced, and the United Church's Division of Mission in Canada (DMC) established an ad-hoc committee on pornography to continue this work. In subsequent years, the General Council continued to receive and respond to petitions regarding pornography.[25]

In addition to pornography, sexual harassment was identified by the mid-1980s as a form of sexual abuse that needed a response from the Church. In 1986, as a result of this concern, General Council approved a policy statement on sexual harassment as proposed by the Women in Ministry Committee (WIM) in consultation with the Standing Committee on Sexism. The theological statement approved by the Executive reads in part:

> Sexual harassment is a sin. We believe that women and men are equal before God and in creation. Sexual harassment is a violation of the integrity of persons based on unequal power relationships. Sexual harassment degrades persons and does not allow their gifts of creativity and wholeness to be used in the Church. Jesus emphasizes mutuality and respect in relationships. To harass is to misuse power and to distort relationships. It leads to alienation and distrust.[26]

WIM explained the importance of the power dynamics in sexual harassment cases: sexual harassment involves the "exploitation of a power relationship"; it is not "an exclusively sexual issue." Sexual harassment was defined to include anything from "verbal innuendo and subtle suggestions to overt demands and physical abuse." Thus, this type of sexual violence was defined primarily as an abuse of power. The adopted "principles and assumptions" were as follows:

- Sexual harassment is unacceptable within The United Church of Canada;
- All complaints of sexual harassment need to be taken seriously;
- The intent of these policies and procedures is to stop the violations of personhood resulting from sexual harassment and to attempt to heal the personal and corporate frailty that we share with all humanity;
- All policies and procedures need to minimize further distress for the complainant;
- Confidentiality needs to be assured;
- Each stage in dealing with a case of harassment needs to involve as few people as possible;
- Everyone dealing with a case should be familiar with the issues involved in sexual harassment;
- At any stage prior to a decision to proceed with a Formal Hearing, the complainant has the right to decide not to proceed with the case;
- Every effort needs to be made to stop the harassment without Formal Hearing procedures.[27]

With the acceptance and implementation of this policy, the UCC took a strong stand against sexual harassment and acknowledged that such harassment occurred both in society and in the Church. This was the first policy statement and set of procedures established by the UCC regarding sexual abuse complaints within the Church.

Sexuality was not the only relevant topic to be addressed in new depth during this decade; children and the family, among other issues, were also the focus of new concerns. These new concerns began with a reconsideration of the role and well-being of children.[28] This attention contributed to a newfound awareness, at an official level, regarding child abuse, including sexual abuse. For example, the United Church's Division of Mission in Canada (DMC) published a series of pamphlets, beginning in February 1985, regarding abuse, sexuality, and families. The first of these pamphlets was entitled "Child Abuse" and addressed types of child abuse, including sexual abuse; suggestions regarding what a congregation could do in response, as well as a list of some resources, were included in the pamphlet. The possibility of child abuse by Church employees, clergy, or volunteers was not identified explicitly in this pamphlet.

In the late 1980s, General Council began to receive petitions pertaining to child and youth sexual abuse. Previous to these years, there was only one petition related to sexual abuse; a resolution was received by General Council regarding "sex offenders" and referred to the Department of Evangelism and Social Service.[29] In 1986, General Council received a petition from Winnipeg Presbytery requesting that the Badgely Commission's report be studied by the United Church, that the Church urge the federal government to implement the main recommendation, and that "the DMC present recommendations to the

1988 General Council to guide the thinking and action of the church on the issue of child sexual victimization."[30] Subsequently, the 32nd General Council (1988) reported that the DMC had established a program unit—"Children, Adults, and Family Ministries"—to "coordinate work in the areas of pornography, prostitution, and family violence." As one example of their advocacy work, this unit corresponded with the federal Minister of National Health and Welfare regarding "violence in the family."[31]

This General Council received two petitions regarding "sexual molestation." One requested that the United Church urge the government to create legislation that would ensure that victims of "intrafamilial and/or incestuous sexual molestation" be given the right to bring charges against their abusers "without time limit."[32] This petition recognized that, for various reasons, a "victim" may not be able or willing to come forward for many years after the abuse began. The second petition was directed primarily at the need to educate and train people in the United Church to become more aware of the dynamics of "sexual molestation" and better equipped to provide pastoral care for those who have been or are being sexually molested.[33] The recommendations of both petitions were carried.

The 1988 General Council received further petitions that were concerned with the "abuse and exploitation of children" in "underdeveloped countries" (partly in response to "the fact that 22 countries have now ratified the [United Nations'] Convention on the Rights of Children"), the availability of child abuse counselling resources, and the issue of confidentiality and reporting of child abuse.[34] The first clear requests at a national level for a comprehensive policy addressing disclosures of child sexual abuse were made at this 1988 General Council. It should be noted that these petitions did not specifically address the issue of child sexual abuse complaints directed at Church volunteers, employees, or officials. Although child sexual abuse had become much more prominent at the General Council level, most of this General Council's energy and time were directed toward the issue of sexual orientation and ordered ministry.

Also in the latter part of the 1980s, greater awareness had been generated in the UCC regarding the damaging effects of Aboriginal residential schools and the need to own some of the responsibility for this damage and make appropriate restitution. Canadian residential schools were "operated in Canada through arrangements between the Government of Canada and the Roman Catholic, Anglican, Methodist, United and Presbyterian churches. Although the Government was no longer officially involved after 1969, a few schools and hostels continued to operate into the 1970s and 1980s."[35] Many Aboriginal boys and girls who attended these schools were abused in numerous ways, including sexually. Lawsuits have ensued. In 1986, the General Council extended a formal apology to First Nations peoples, saying, in part, "In our zeal to tell you of the good news of Jesus Christ we were closed to the value of your spirituality.... We imposed our civilization as a condition of accepting the gospel.... We ask you to forgive us and to walk together with us in the Spirit of Christ so that our peoples maybe blessed and God's creation healed."[36] The apology was "received" as a beginning, but not accepted as a sufficient response in and of itself, by the newly created All-Native Circle Conference in 1988.[37]

The UCC has been clear that it has a "moral responsibility" to the survivors, regardless of court judgments. Many financial legal judgments and out-of-court settlements have been paid. The Healing Fund, created by the General Council in 1994, was intended as a five-year campaign "to address the impacts of residential schools on Aboriginal people. It now continues as one facet of the United Church's ongoing reconciliation work with Aboriginal people." The UCC has now raised over $1,200,000 for this project and its healing work.[38] In addition to breaking more of the silence concerning child sexual abuse in relation to the Church, the residential school crisis contributed much to the use and development of alternative dispute resolution processes regarding child sexual abuse complaints. In particular, healing circles have been very helpful to some complainants.[39] The Mennonite Church has done most to develop this aspect of restorative justice, as it applies to sexual offenders, through their use of circles of accountability.

At the end of the 1980s in the United Church, child abuse was understood primarily as part of family violence.[40] As awareness of child abuse increased, the need to respond to such abuse perpetrated by people outside as well as inside the child's family became increasingly important. This new awareness was related to a changing understanding of the family as a system that could be destructive as well as nurturing.

On April 19, 1991, a motion at the General Council Executive was passed to create the Moderator's Task Group on Sexual Abuse, Exploitation, and Harassment. The mandate of the task group was approved as follows:

I   Sexual Harassment
   a Gather existing policies on Sexual Harassment.
   b Determine areas of deficiency in the present policies.
   c Prepare recommendations for filling deficiencies in present policies and practices....
II Other Forms of Harassment/Abuse
   a Prepare a theological statement on such matters as ... dissent, means of dealing with conflict, et cetera appropriate to the polity and tradition of The United Church of Canada.
   b Define the forms of Harassment/Abuse to which the Church needs to address itself.
   c Develop guidelines for grievance procedures and conflict resolution.[41]

The task group had its first meeting in October 1991. At this meeting it was determined that parallel subgroups needed to be formed in order to address adequately the mandate. The task group recorded the following rationale for the formation of two subgroups: "Group members recognized the need for the church to address these issues [i.e., harassment and abuse] from the perspective of those who have experienced harassment and/or abuse in terms of sexuality, discipline within the life of the church, and culture/race."[42] Accordingly, one group focused on sexual harassment/abuse, and the other looked at discipline within the Church.

At its second meeting in November 1991, the group as a whole agreed on their main objective: "our task is to address the result of sexual abuse, exploitation and harassment within the United Church of Canada from the point of view of the victims."[43] This focus on the voices and empowerment of victims was to continue.

Approach to Child Sexual Abuse, Including Relevant Statements, Policies, and Practices: 1992–2009

The Moderator's Task Group on Sexual Abuse, Exploitation, and Harassment presented its first report to the General Council Executive in February 1992. Although this group had been functioning for only five months, it had authored three reports for presentation to the Executive. The first report included a faith statement reading, in part:

> as a faith community we have not heard the cry of the abused, exploited and harassed in our midst nor have we acknowledged the truth of their experience and pain; we have failed to respect one another's worth as children of God who have been created as equals in God's image; we have violated our sacred trust through acts of sexual, racial and cultural oppression; we have failed to sustain and inspirit those who have stood with the abused. We acknowledge the growing sense that we must hear and act now. We ask God's forgiveness and the forgiveness of those who have suffered. We call for the Church to repent and respond to our recommendations....[44]

Addressing sexual abuse had become a priority in the United Church.

There were many factors leading to this new attention to abuse, including child sexual abuse. As outlined in the previous pages, part of the reason was the gradual shift from a primarily act-centred sexual ethic to a primarily relational sexual ethic; a priority on the quality of relationships as compared to sexual acts as good or bad meant that sexual expression came to be evaluated more in terms of the well-being of the people involved. Other significant causes included the media reports on clergy sexual misconduct and child abuse, particularly regarding the Mount Cashel cases and the Gallienne abuses at St. George's Anglican Cathedral in Kingston, and the federal government's 1984 Badgely Commission Report. In general, the increasing awareness generated by the media, lawsuits, and by the emergence, in the 1980s, of theological publications regarding abuse and clergy sexual abuse helped to break the silence and the belief that clergy and Church officials were beyond reproach: "During the past six years the awareness of issues related to sexual abuse in society has increased dramatically. Churches have been slower to accept the reality of sexual abuse within our midst, particularly abuse which is perpetrated by those to whom we have entrusted positions of leadership."[45]

The three reports presented by the Moderator's Task Group on Sexual Abuse, Exploitation, and Harassment addressed a broad understanding of those subjects. One subgroup examined abuse, exploitation, and harassment regarding race and cultural issues. The work of this subgroup recognized and drew attention to the systemic relationship between racial and cultural prejudice,[46] and a higher incidence of abuse not only in wider society but also within the UCC.[47] Another subgroup considered abuse and harassment experienced by some as a result of their differing views or theologies: "The 'harassment' with which this group has been concerned has its roots in theological differences and differences in perspective on the nature of the church and its role in the world."[48] In particular, this subgroup identified the controversy regarding same-sex issues in the UCC as a problem that had left some feeling persecuted or harassed. The remaining subgroup looked at sexual abuse. This subgroup interviewed several people with various roles in the UCC who discussed their experiences of sexual abuse, harassment, or exploitation within the Church. Based on these stories and some pertinent secondary writings on abuse, the subgroup found "indication[s] of widespread sexual abuse within the United Church."[49]

Each of the subgroups presented a series of recommendations to the General Council. The recommendations of the last subgroup are most relevant to this book. Their recommendations included: the need for the UCC to "adopt a standard procedure for abuse/harassment allegations"; to insure that "victims" receive as much care and protection as do "alleged perpetrators"; to hear the "stories of harassment and abuse" and ensure that the wider Church knows of the abuse in its midst; to address the dangers around "confidentiality and secrecy" regarding abuse; to build in, as part of policy, "standard procedures for the immediate suspension ... with full pay and benefits, of a staff person when a Formal Hearing is called on harassment/abuse allegations"; to develop "a clear re-entry process" "whenever a person in paid accountable ministry is reinstated or continues in that position after having been found guilty of charges of harassment/abuse"; to both protect and educate students training for ministry regarding potential harassment and abuse; and to educate people in paid accountable ministry regarding harassment or abuse. General Council received the report "for information" and responded to each of the recommendations. Most of the recommendations, it was determined, were dealt with by the Division of Ministry Personnel and Education (DMPE) Report as discussed below. General Council passed two motions addressing the points raised regarding candidates for ordered ministry and their educational experiences.[50] Finally, the report as a whole was referred to "the Division of Ministry Personnel and Education in cooperation with [the] Committee on Sexism" to "continue to extend the work begun by the Moderator's Task Group on Sexual Abuse, Exploitation, and Harassment" and to follow up on the task group's recommendations.[51]

The DMPE approved and presented a report and policy by the Women in Ministry Committee "with later involvement" of the Pastoral Relations Committee entitled "Sexual Abuse: Harassment, Exploitation, Misconduct, Assault, and Child Abuse" to the 1992 General Council for discussion and approval. This team of writers and the Moderator's Task Group on Sexual Abuse, Exploitation, and Harassment conferred, and the latter sent a response to the policy document before it went to General Council.[52] The writers also consulted with others in the UCC as well as "a number of ecumenical colleagues."[53]

After the policy was approved for official use in the UCC, and "experience was gained" in its application, future General Councils and, regarding more minor revisions, the Executive of General Council,[54] approved policy revisions accordingly.[55] In 1996 a National Committee on Sexual Abuse (Sexual Harassment, Sexual Exploitation, Pastoral Sexual Misconduct, Sexual Assault) and Child Abuse was established in the Division of Ministry Personnel and Education to replace the initial groups with the following mandate:

- monitoring the Church's policy on sexual abuse,
- advising the Pastoral Relations Policy Specialist with regard to policy and procedures, and
- making recommendations to the Division of Ministry Personnel and Education for the development and redevelopment of the Sexual Abuse Policy[56]

This mandate was updated in March 2003 to more accurately reflect the expanded work of the committee:

1 monitoring the Church's policy on sexual abuse
2 advising the pastoral relations policy specialist with regard to policy and procedures
3 making recommendations to the Division of Ministry Personnel and Education for the development and redevelopment of the policy
4 reviewing and approving requests for funding for applicants to the Fund for Survivors of Sexual Abuse
5 maintaining connections with the network (such as gathering additions to the bibliography and distributing and assisting with resources)
6 gathering conference committee representatives for ongoing education and updates about the policy during the fall prior to the next General Council meeting

The committee's terms of reference directed that membership include "three to four people with extensive knowledge of issues related to sexual abuse, at least one of whom has experience in working with the United Church's policy. All members of the Committee should understand the pastoral, ethical and theological issues involved in the work of the policy."[57] The membership of this committee retained significant continuity until 2004, when it was decided that existing members had fulfilled their commitment and new people needed an opportunity to continue this work.

Complaints of Child Sexual Abuse and Complaints by Adults of Historical Childhood Sexual Abuse

The document *Sexual Abuse: Harassment, Exploitation, Misconduct, Assault, and Child Abuse* was amended and approved for official use by the 1992 General Council and so became the first set of policies and procedures in the UCC that specifically addressed child sexual abuse complaints as well as other forms of abuse. This policy has been built upon in the years following 1992 with changes made in response to lived experiences, legal cases, and an ongoing desire to seek the best possible justice and care.

The policy begins with a theological statement outlining the Church's commitment to the vulnerable. Such a statement has been included in all revisions. Definitions of the terms in the document's title are also included and thus far have remained constant apart from the following revisions: "Sexual Exploitation" was removed from the list of definitions and the policy title in 1997 since "the term is more descriptive of a power dynamic (present in all categories of sexual abuse) than it is definitive of a category of abuse"; and the definition of "Sexual Harassment" was expanded to include "harassment based on marital status and sexual orientation" to more accurately reflect the consultants'[58] experiences of complaints.[59] The well-being and healing of all involved, including the "victims" and "offenders," are identified as a primary goal of this first policy.[60] This document uses the terms "complainant" and "responder" when referring specifically to those who are using the UCC process for addressing a complaint.[61]

Concerning current child sexual abuse, the report outlines specific instructions in accordance with Canada's laws: "When a complaint of sexual or physical abuse of a child designated by provincial law as a legal minor is disclosed or where there are reasonable grounds to suspect such abuse, the person to whom the disclose is made or who suspects such abuse shall immediately report the suspicion and the information on which it is based to the authority or agency as defined in the provincial statutes...."[62] The document is clear that the legal duty to report outweighs any commitment to confidentiality whether in an informal setting, counselling setting, or confessional setting.[63] The authors advise the person who reports child abuse to keep careful notes regarding the incident. Further, "[w]hen the alleged perpetrator in a case involving a legal minor is in an accountable relationship to a court of The United Church of Canada the matter shall be reported to the appropriate court of the Church by the person who has taken the allegations to the authorities. This shall be done as soon as it is permitted by provincial/territorial legislation...."[64] The Church was not to interfere by interviewing the people involved, but offering pastoral care to all involved was strongly encouraged.

The UCC's revised policy of 2007 does not differ substantively regarding the process involved for cases involving legal minors. Aside from some editorial adjustment, the difference is one of tone; the 2007 version uses more of a legal tone and terms, whereas the previous policy versions were written with a more pastoral tone or simply with less attention to legal terms and criteria. However, the newer policy retained the model of opening with a theological statement regarding the theological imperative to seek justice and resist abuse.

The original and revised policy documents are clear that it would be inappropriate for the same person "to offer pastoral care to both the victim and the alleged offender."[65] In 1997, the policy was amended to refer policy users to updated information regarding the reporting of child abuse, which was added in a "Resource Packet" supplementing the policy.[66]

While the Church policy directs complaints of current child abuse first to the legal system, the UCC sexual abuse policy can be used by legal guardians after the legal investigation: "In order that such investigation is not hindered, no representative of The United Church of Canada will question the alleged victim, the alleged perpetrator, or any potential witness concerning the investigation by the provincial or territorial agency, authority, and/or police is being undertaken or until such time as those authorities indicate such questioning may proceed."[67]

Further, if a person serving as ministry personnel is charged with a criminal offence, there are procedures, outlined in another section of *The Manual*, which the sexual abuse policy follows.[68] At the time of this writing, only once in the UCC's history has a complainant of child sexual abuse immediately used the Church procedure following legal permission to proceed.[69] Normally the UCC will not agree to proceed without the child's assent in addition to the request of the legal guardians. The 1992 policy includes the following statement in this regard: "If the complainant is a child/teenager, a parent/guardian responsible adult could be involved in the initial consultation and throughout the process. Such situations need to be treated with particular sensitivity with the well-being of the complainant being given utmost consideration. All cases involving allegations of abuse of a legal minor should be referred to the required authority as designated by provincial law."[70] The 2007 policy does not include s similar statement, but it is understood that the requirements of the law will protect the "legal minor."

Regarding child sexual abuse, the UCC policy most often has been used by adult complainants of historical child sexual abuse: "there shall be no time limit regarding the filing of a complaint," although the policy also states that incidents of historical child abuse need to be reported to the legal authorities.[71] Further, in 2002 an addition was made to the policy regarding complaints involving respondents who are deceased: "In cases where the respondent has died subsequent to a complaint, a Formal Hearing cannot proceed after the death of a Respondent. In these situations, an alternative process will be offered to the complainant by the church court (e.g., Listening Team) ... [and] in cases where the respondent is dead, an alternative process will be offered to the complainant by the church court (e.g., Listening Team)."

Each conference executive appoints at least five people, including both men and women, "with a majority of the consultants being women."[72] A "complainant may approach any of the consultants."[73] The consultant's primary role is to listen, explain the options, determine "if the complaint is one to which the policy applies," and ensure that the complainant understands the policy.[74] In 1997 the consultant's role was further clarified by stating that "the Consultant may not also function as the support person, pastoral caregiver or Advocate in relation to the Complainant."[75] Someone else outside formal policy roles would be designated to provide this care and/or advocacy in the interest of maintaining appropriate boundaries. It was also made clearer that Consultant A would be the complainant's consultant and a different consultant—Consultant B—would be designated to ensure that the respondent had "access to information and ongoing consultation" in a way similar to the complainant.[76] In the most recent version, the policy does not use the terminology of "Consultant A" or "B"; rather, the reference is simply to a "consultant" who is contacted by the complainant and a consultant who is assigned to the respondent.[77]

The 1992 policy was designed as a complainant-driven process, stating that "at no point can action be taken without the complainant's permission to proceed."[78] The 2007 policy changed this and provides for the possibility of the consultants filing the complaint themselves or based on an evidence-substantiated third-party report: "In the event the complainant chooses not to put the complaint in writing the notes made by the consultant of the conversation with the complainant will serve as the written record of the complaint. A complaint by a third party must be made in writing" (see "Third-Party Complaints" section below).[79]

Under the original policy the complainant had the following options before signing a written complaint: attempt to resolve the issue informally by, for example, asking the respondent to stop "the offensive behaviour"; not to proceed further through UCC sexual abuse procedures (for one of the following reasons: the issue is resolved informally; it is determined not to be a case of sexual abuse; the complainant decides, for any reason, that he or she does not want to proceed; or the complainant chooses to proceed through "external routes"); to proceed directly to a formal hearing ("in cases where the harassment/exploitation/abuse is extreme"); or to proceed by writing a signing a complaint form and giving it to Consultant A.[80] Under the 2007 policy, it may be that the complainant, in consultation with the consultant, decides: to address the issue outside of the policy; that the policy does not apply to the issue; or not to proceed for any reason.

However, the consultant is required to file a third-party complaint regardless of the person's decision if the consultant can identify the potential respondent and has reason to believe the allegation may be true. Because of this potential, the consultant is to advise any person who wishes to consult with him or her that the person ought not identify the potential respondent unless the person is prepared to have the consultant file a third-party complaint with or without the person's agreement. This caution is an attempt to preserve the person's power to decide while providing another option if the person would like someone else to pursue the complaint. The danger is that the consultant may forget to advise accordingly or the person may forget and inadvertently use the alleged perpetrator's name or otherwise identify him or her unintentionally. Further, another party may choose to file a third-party complaint without having provided due notice to the person communicating an abuse experience. On the other hand, the older policy did not provide an alternative option for people who did want their complaints pursued, but not by themselves.

If a written complaint is submitted, the conference personnel minister (CPM) is notified by the consultant of the complaint and receives the written complaint. After this, the 1992 policy included a "fact-finding" step—which was renamed "The Response" in 1997 (please see the subsequent section regarding "investigative procedures" for further explanation)—and notification of the respondent and appropriate Church court. The updated 2007 policy is different and includes an investigation, as explained in the next section regarding "investigative procedures." Relevant parties in the UCC are notified and the respondent is contacted by a consultant and provided with a copy of the complaint. Pastoral care and the policy are both discussed with the respondent.[81]

Under the original policy, there were four subsequent possible courses of action: (1) not to proceed; (2) the consultant could assist in finding an agreeable way in which to settle the case (for example, the respondent might write a letter of apology to the complainant) (this option was later, in April 2000, revised to read "to consider an offer from the Respondent to seek a negotiated settlement [6(a)]"); (3) to proceed to an informal hearing; or (4) to proceed to a formal hearing.

The same procedures outlined in section 73 of *The Manual* for informal hearings in general are followed with two additional requirements: "at least half of the Informal Hearing Committee shall be of the same sex as the complainant," and both men and women shall be on the committee. Further, all committee members must be "fully knowledgeable of the policies and procedures of The United Church of Canada in relation to sexual abuse...."[82]

When informal "efforts at resolution have not succeeded in stopping the sexual abuse [in the case of adult complainants] ... or that ... the abuse is so severe and/or the possibility of resolution [is] ... remote," or if either the complainant or the respondent request it, formal hearing procedures are begun as outlined in section 74 of *The Manual*, with the same two additional requirements included in informal hearings.[83] To summarize:

> The term "formal" is a good descriptor. This is a formal process like a court of law. There is a Complainant and a Respondent and the "judge" is a panel of 3–5 United Church members. Often one of the members of the Formal Hearing Committee (panel) is a lawyer. Where this does not happen, the panel will usually have legal counsel.
>
> A Formal Hearing will receive and consider material in evidence. There will also be a time to hear testimony and to cross-examine witnesses. The Rules of Evidence for the provincial jurisdiction apply.
>
> Usually, the Complainant and Respondent are represented by legal counsel. It is for the Complainant (and counsel) to present the case and for the Respondent to defend.
>
> A verbatim record ... or a tape recording is taken of all the proceedings. After the panel has received the evidence and heard the testimony, there are closing arguments by each of the parties and the panel is left to make a decision. When the Formal Hearing Committee makes its decisions, they become the decisions of the court that appointed them. They may also make recommendations which the church court will need to consider, debate, amend and/or accept. Decisions of a Formal Hearing are subject to appeal to the next higher court.[84]

In April 2000, the General Council Committee on Sexual Abuse began to draft a proposal for an investigative piece that was approved by the 2003 General Council. Additionally, in 2003, the option of an informal hearing was removed since it was decided that the alternative dispute resolution process was an adequate alternative.[85]

Under the newer 2007 policy, the next step following the initial discussion with the respondent is to make a decision regarding the possible suspension, with full pay and benefits, of the respondent; suspension is not automatic and this remains a controversial part of the policy (see section below regarding "Responses to Involved People"). Next, a qualified investigator is assigned. After the investigator's report and recommendations are received, the court makes a decision about accountability (e.g., "For the purposes of this policy the appropriate Church Court is the Court of the United Church of Canada to which a respondent to a complaint of sexual abuse or child abuse has a primary accountable relationship") regarding the subsequent step.[86] There are three such possible steps: (1) it is determined that there are no grounds for a hearing and no further action under the policy is taken; (2) informal procedures toward resolution are pursued "on agreement of the complainant and the respondent"; or (3) it is determined that there are reasonable grounds to proceed with a formal hearing where the complaint will be heard by the next higher court.[87] It is estimated that at least nine out of ten cases are resolved before reaching a formal hearing.[88] The court of accountability is responsible for all costs associated with a formal hearing, as part of the implementation of the investigative piece, "except for costs for legal counsel for individuals."[89]

Investigative Procedures Regarding Complaints

The 1992 policy did not include a formal investigative piece, but did include a less formal "fact-finding process." This step was proposed and approved by General Council in 1992 with a significant amendment; the proposed policy directed a fact-finding process to be undertaken by a second consultant "named by the Conference Coordinating Committee ... who accompanies the initial consultant [who was approached by the complainant] to a meeting with the respondent" at which the consultant would gather "information" from the respondent.[90] The amended and approved policy instructed that the "fact-finding process shall be the responsibility of the court to whom the respondent is accountable; and shall be undertaken by an officer of that court, assisted by a Conference consultant on Sexual Abuse (Harassment, Exploitation, Misconduct, Assault), and Child Abuse who has not been in communication with either the complainant or the respondent regarding the charge or complaint."[91]

In 1997, the National Committee on the sexual abuse policy recommended a change to this process that was approved by General Council: the fact-finding step was renamed "The Response" because "fact-finding" inaccurately led people to interpret this as a formal investigative step "rather than one in which a response was elicited from the Respondent."[92] Consultants and coordinating committees had found that the term "fact-finding" tended to imply that "facts" were revealed by the respondent in telling his or her side of the story rather than being simply the respondent's "response." Therefore, the name change was understood to more accurately reflect the purpose of this step. In addition to the response meeting, there was also a clarification meeting with the respondent during which the process was clarified and discussed. At this time, there was no investigative piece.

As noted in the preceding section, the National Committee began to create a proposal for a formal investigative step in 2000 that was to be approved by the 2003 General Council, but not implemented until July 1, 2007. This investigative step and the provision for third-party complaints are the first significant substantive changes to the original 1992 policy procedures. The National Committee was motivated to create this investigative piece in the interest of making the policy as just as possible by increasing the Church's responsibility to support the complainant financially, morally, and procedurally in the cases of complaints that have reasonable grounds. As is recorded in the minutes of the December 1–3, 2000 Sexual Abuse Committee meeting:

> In the light of the changes recommended through petitions to the 37th General Council, we want to be pro-active in suggesting changes to the policy that will

reflect the growing experience of the church in its implementation. To that end, we are determined to keep the policy complainant driven but we want to explore possibilities of changes to the Formal Hearing procedures by including an investigative procedure. Moved that we begin with conversations with GC Legal Counsel and perhaps the judicial committee. Our primary concern is to develop ways for complaints that go to Formal Hearings to go forward without the sole financial burden being borne by the Complainant. Linda Murray/Tracy Trothen <u>CARRIED</u>.

Petitions regarding the policy that were approved by General Council in 2000 were relevant to the development of both an investigative procedure as well as the issue of third-party complaints.[93] These are discussed later in the "Third-Party Complaints" section.

Under the proposed investigative procedure, after the results of an investigation are determined, the Church court could "assess if there is merit in lodging a complaint on behalf of the Complainant (with the Complainant's permission). This would include moral and financial support, if the decision of the court is to proceed."[94] If the court decides, on the basis of the investigation, that there is sufficient merit to proceed, then the appropriate Church court (e.g., the court "to which a respondent to a complaint ... has a primary accountable relationship") would pay the costs, not the complainant.[95] The function of this investigative component is to ameliorate both the financial and emotional costs to the complainant. Further, it was seen by the then committee members as a more empowering alternative to the potential provision of a third-party complaint system.

The General Council Committee on Sexual Abuse Policy held a consultation in October 2002 for the Conference Personal Ministers and Conference Coordinating Committee Chairs to review the revised policy, discuss and share experiences and concerns, and consult regarding the proposed investigative piece.[96] The feedback was largely supportive of the proposed investigative piece with some minor adjustments.

Accordingly, in April 2003, the Sub-Executive of the General Council adopted the recommendation of the Sexual Abuse Committee regarding the implementation of an investigative step, with the amendment that "all information obtained by the investigator, including any written report prepared for the church court, will be kept confidential, unless required by law to disclose it in a legal proceeding."[97] The Sexual Abuse Committee then addressed the implementation of the new procedural step, which was initially planned for 2004 but was delayed until 2007 due to a need for more preparation.[98]

The 2007 version of the policy describes the investigative step.[99] After it is determined that the complaint is appropriate to the policy, the written complaint is submitted and parties are informed of the complaint. Next, a consultant is assigned to the respondent and the complaint is communicated to the respondent, after which a decision is made regarding the possible suspension (with pay and benefits) of the respondent. This decision remains rather subjective unless the evidence is overwhelming. A concern is that in the case of unsubstantiated complaints, the respondent's reputation will be unduly compromised if he or she is suspended. However, on the other side, the potential harm to the complainant if the respondent remains in his or her position is significant. At the very least, the complainant would be unable to safely access the church.

At this point, a qualified investigator is assigned to the case. The investigator's written report forms the basis on which the Church court of accountability decides how to proceed; it will be decided if there are reasonable grounds to proceed with a formal hearing, or an informal resolution approach, or "no reasonable grounds to proceed with the complaint ... under this policy." There is no provision for appeal.[100]

Complaints Regarding People Who Are Not Church Personnel and Complaints Regarding People Who Are Church Officials and/or Employees

Complaints may be brought against a United Church "member, adherent, candidate for the ministry, or member of the Order of Ministry."[101] The 2007 policy reads almost the same way with one change: instead of "member of the Order of Ministry," it reads, "a person who is Ministry Personnel."[102] Further, "any person who is not a member or adherent who has sought out the professional or pastoral services of The United Church of Canada's employees as cited above for purposes of pastoral care, counselling, marriage workshops, day care, et cetera, has the right not to be abused in any way. Such person is also extended the right to full protection of the denomination's policies and procedures for the addressing of such matters, and may therefore lay a charge within the courts of The United Church of Canada."[103] In 1997, General Council approved an addition to the beginning of the policy that is explicit regarding against whom a formal complaint may be made under the policy:

A formal complaint may be made against:
- a person serving as Ministry Personnel
- a member of the Order of Ministry
- an Inquirer
- a Candidate
- a lay member or adherent of The United Church of Canada who is not currently serving as Ministry Personnel and who is not an Inquirer or a Candidate.[104]

Complainants may choose to avail themselves of the sexual abuse policy. It is also possible for people to use other relevant provisions of *The Manual*:

iii. When a question is raised by a Pastoral Charge or by the Presbytery regarding: (1) the efficiency of a member of the Order of Ministry or person under

Presbytery Appointment; (2) the failure of a member of the Order of Ministry or person under Presbytery Appointment to maintain the peace and welfare of the church; or (3) a member of the Order of Ministry or person under Presbytery Appointment who refuses the authority of Presbytery.[105]

The most recent version of the policy makes clear that this "policy does not apply and is not intended to be used for complaints which may be brought between members or adherents in a congregation."[106]

Third-Party Complaints

Until 2007 the UCC was committed to a complainant-driven policy: "no action involving any third party or court of the church will be taken without a formal written complaint signed by the complainant. At no point can action be taken without the complainant's permission to proceed"; and "When the charge is one of sexual abuse (sexual harassment, sexual exploitation, pastoral sexual mis-conduct or sexual assault), only the person experiencing the unwanted sexual attention may lay the charge."[107] This did not apply to current cases of suspected child abuse, which must be reported by law. From the policy's initial implemen-tation, third-party complaints were raised as an issue: the 1992 General Council referred further questions back to the Women in Ministry and Pastoral Relations Committees, including "readiness to return" to ministry positions after a charge had been processed, and "clarification of the possibilities and the limits of third party complaints."[108]

Petition 45, approved and referred to DMPE by the 2000 General Council, paved the way for a very significant policy change that was to occur in 2006 and be implemented in 2007. The petition, received from the Hamilton Conference, reads:

> WHEREAS the current procedures for dealing with a complaint of sexual abuse depend heavily upon the abilities of the Complainant and Respondent to pres-ent their case; and
>
> WHEREAS the current procedures for dealing with a complaint of sexual abuse are very costly emotionally, physically and monetarily for the Complainant and Respondent; and
>
> WHEREAS the United Church has provided the mechanism for a court of the church to lay a charge where it has reasonable and probable grounds to believe that an offence has occurred (s. 72(b) of *The Manual*, 1998); and
>
> WHEREAS there may be occasions where a church court is aware that abuse may be taking place and therefore has an obligation to maintain and keep a safe environment for worship, work, and study;
>
> THEREFORE BE IT RESOLVED THAT Hamilton Conference petition the 37th General Council to make provision for a court of the church to be able to inves-tigate allegations of sexual abuse brought by an individual who believes that they have experienced sexual abuse as defined in the United Church's Sexual

Abuse (Sexual Harassment, Pastoral Sexual Misconduct, Sexual Assault) and Child Abuse Policy and if there are reasonable and probable grounds for the allegations and, with the consent of the individual who believes that they have experienced sexual abuse, to bring a complaint under the sexual abuse policy.[109]

As was reported on the website's news page for the United Church, the petition generated significant division among those familiar with the policy; some argued strongly for a change that was believed to be supportive of the adult complainant, while others argued that the petition was going too far toward a third-party complaint system that would further disempower the complainant.[110]

The executive of DMPE responded to the referred petition by first noting that the policy document does not currently "allow for a complaint initiated by a third party." Further, the executive pointed out that there were already provisions in *The Manual* to address an unsafe Church environment:

> The Division Executive believed that the intent of the petition was not clear; how could a church court bring forward a complaint based on allegations? (The Presbytery already has the authority to conduct a review of the conduct of ministry personnel and recommend remedial action under Section 363 of *The Manual*.) ... The Division Executive was concerned that this lack of clarity could lead to an action where the Complainant is disempowered or the Respondent is put at risk due to rumours. The Division Executive requested the General Council Executive refer Petition 45 back to the next General Council for clarification as per *The Manual* Section 524(d). The GCE agreed to this request.[111]

No further action was taken in response to Petition 45.

However, the push to institute a mechanism to review third-party complaints continued until such a provision was approved first by the Executive of the General Council (April 28–May 1, 2006) and subsequently by the 39th General Council (2006) for implementation July 1, 2007. The 2006 General Council referred the following changes to allow for third-party complaints to the Executive, who subsequently approved them: "072(a) Delete the final sentence of this section which is the provision that only the person experiencing the sexual abuse may make a complaint; 072(b) Delete the clause which prohibits a Court from making a complaint of sexual abuse."[112] The new policy reads in part:

> A complaint may be made by an individual who has been sexually abused by a person to whom this policy applies, by a third party who has first-hand knowledge (has observed or has evidence) of sexual abuse by a person to whom this policy applies, or by a court of the church. In the case of the abuse of a minor, a parent or guardian may initiate a complaint as third party.

Similarly to RCC dioceses, anonymous complaints are not acted upon under this policy.[113]

Concerns continued to be raised regarding the possibility of an adult complainant being further disempowered or re-victimized if their consultant filed a third-party complaint against the complainant's wishes. All were interested in a policy that would best support the vulnerable and uphold justice; how to best do this was the point of contention. As is stated in the preface to the 2007 policy:

> The United Church seeks to ensure that the voice of the complainant is listened to and heard, and that pastoral care and support are provided to that individual and her or his family. It recognizes that sexual abuse occurs when one uses her or his power to take advantage of the vulnerability of another. Consent to a sexual relationship or act can be given only by an individual who is in a position to make such a choice, and that choice cannot be made by an individual who acts out of fear or who is taken advantage of by a person in a position of trust. While seeking to respect the difficult decision a complainant makes when deciding to initiate a complaint, the church also seeks to honour the duty of care that it has to its members, adherents, employees, and those who avail themselves of our services.[114]

The 2007 policy seeks to address these concerns by providing for the possibility of a consultant carrying a complaint forward with the permission of the one who has claimed the experience of abuse and who may not want to shoulder that burden. Accordingly, information in the resource package, which is appended to the policy, directs the consultants to advise any potential complainant to refrain from using the respondent's name or identifying him or her in any way until the complainant decides whether or not to go forward with the complaint. How successful the Church will be, through this revised policy, in balancing a duty of care and empowering those who experience abuse will be learned through experience. Regardless, the commitments to seek justice and to protect the vulnerable remain guiding principles for the UCC.

Responses to Involved People

The Manual had stated previously that when a criminal charge is laid against a member of the Order of Ministry or other ministry personnel, the minister may or may not be permitted to continue to function in that position "pending the final disposition of the matter."[115] Due largely to "the judgment of the Ontario Division Court regarding two cases in Bay of Quinte Conference," the Judicial Committee/the Manual Committee proposed an amendment to "suspend the minister immediately" in the case of a criminal charge of child abuse or aggravated sexual assault.[116] General Council approved a much more lenient amendment that stated that in the case of a criminal charge of "child abuse or sexual assault," the decision of whether or not to suspend must be made within "7 days of receipt of notification that a charge has been made" and conveyed to the pastoral charge at a meeting chaired and called by an appointee of the

Presbytery.[117] The only significant change was that a specific timeline became required; the respondent could remain active in his or her position pending the outcome of the charge, if a preliminary hearing so decides.[118] The decision to suspend or not is made at a "preliminary hearing ... convened by the Chairperson of the appropriate court, or acting designate of the same, who with two other officers of that court, shall determine whether the respondent should be relieved of all responsibilities pertaining to their office(s) or position(s)...."[119] As the 2007 policy explains, this "is a Decision to be made in the best interests of the community served by the church court. It is not, nor is intended to be, a Decision with respect to the innocence or guilt of the respondent."[120]

Further, if "the respondent is understood to be in the employ of The United Church of Canada, then full pay and benefits shall continue pending the outcome of the Formal Hearing." If the respondent is placed on leave pending the outcome of a formal hearing, the "cost of salary and benefits" is the continuing responsibility of the "pastoral charge/employing unit budget."[121] The rationale for a rejection of the committee's proposed change was that "automatic suspension tends to presume guilt ..., even though in many/most cases a suspension will happen, it needs to be the result of a 'preliminary hearing' within seven ... days."[122]

Regarding the issue of costs incurred by the complainant, the 1992 General Council raised the issue of restitution "so that the victim may not have to resort to civil court processes," but no conclusion was recommended at this time.[123] Later, with the implementation of the formal investigative step, the court of accountability assumed any costs apart from the costs of legal counsel, if chosen by either party. Further, the policy has stated since 1992 that "It is normally inappropriate to assess costs against complainants of sexual abuse."[124]

Later, the 1994 General Council received three petitions requesting that the Church provide financial support for the counselling needs of United Church members or personnel who are survivors of sexual abuse, and for those who claim to have been abused by anyone representing the United Church. General Council agreed to refer the matter to appropriate committees to "develop a plan for an Employee Assistance Program."[125] Two assistance funds subsequently were created and funding became available in 1998: the Survivors of Sexual Abuse Fund and the Ministry Personnel/Survivors of Sexual Abuse Fund. The only stipulations for eligibility for up to $1,000 per calendar year are a letter from a therapist attesting to the importance of therapy to address a history of sexual abuse that occurred in the United Church of Canada context (it is not necessary to have the incidence of such abuse proven or supported except by the therapist and applicant), and the approval of the National Sexual Abuse Committee in consultation with the relevant Conference Coordinating Committee on Sexual Abuse. "Applications can be from lay and non-United Church individuals." There is a maximum of $25,000 available for disbursement each calendar year. The purpose of the second fund is "to help ordained ministers who are survivors of sexual abuse to stay in active ministry while participating in therapy to deal with sexual abuse issues that are part of their history."[126]

In 1992 it was stated that if a formal hearing proves the complaint, consequences to the respondent may include "monetary payment or other form of symbolic restoration" on the part of the respondent.[127] It was also moved and carried "that the 34th General Council direct the Division of Ministry Personnel and Education in consultation with the Division of Mission in Canada to develop guidelines to assist Formal Hearing committees in determining the nature and extent of restitution."[128] Financial contribution toward "counselling expenses of the complainant" was suggested as one appropriate form of restitution. Formal hearings, in general, "when the charge has been proven ... [result in] a Decision to admonish, rebuke, suspend, depose or expel" the respondent.[129] Provision for restitution, as mentioned above, was added to *The Manual* specifically in response to the sexual abuse policy.[130]

Since the policy's inception, disciplinary actions have been recommended, if the hearing committee finds the complaint is credible, including a "directed programme ... for the respondent." Further, "an oversight committee shall be appointed to monitor the respondent's progress in the directed programme, to receive a report from the director of the programme, and to make a recommendation to the respondent's court of accountability regarding readiness to return to church leadership positions."[131] If the respondent is not placed on the discontinued service list (and therefore may return to ordered ministry) or terminated, his or her "readiness to return to positions of authority" is assessed based on the following "minimal requirements": "letters of apology" are to be written and sent to affected people; "evidence of genuine remorse," "evidence of repentance," "undertaking of some form of restitution," and "satisfactory progress in a directed programme."[132] Further, the respondent must be supervised for "at least one year following return to a ministry position."[133]

The new policy identifies possible consequences, in accordance with *The Manual*:

> (a) If the Formal Hearing panel determines the complaint is proven it may make a Decision that any of the actions provided for in section 075(k) and (l) of *The Manual* be taken as the panel determines appropriate. These actions include but are not limited to Admonition, Rebuke, Suspension, Deposition, Discontinued Service List (Disciplinary) or Discontinued Lay Ministry Appointment List, Expulsion, and other actions as provided for. The Decision of the Formal Hearing panel is to be implemented as provided for in section 075(m) of *The Manual*.
> (b) If the complaint is not proven, the Formal Hearing panel shall dismiss the complaint.[134]

All records of the complaint are kept confidential and are retained using an anonymous coding system so that the files can be located in the event that future complaints are filed against the same respondent.[135] In the original policy, the conference personnel minister was to "ascertain whether there was confidential material related to previous complaints of sexual abuse" against the respondent immediately after receiving the signed complaint. In 1997 this step was delayed until after the charge had been proven at the end of a formal hearing process. This change was made in order to better ensure that such information be used only in the development of the formal hearing committee's recommendations, and is consistent with secular law.[136] Further, "in accordance with principles of natural justice," the respondent is to be informed in writing "in the event that confidential information relating to action taken on previous complaints of sexual abuse brought against the Respondent is obtained by the Formal Hearing Committee for use in developing its recommendations" so that he or she can have "an opportunity to address the Formal Hearing Committee in regard to the information."[137]

Throughout the process, the policy states that "Presbytery (or other appropriate church court) needs to ensure appropriate pastoral support to the complainant, the respondent and their respective families, and to the Pastoral Charge/employing unit."[138] The 2007 policy maintains this concern for the provision of pastoral care to the complainant and the respondent and family.[139] However, concern for the provision of such care to the pastoral charge led to petitions to the 2000 General Council requesting that a "consultant be appointed for the Pastoral Charge."[140] These petitions and other feedback to the General Council Committee led to discussion regarding the creation of a Consultant C, one assigned specifically to the involved pastoral charge. The Hamilton Conference proceeded with their creation of a Consultant C, although it is not part of the policy. The General Council Committee understood that part of the reason for this independent action was because the committee was not sufficiently proactive—the committee needed to meet more often and do more; this is a demanding and important subject area not yet addressed in the policy.[141]

The UCC recognizes that congregations and other involved parties need pastoral care throughout and after the process of addressing a complaint, regardless of the outcome. More work in terms of policy and education must be done to ensure that such care is adequate.

Screening Policies and/or Mandatory Education for Church Volunteers, Employees, and/or Officials (in Positions of Responsibility Regarding Children and Youth)

Faithful Footsteps—Screening Procedures for Positions of Trust and Authority in the United Church of Canada: A Handbook[142] is the result of the mandate given by the 1997 General Council to the Division of Ministry Personnel and Education and the Human Resources Committee "to develop policy, protocol and educational resources for the screening of people in positions of trust and authority in the United Church of Canada."[143]

Two supplementary brochures, "A Tender Trust" and "Trustworthy Care," were also designed as educational aids. This mandate was understood to build upon the 1992 *Sexual Abuse Policy* document and also to respond to "recent court rulings on vicarious liability [that] have underscored that institutions can and will be held responsible for the actions of their employees and volunteers."[144] In 1998 a task group was created comprised of members from the two mandated groups that began work on the project. Coincidentally, "the Ontario Screening Initiative, a project of Volunteer Canada, was meeting with faith groups to begin work on resource development and education for the screening of volunteers within the faith communities" in which the UCC participated through the task group.[145] Volunteer Canada developed a thorough resource entitled *Safe Steps: A Volunteer Screening Process for the Faith Community*. The UCC drew heavily on it, but created a slightly different resource that included a faith statement and was tailored to the particular context of the UCC.[146]

A news release on June 17, 1999, from the UCC stated "that the Supreme Court decision regarding vicarious liability in the Children's Foundation appeal could have wide ranging ramifications for many community groups, including church related programs involving children and youth. Further study of the decision is needed before the church is able to offer advice as to what this ruling may mean for a wide variety of church programs, including camps, youth groups and other outreach ministries of the United Church." Church spokesperson Rev. David Iverson, then general secretary of the Division of Mission in Canada, further explained that the UCC has "very clear policy guidelines" established in the 1992 *Sexual Abuse Policy*, and these will be built on to address the more particular issues related to the Supreme Court decision. As is explained in the introduction to *Faithful Footsteps*:

> The United Church of Canada has a legal, moral, and spiritual duty to care for and protect participants in our church programs. This is a legal principle called "Duty of Care," and church groups have been, and will be, held legally responsible for ensuring reasonable measures are taken to ensure safety.
>
> This handbook is provided by the United Church of Canada to help our institutions, organizations, ministries, camps and congregations understand the principles of screening, as one measure of our "Duty of Care," and to put these procedures into practice in the recruitment and selection of both staff and volunteers. Screening is a process designed to create and maintain a safe environment. The process involves identifying any activity or aspect of a ministry program which, by virtue of the position, could bring about harm to vulnerable individuals.[147]

The authors of this UCC document described the relationship of this set of guidelines to the Church's faith claims: "The principle which supports this statement on 'Screening Procedures for Positions of Trust and Authority in the United Church of Canada' is that followers of Jesus must demonstrate love, respect and honour for one another as members of the body of Christ. For Jesus reminds us that as we do to the most vulnerable among us we do unto him" (Matt. 25:35–40).[148]

The document is divided into four parts: an introduction, an explanation of risk and risk assessment, an outline of concrete screening procedures, and a conclusion. This handbook is meant to serve as a guide in screening UCC volunteers and employees in "many contexts," including: "Christian Education committees selecting Sunday School teachers, mid-week children's program leaders, etc.; Sexual Abuse Policy Committees selecting Sexual Harassment/Abuse consultants; Church boards responsible for the oversights of volunteer pastoral care visitors; Church Camp Boards; Presbytery or Conference Youth event planners; [and] Ministry and Personnel Committees."[149]

Determining the level of risk in a particular ministry setting and role is the first step in screening, and the document outlines criteria for this determination. Relevant factors identified are: the age of the participants (for assessing vulnerability); the setting (if it is physically safe for vulnerable participants); the activity; the "supervision provided"; and "the nature of the relationship between participant and leader," including the power differential.[150] Each factor is evaluated on a scale of 1 to 10 (1 indicating the lowest level of risk and 10 the highest). Accordingly, each position is assessed as a low, medium, or high risk:

- Low Risk: minimal or no contact with children or other vulnerable people or programs take place in large groups
- Medium Risk: activities with vulnerable people, but no private or one-on-one sessions
- High Risk: position presents opportunities to be alone with children or vulnerable persons, or opportunities to exert influence over youth or seniors[151]

Perhaps most helpful is the example case assessment that illustrates how to apply the risk-assessment scale.[152] This second section concludes with "options for reducing risk," ranging from eliminating the risky activity to minimizing the risk.[153]

The third section outlines the concrete steps involved in screening *all* people who are candidates for positions involving some level of risk. The ten steps are described in detail:

1 design an appropriate and clear job description that "formaliz[es] roles and ... send[s] a clear message to any potential abuser that safety of participants is a primary value"
2 engage in the risk-assessment process as outlined

3 be careful regarding how recruitment is undertaken and emphasize that
   you have a diligent screening process
4 design thorough, non-discriminatory application forms that include, if
   needed, the possibility that if an offer is made, a police records check will
   apply
5 use an interview to assess fairly the candidate's "fit," explain your screening
   process, and develop a written record of the interview team's assessment,
   which will be kept confidential or, if the candidate is unsuccessful, destroyed
6 complete thorough reference checks
7 complete a police records check (PRC) if the position involves sufficient
   risk, consider what types of offences are relevant to the position, and know
   the limitations of information attained via a PRC
8 understand that screening is ongoing: orientation and training offer opportunities to confirm (during a probationary period) that the person is suited
   to the position
9 implement ongoing supervision and evaluation as monitoring and support tools
10 gather evaluative feedback from program participants, staff, and
   volunteers[154]

Lastly, concluding words and appendices with references to additional
sources, further case examples, and template forms and letters are offered.

There are some peripheral but significant documents extending from this
guidebook. Immediately prior to the release of *Faithful Footsteps*, the General
Council Executive passed a motion stating that "all camps, schools, residences,
outreach ministries, and congregations using the name of 'The United Church
of Canada' and all groups incorporated under Appendix IV of *The Manual* shall
follow the national standards of the church in relation to the protection of vulnerable people served by church ministries."[155] For example, the UCC developed
(in 2004 and revised slightly in 2005 and 2006 to make the questions clearer) an
"accreditation site visit tool" for United Church associated camps. The extensive checklists are consistent with the screening procedures outlined in *Faithful
Footsteps*; all staff and volunteer positions are treated as positions of authority
and trust. Further, clear policies regarding "sexual conduct" at the camps are
required. Child abuse is identified and explained in camp policies, procedures,
and education for staff and volunteers. Additionally, the United Church has had
a *Camping Standards Manual* since 1982 and revised it in 2007 (previous revised
versions were released in 1993 and 2002). The rationale for such a manual is
described in the introduction: "it is our privilege and obligation as a church to
ensure that all United Church camps continue to offer safe and high-quality
programming for the thousands of people who come to camp each year."[156]

The UCC also requires education and screening of ordered and lay ministry
personnel. The work on *Faithful Footsteps* gave rise to further discussion among
the relevant UCC groups regarding the creation of "a comprehensive plan for

ongoing screening for all Ministry Personnel indicating the importance placed on making our church a safe place."[157] This 2000 General Council resolution affirmed current screening procedures and added a police records check (PRC). All candidates for UCC ordered ministry, all ministry personnel, all staff associates, all candidates for lay pastoral ministry in training, all seeking UCC endorsement, and all others retained on the roll of presbytery/district, must provide up-to-date (within three years) PRCs.[158] As of the 2006 General Council, there have been some substantial changes. Anyone seeking candidacy for ordered ministry or designated lay ministry, anyone seeking appointment as congregational designated ministers (these latter two terms incorporated the positions previously identified as lay pastoral ministers and staff associates, plus other paid accountable ministry positions, including parish nurses and paid youth workers), and anyone seeking admission to the UCC ministry must have a current (i.e., issued within the past twelve months) level 2 PRC. Also, all candidates for ordination, commissioning, recognition as a designated lay minister, and admission must have a level 2 PRC that has been issued within the twelve-month period prior to his or her final interview by the Conference Education and Students Committee. Anyone seeking a call or appointment in a presbytery accountable ministry in the UCC must have a current (i.e., issued within the past twelve months) level 2 PRC at the time the call or appointment is approved by the presbytery/presbyteries involved. Further, all ministry personnel who are currently serving a UCC call or appointment or who are on the roll of presbytery must obtain the vulnerable sector check (level 2) PRC at least every six years.[159]

Chapter Summary

The UCC has a history of commitment to social justice. One manifestation of this commitment has been a more progressive approach to sexuality-related issues than was reflected in the laws of the land at times. For example, contraception was approved by the UCC in 1932 primarily due to concern for the economic pressures that families experienced during the Depression years, whereas contraception was not legally available until 1969. Further, the UCC began ordaining women in 1936, and by the 1960s recognized that not all marital sex was consensual, whereas rape within marriage was not recognized by the law as a crime until 1983.

The protection of the vulnerable, particularly women and children, have been long-standing concerns of the UCC. For some years, this was expressed primarily by encouraging women to remain in their traditional roles of wife and mother. The image of the nuclear family as all good began to be challenged in the 1960s, as did the sole image of women as wives and mothers. This challenge was due largely to women claiming voice within the UCC and task groups and committees dedicated to examining the changing roles of women throughout the late 1970s and 1980s. In 1984 the UCC formally confessed its complicity in sexism, thus deepening the Church's willingness to be self-critical and confess its participation in systemic patterns of oppression.[160]

The same years brought a new focus on human sexuality; a move from a primarily act-centred sexual ethic to a primarily relational sexual ethic was well underway in the 1980s. Sin became much more clearly understood as a violation of right relationship, and particularly as harm to the vulnerable.

Children and children's voices emerged more loudly throughout the 1980s. Liturgically, the UCC took more official steps to encourage the inclusion of children in the celebration of the Lord's Supper, for example. Most notably, by the later 1980s abuse began to be discussed in relation to the family in general and children in particular.

The first policy and set of procedures regarding any form of sexual abuse allegations were developed in 1986 regarding sexual harassment; it had become recognized at an official level that sexual harassment occurred within the UCC.

The 1980s saw the results of the Badgely Report (1984) regarding child sexual abuse, the media exposure of the Mount Cashel traumas, and the revelation of the abuses at residential schools. These events combined with other factors, including the gradual emergence of the internal recognition that the Church as not immune from abuse; the greater voice taken by women and children; a newfound engagement throughout the 1980s with human sexuality; and the emergence of feminist and liberation theologies all paved the way for the development of a sexual abuse policy in the UCC.

Because of the United Church's conciliar structure, it has been possible for one overarching binding policy to be developed. Created in 1992, the policy has undergone revisions. The language of the policy has become increasingly legal in tone. Notably, an investigative step and a provision for third-party complaints were implemented in 2007. The latter has been particularly controversial; it will be important to assess this in the light of experience.

Chapter 4

The Anglican Church in Canada

THE ANGLICAN CHURCH IN CANADA (ACC) is a diocesan Church and, as such, does not have one binding sexual abuse complaint policy.[1] The ACC's National Executive Council (NEC) established their first policy addressing sexual abuse complaints in 1992. This policy was binding on all General Synod employees and volunteers; individual dioceses could choose to implement the same or similar policy, or not.

Church Structure and Description of the Context

After the United Church, the ACC is the next largest Protestant denomination in Canada, and has existed within what is now known as Canada for over two hundred years. At the time of the writing of this book, there are over 800,000 worshipping members and 2,035,500 people who affiliate themselves with the ACC.[2] The ACC is episcopalian with a national superstructure.

The wider Anglican Church is structured either nationally (e.g., by country) in most cases (for example, Canada, the United States, Nigeria), or regionally (e.g., covering more than one country) in some cases (for example, Southern Cone, Europe). Each national or regional Anglican Church is administratively independent. However, each is "in communion with the Church of England's Holy See of Canterbury and its Archbishop, and thereby in communion with other national Anglican churches." Member churches exercise jurisdictional independence, but share a common heritage. Churches in the Anglican communion continue to reflect the "balance of Protestant and Catholic principles that characterised the via media of the Elizabethan Settlement."

Member churches of the global communion do not exercise jurisdiction over each other, but seek to work co-operatively through a variety of international forums.[3] Bishops within the Anglican communion operate within a persuasive rather than a monarchical governance system; the power of the bishop is not absolute.[4] In each national or regional Church the constituent dioceses are subject to the oversight of the national bishop (called the primate) and a legislative body (General Synod) composed of three orders (bishops, clergy, laity) representing the various dioceses.[5] For legislation to pass at a meeting of the General

Synod, it must receive assent by both the Order of Bishops and the Orders of Clergy and Laity (who usually vote as one body).[6]

There are thirty dioceses in the Anglican Church of Canada, each of which mirrors the national structure. A diocesan bishop, who may be assisted by assistant, associate, or coadjutor bishops, is elected by a diocesan synod to govern each diocese. Assistant bishops are "appointed by the diocesan bishop to assist" in fulfilling diocesan duties, but do not have the right of succession or jurisdiction.[7] Suffragan and coadjutor bishops are elected by their respective diocesan synods "to assist a bishop of a diocese," with coadjutor bishops having the right of succession and suffragan bishops "having no right of succession."[8] "The Bishops' role is to exercise Christian authority, preside at the Sacraments, and preach the Gospel, as well as to exercise responsibility for Doctrinal matters and the unity of the Church."[9] Although bishops are elected, they must be ordained clergy of the ACC and, once elected, serve a term without limit.[10] The bishops of the ACC meet twice annually as a House of Bishops, with the primate (the head bishop of the ACC) presiding.[11] Although the bishops work toward consistency among diocesan canons (i.e., Church governing law) and administrative practices, variations between dioceses exist. The following is therefore only a general picture of the structure of each diocese.

Although not originally required, a diocesan synod governs each diocese. The synod meets annually or biannually, with special meetings occurring at the call of the bishop.[12] Synod is the policy-setting legislature of the diocese, and as such must approve all canons and other major diocesan policies; it also receives reports from the various committees and working units of the diocese.[13] In order to be approved, a measure must have the support of the majority of the Order of Clergy (which includes coadjutor, suffragan, and assistant bishops), a majority of the Order of Laity, and the approval of the bishop of the diocese.[14] In effect each order and the bishop hold veto power over each measure. When a measure calls for "the enactment, amendment or repeal of any part of the Constitution or Canons," it requires support of two-thirds of each order and the approval of the bishop before it can take effect.

In the interim between meetings of the synod, an Executive Council (or equivalent body) will "generally exercise all the powers and function of the Synod," as well as manage and administer "all the funds, lands and property of the Synod." For example, in the Diocese of Huron, the council consists of the bishop, coadjutor, suffragan bishops, members of the legal council, officers of the synod, archdeacons, one clerical and one lay member of each deanery, and a number of other clerical and lay members elected at large from the members of synod.[15]

Most dioceses also have a number of subsidiary levels of administration, usually called archdeaconries and deaneries.[16] An archdeacon, appointed by the bishop, heads an archdeaconry. Each archdeaconry is divided into regional deaneries, which are comprised of parishes. Each parish consists of one or more congregations. All parishes within the archdeaconry are under the supervision of the archdeacon.[17] Regional deans are responsible for ensuring that the bishops' administrative functions are carried out within their particular deaneries.[18]

For example, in the Diocese of Nova Scotia and Prince Edward Island, the archdeacon has the following responsibilities:

- [To] interact with [the] Regional Dean in supporting the pastoral and administrative roles of the episcopacy in the Diocese and in their Regions [with a greater focus on supporting the Bishops' pastoral role];[19]
- [To resolve concerns that] … cannot be resolved at the parish level;[20]
- To examine the ministry of the parish with reference to Diocesan Canons and Guidelines;[21] [and]
- To advise and assist clergy in all matters relating to their pastoral duties [and] provide real and moral support to clergy in times of personal difficulty.[22]

In this diocese, the regional deans' responsibilities include the following:

a   To make certain that parish business is being conducted properly, that proper records are being kept and that properties and buildings are being maintained in accordance with Diocesan policies and guidelines;[23]
b   To encourage and assist the Regional Council [deanery council] in providing adequate training for all parish and church officials in the fulfilment of their duties;[24] [and]
c   To ensure that every parish … observes the Canons and Guidelines of the Diocese.[25]

Regional deans also oversee meetings of the clericus—that is, all clergy of the deanery—and preside over meetings of the deanery council.[26] Deanery councils consist of the regional dean, "all Clergy, all Churchwardens, all Deputy Churchwardens, all Lay Representatives to Synod, all Substitute Lay Representatives and all Youth Representatives."[27] Deanery councils function as educational bodies, provide communication links between different parts of the diocese, and discuss matters placed before them.[28]

Dioceses are grouped to form four ecclesiastical provinces. These provinces predate the formation of the national General Synod of the Anglican Church of Canada.[29] A metropolitan, who is also a bishop of one of its constituent dioceses, governs each province along with its synodical structure, which is similar to that of a diocese. The limited functions of the ecclesiastical province include: the setting and amending of diocesan boundaries; the provision of oversight of diocesan bishops by the metropolitan; and the provision of a court of appeal for disciplinary decisions of diocesan bishops.

Although the Anglican Church has existed in Canada since 1788, the national General Synod of the Anglican Church (then the Church of England in the Dominion of Canada) did not come into being until 1893.[30] The General Synod consists of all bishops (diocesan, coadjutor, suffragan, and some assistants) and representative lay and clergy members elected by each diocese proportionate to the number of church members resident in that diocese.[31] The General Synod has "responsibility for matters of doctrine and discipline" with "undesignated powers rest[ing] with the diocese and/or diocesan bishops."[32]

Of particular relevance to this book are the General Synod's powers related to residential schools, and the discipline of clergy, staff, and Church members. In 2007 the ACC consecrated its first bishop responsible for First Nations peoples.[33] Although the General Synod has passed resolutions related to residential schools and took a lead in negotiating with the Government of Canada for the Comprehensive Settlement Agreement, the individual dioceses bear the financial responsibility. This is similar to the Roman Catholic Church, which is also structured as a diocesan Church. For this reason, although one diocese declared bankruptcy as a result of mounting claims, the entire Church was not forced into bankruptcy; likewise, all dioceses were required to affirm the Comprehensive Settlement Agreement before it could be declared that the Anglican Church of Canada was a party to the agreements.[34]

Similarly, the General Synod has responsibility for establishing a canon regarding discipline. Individual dioceses appear to either refer to the national canon or to have adopted a similar canon locally, thus preserving the ecclesiastical autonomy of each diocesan bishop.[35]

Approach to Child Sexual Abuse, Including Relevant Statements, Policies, and Practices: 1960–80

Issues of child sexual abuse were not very visible at an official level prior to 1980. Similar to the Roman Catholic and United Churches, engagement with other issues related to human sexuality and gender, including divorce and remarriage, the ordination of women, and sexual orientation, preceded concerted discussion of child sexual abuse.

Throughout the 1960s the ACC was very interested in divorce and remarriage. In 1962, the House of Bishops, when discussing the "solemnization of marriage by the clergy on a more liberal basis than at present," reported that "parents who have married following divorce ... regard themselves as excommunicated by the Church," although they may have children in the Church's confirmation classes; the bishops asked that this matter be studied further.[36] At that time individual dioceses set their own policies regarding the participation of divorced and remarried people in the life of the Church, with some dioceses banning them from the eucharist.[37] Accordingly, in 1964 the bishops recommended "that the marital status of the parents should not be a barrier to the admission of their children to baptism and confirmation." The bishops noted that in "the Province of Quebec, if a child is of such a union, when baptized it is recorded for life as an illegitimate." To avoid this stigmatizing, the bishops advised that "baptism [be] ... delayed" until after adoption takes place.[38]

At the 23rd Session of the General Synod, the "Theme of the Day" was the "The Church and the Family."[39] So moved were the delegates by the theme presentation of Rt. Rev. E.W. Scott that it was published in the *Journal of Proceedings*, providing a glimpse of how the Church viewed the family in 1967. At this meeting, the General Synod considered a major revision to its marriage canon in order to meet the increasing need to address divorce and remarriage. The purpose of marriage was seen as threefold: "the hallowing aright of the natural instincts and affections implanted by God; the procreation and nurturing, if it may be, of children; and the mutual society, help and comfort that one ought to have to the other in both prosperity and adversity."[40] However, the Rt. Rev. Scott noted that change was taking place within the family, particularly with respect to the role of women. Women had come to be seen as "much more concerned about inter-personal relationships within the marriage than simply with status and security." Both the ability to limit the size of the family through contraception and the lack of extended family relationships were mentioned, as were the changes in the status of women in society and the resulting need to re-evaluate the role of women in the Church.[41] The Rt. Rev. Scott noted, in 1967, that many "women hold professional positions in the secular world and know their ability to give leadership and desire a wider range of activities within the Church than is usually provided."[42]

Linked to this was the perception of the nuclear family as pure and therefore foundational to society. As a result, avoiding family breakdown was a priority.[43] Motions were centred on "Family Life," including the provision of adequate housing for families and women. Women's changing role in Church and society, it was concluded, needed to be accommodated to a greater degree if the family was to be preserved. Specifically, there were motions to form a unified Commission on Women to examine the role of women in the Church, and another calling for a policy to recruit, train, and employ more women in the Church.[44]

It was also at this General Synod that major changes to the ACC marriage canon were affirmed. The canon agreed to consider granting permission to remarry when: one's previous marriage(s) had been "validly dissolved or terminated in accordance with the law of property applicable thereto"; a divorced man's ex-wife and any children were supported according to his ability; and that the remarriage was not "a mere pro forma marriage to legitimate a child or children," among other criteria.[45]

In a landmark decision amid heated debate, the 27th General Synod voted to ordain women (1975). Although the General Synod resolved in favour of the ordination of women, it also resolved "that no bishop, priest, deacon or lay persons ... should be penalized in any manner, nor suffer any canonical disabilities,

nor be forced into positions which violate or coerce his or her conscience as
a result" of the affirmation on the ordination of women.[46] This meant that
ordained women could be denied appointment at any church if her appointment
contravened the relevant bishop's, priests', deacons', or the parish's conscience.
However, over time, this clause has become more limited through subsequent
actions of the House of Bishops.[47] In the years following, the synod advocated
for greater "progress towards sexual equality of opportunity in filling senior
positions at the national and diocesan levels of the church."[48]

In the late 1970s the House of Bishops examined the issue of the inclusion
of "homosexuals" within the life of the Church. Although much of the bishops'
discussions would not be made public until the mid-1980s, they affirmed that
homosexual people are "children of God, [and] have a full and equal claim, with
all other persons, upon the love, acceptance, concern and pastoral care of the
Church." The bishops acknowledged that homosexual people were entitled to
the same protections under the law, but also noted that the biblical purpose of
sexuality was for the completion of the male and female through heterosexual
unions and for procreation.[49]

The 1960s and 1970s were decades during which the ACC engaged in critical work and debate regarding marriage, divorce, women's roles, and sexual
orientation. Future years would see the expansion of this work and with this a
greater ability to critique the supposed priority of both the nuclear family and
the Church family. Child sexual abuse would not be addressed in any depth until
the mid- to late 1980s.

Approach to Child Sexual Abuse, Including Relevant Statements, Policies, and Practices: 1981–91

The 1980s saw the ACC further its work on violence against women and begin
to address child abuse in the latter part of the decade. In 1983, motions related
to violence and the abuse of children were passed by the General Synod, including Act 109, which called for "this General Synod [to] initiate ... steps towards
the elimination of pornography and depictions of sexual violence, particularly
toward women and children by enlisting where possible the co-operation of
other churches, pressing governments for stricter enforcement of existing laws,
and if this is inadequate, for passage of such further legislation as may be necessary to achieve this objective, and that this General Synod request the Program
Committee to give consideration to this important issue and make appropriate
recommendations to the Church."[50]

Pornography continued to be an abuse issue for the ACC, with the House of
Bishops issuing a statement in 1983 addressing "our understanding of human
sexuality and our deep concern for the impacts of pornography upon our people
and upon the whole of society."[51] Significantly, the bishops recognized that the
Church was not pure and had "sometimes failed both in its attitude and its

teaching to help its members understand and express these Biblical truths," and that "this failure has contributed to some of the negative attitudes to human sexuality which exist today." Because of their "belief in the beauty and the sacredness of human sexuality [they] are deeply concerned by the perversion of that sexuality in the form of pornography," noting that these materials have become more explicit and available. Further, pornography "victimises and debases women by portraying them as mere object, and degrades men by portraying a stereotype of aggression," and "pornography increasingly uses children as subjects, and increasingly depicts and incites to violent behaviour," thus distorting God's purpose for sexuality.[52] The bishops pledged themselves to work against this evil with like-minded Churches, institutions, and people of other faiths, and called upon members of the ACC to do the same.[53]

Significantly, this General Synod also requested that every diocese and parish "commit itself to using its own resources and to working with community groups to eliminate violence against children and youth" by stating "that violence and abuse is wrong and must stop"; supporting "emergency and longer term services necessary to protect abused children and youth"; and "foster[ing] the use of education material covering the theological, social and legal aspects of all forms of violence and abuse in the family."[54] Thus, the issue of child abuse was first framed as a component of "family violence," similarly to the United Church of Canada's initial approach to this issue.[55]

The Taskforce on Violence against Women was established in 1981 "with a mandate to encourage (1) the church to recognize and own that violence against women exists, that it is wrong, and that the church must be involved in necessary action to alleviate and prevent it; and (2) to get the church to address the problem as a structural and societal one."[56] In 1983, in accordance with the task force's request, the General Synod of the ACC passed a motion (Act 27) requesting that "every diocese and parish commit itself to using its own resources and to working with community groups to eliminate family violence," focusing on "the battering of women."[57] Additionally, the dioceses and parishes were asked:

1 To declare publicly that violence is wrong and that it must stop;
2 To support the emergency and longer-term services necessary to protect battered women and to enable them to re-establish their lives;
3 To lobby, where necessary, for changes in law, and in police, court, and social service procedures to ensure that women and men are treated justly;
4 To undertake preventative work in areas of marriage preparation and family life by exploring the issues related to wife-battering, e.g., isolation and dependence for the wife, and the husband's authority over his wife;
5 To provide further education for the clergy and laity in their roles as counsellors in this area.[58]

The resolution framed violence against women as a social issue relevant to the Church.

At the General Synod in 1986, the Taskforce on Violence against Women presented their report *Violence against Women: Abuse in Society and Church and Proposals for Change*; the report was published in book form in 1987. The report not only explored the causes of violence against women but also examined the role of the Church in sanctioning such violence; this awareness of complicity at an official General Synod level was new to the ACC. This recognition assisted the wider Church in addressing the possibility of child sexual abuse perpetrated by Church leaders. Because it lays significant groundwork for the emergence and analysis of child sexual abuse in the Church, this report will be examined in some depth.

Violence against Women documented the complicity of both Church and state in violence against women. "Historically both the church and state gave husbands the absolute right to appropriate and control, if necessary by force, the personal services of their wives, which included sexual services," wrote the task force, noting that until 1983, under Canadian law "husbands could rape their wives with complete legal impunity."[59] In addition to connecting violence against women to both the structure of modern capitalism and social arrangements that codify gender inequality, the authors also acknowledged that the Church had participated in this patriarchal systemic oppression by unduly using women's free labour.[60]

The task force urged the ACC to look critically at its conception of family, its theology, and its pastoral responses to domestic assault. In identifying the privatization of domestic violence and the attitude that saw the family as sacrosanct, the task force began to break the Church's silence. For example, the task force critiqued the Clapham Sect for perpetuating violence against women; the Sect was a group of British Anglicans who had proselytised "'the cult of true womanhood' in which male dominance and female submission were systematically elevated as cardinal Christian virtues."[61]

The authors understood sin primarily in relational terms as a breaking of mutual love, and called the Church to acknowledge its participation in violence against women through patriarchal theologies, its use of exclusive language, and an historic tendency to support "a pattern of dominance and submission."[62] They supported this claim through anecdotal examples. One woman, quoted anonymously, described her experience: "My pastor's reaction was to call and confront me. I hoped for some help, or at least some consolation and advice, but I received only a lecture on having deceived him and the community into thinking we had a Christian marriage. So in my shock and loneliness I was given no help. In fact my pastor contributed to my isolation and shame."[63]

The report identifies child abuse and violence against children and youth, but does not explain or explore these issues in any depth, aside from noting that male images and parental images of God are relevant to child abuse.[64] The authors stated that attention must be drawn to violence against women over child abuse because child abuse was more widely acknowledged: "child abuse is now widely recognized by the state and the helping professions, whereas assaults on wives still tend to be denied or disguised."[65] However, although wider Canadian society had begun to discuss child abuse, religious institutions, including the ACC, had yet to confess their complicity in terms of acknowledging and creating policies to respond to child abuse by their own leaders and employees.

Upon receiving the report of the Taskforce on Violence against Women and its recommendations, the General Synod of 1986 commended the report for study and action to the whole Church. Dioceses were asked to provide appropriate resources and to report progress and provide suggestions to the Women's Unit of the General Synod offices for the use of the General Synod's national executive prior to the 1989 meeting of the General Synod. The Committee on Ministry was asked to bring the report's relevant recommendations to the attention of ACC theological schools for implementation in the theology curricula.[66]

Between the 1983 and 1986 General Synods, the National Executive Council of the General Synod (NEC) considered two resolutions concerned with sexual offences against children and youth.[67] In response to the report *Getting on the Agenda: Informed Responses to the Report of the Committee on Sexual Offences against Children and Youths*, the NEC resolved to petition the federal minister of Health and Welfare to consider the report's recommendations and amend applicable legislation.[68] The Children's Unit of General Synod was asked to continue monitoring the subject matter and "hold a joint discussion of the report" with the ecumenical Churches' Council on Justice and Corrections as soon as possible.[69] Act 63 of the 1986 General Synod continued with the theme of sexual offences against children and urged provincial and federal governments to "pursue: a) a program of treatment for convicted pedophiles and their victims; and b) a concerted effort to apprehend and convict publishers, distributors, and possessors of child-pornography so as to uphold the law as it now stands"; to examine children's rights legislation in connection with the United Nations' *Declaration of the Rights of the Child*; and to educate "children to help them learn how to avoid becoming victims of abuse."[70]

Many of the above themes were continued at the 1989 meeting of General Synod, held in St. John's, Newfoundland, at which a resolution was passed (Act 144) without debate, urging the provincial and federal governments "to provide the necessary resources and combat the serious problem of sexual abuse of children across the country." Those at the meeting also expressed "deep concern about the frequency of domestic violence and the sexual abuse of children" and asked "Christian leaders to be explicit about the sinfulness of violence and sexual abuse whether of children or adults, and to devise means of providing support for the victims and perpetrators of such exploitation to enable them to break the cycle of abuse."[71]

During this period of time, the study document *A Study Resource on Human Sexuality* was released for use in ACC parishes. The document included some earlier statements from the House of Bishops and articles regarding theology and sexuality, including "homosexuality."[72] The 32nd Session of the General Synod emphasized the need for continued reflection on sexuality, encouraging "each diocese and parish [to] increase by study, prayer and action their understanding of sexuality, supporting the Church in enabling all persons to develop a richer awareness of their gifts of sexuality and the dignity of all before God."[73] At the end of this period, in 1991, the House of Bishops reaffirmed the 1979 requirement that homosexuals who wished to be ordained must abstain from sexual activity through celibacy.[74]

Sexual orientation continues to be debated within the ACC. For a number of Anglican parishioners, child sexual abuse issues have been linked and confused with sexual orientation issues. A General Synod-commissioned national ACC study found that "in many smaller communities, homosexuality and sexual abuse has become a single 'hyphenated topic'" among both ordained and lay members.[75] For example, reporting on the results of interviews with parishioners from urban Toronto parishes, researcher Sally Edmonds Preiner states that discussions of homosexuality blend into other issues, including residential schools and sexual abuse of children: "these murky discussions are issues and concerns around 'the protection of the most vulnerable,' by which they mean sexual abuse of young children, in particular, boys."[76] This conflation can prevent awareness of child sexual abuse when the offender is heterosexual, which is most often the case.

In 1990, the House of Bishops received a report from the Paedophilia Task Force. In discussing the working paper, Bishop Conlin said, "there is a need to raise our consciousness on the issue. In the event of a reported case, the first step is confrontation, not avoidance."[77] This House of Bishops record also states that "clear policies which describe inappropriate sexual behaviour" must be developed, and relevant "education, particularly among bishops and clergy" provided.[78] Accordingly, the bishops requested that the primate "appoint a task force to establish sexual abuse policies and guidelines for use" across the Church, "taking into consideration the work that is already in progress."[79]

Approach to Child Sexual Abuse, Including Relevant Statements, Policies, and Practices: 1992–2009

In 1992, the General Synod referred a resolution on the "Sexual Molestation and Abuse of Children" to the NEC. This significant resolution was the first to claim formally the possible perpetration of child sexual abuse by ACC personnel; the General Synod moved to "recognize that sexual molestation and abuse of young persons by some church personnel while administering church programs has occurred and deeply regrets that the pastoral needs of some victims and their families have not been met." It further asked the Program Committee to create a protocol for use by the whole ACC: "a comprehensive protocol [is needed] for responding to reports of sexual molestation and abuse of young persons by some church personnel and that this protocol be circulated to all dioceses."[80] This resolution marks the start of development of specific policies to deal with child sexual abuse complaints.

In 1992 the ACC National Executive Council (NEC) adopted its first *Sexual Assault and Harassment Policy*. The policy affirmed "that every human being is created in the image of God who has made us for loving, covenantal relationships with our Creator, others and the world," and that "our personal dignity, freedom and bodily integrity are ensured by faithfulness to just covenants of mutual entrustment care and respect." It acknowledged systemic vulnerability: "that children, adolescents, the infirm and elderly are particularly vulnerable to the tragic consequences of broken covenants and abuse," and that "special care must be taken to protect their individual rights and personal integrity." Sexual abuse was described as "self-gratification by exploitation." The resolution called on the Church to be "clear about these violations of sexual intimacy; ... explicit in its teaching about these particular aberrations of sexual relations; aggressively proactive about its social policy and action touching on these areas; and forthright in dealing with violations in its own community."[81]

The policy guidelines developed are binding only to employees and volunteers of the General Synod and its national office; dioceses may choose to adopt the policy as is, in part, or not at all. The policy stated that the ACC's national office would not tolerate "sexual assault, sexual harassment, or sexual abuse of any kind, whether to adult, adolescent or child, male or female, by or to any staff person, contract employee or volunteer...." Accordingly, the national office was to "deal with any accusations promptly, seriously and systematically, [and] where appropriate, in co-operation with proper authorities." It was expected that the greatest care would be taken "to avoid taking advantage of trust, or abusing power and the responsibility of authority" in relationships of trust.[82]

After the policy was adopted, implementation guidelines were developed. The first guidelines were adopted in November 1992, and revised in November 1993.[83] In 1997 the officer of the General Synod appointed a committee to review the policy. In addition to examining difficulties encountered in a "harassment case involving national staff members," the committee, more generally, was to "ensure that the guidelines provide a just, speedy, streamlined and efficient structure to handle sexual harassment and abuse complaints."[84] The review resulted in amendments to the policy in 1998. The policy was revised again in March 1999 and March 2001.[85] Many of these revisions dealt with technical matters. For example, the March 2001 revisions concerned the timing of training, and the March 1999 amendments were directed primarily at affirming that "adherence to this policy is seen and understood as a mandatory and vital component of our life and work together as employed staff members and volunteers of the General Synod of the Anglican Church of Canada."[86]

The availability of a national-level sexual abuse and harassment policy has been seen as a needed foundation, but some Anglicans have since requested more direction at the diocesan level. At the General Synod of 2001 a motion was approved stating "that this General Synod direct the Council of the General Synod to develop comprehensive sexual abuse and harassment guidelines for use throughout the Anglican Church of Canada."[87] The following year, the House of Bishops discussed the need "for a national policy on sexual misconduct."[88] Bishop Jenks stated that "he felt strongly about the need for a national policy," saying that "it should be included in the General Synod Handbook, and that it should even be a canon"; the provision of a policy for national-level staff and volunteers that is offered as only a guide to the rest of the ACC was insufficient from the perspective of such proponents.[89] Later in 2002, at a meeting of the Council of General Synod, it was moved that there be an investigation of the "canonical ramifications of some of the present diocesan sexual misconduct policies as a preliminary step to the development of national guidelines for the Anglican Church of Canada." National-level units were asked to work co-operatively on this matter.[90] By 2004, the Handbook Concerns Committee was asked to work in consultation with the general secretary and others to review the existing national-level *Sexual Abuse and Harassment Policy and Guidelines* and report any recommended changes back to the Council of General Synod by November 2005.[91] Newly revised guidelines, titled the *Sexual Misconduct Policy Applicable to National Staff and Volunteers*, were prepared for May 2005, and at the November meeting, council adopted the new document in place of the previous policy and recommended it to other organs of the national body for adoption.[92] A nationally binding policy applicable to all dioceses was not an outcome.

This revised policy maintains continuity with the earlier policy, but is more clearly written. The policy states the council's commitment to ensure:

- That all our work places and endeavours are free from violence, coercion, discrimination and sexual misconduct,
- That no one is subjected to sexual misconduct of any kind,
- That we deal promptly, seriously and systematically with all complaints of sexual misconduct,
- That those who hold positions of trust or power in the church do not take advantage of, or abuse, that trust or power,
- That we practice an ethic of mutual respect, responsibility and caring,
- That we model wholeness and healthy sexuality in or relationships.[93]

Sexual misconduct is construed broadly and includes behaviours that include "sexual harassment, sexual exploitation and sexual assault."

This revised policy requires that all national-level employees and volunteers "agree in writing to comply with" the policy and review it as changes occur.

Specific responsibilities for ongoing orientation and administration of the policy are assigned to the officers of the General Synod, the Council of General Synod, and the human resources coordinator.[94]

Complaints of Child Sexual Abuse and Complaints by Adults of Historical Childhood Sexual Abuse

Although the national ACC and individual diocesan policies tend to focus on current rather than historical cases of abuse, complaints of historic child sexual abuse can be addressed. Each diocese is to make that decision autonomously. The national policy advises that complaints must be "made within six months after the incident given rise to it in order that it may be fairly and thoroughly considered and investigated"; however, the general secretary of the ACC "may extend the time for making a compliant if no one will be prejudiced by the extension."[95] This instruction may have been written implicitly with adult-to-adult sexual abuse complaints in mind. Ultimately, decisions regarding whether or not to proceed with a historical complaint are at the discretion of the bishop. The diocesan bishop can make use of a local diocesan sexual abuse or crisis response team to discern the appropriate actions to be taken in a case of historic abuse.

In all cases of child sexual abuse, historic or current, *Canon XVIII* applies and is used to discipline guilty parties. Also, in some cases where complaints of historic child sexual abuse have been pursued unsuccessfully in criminal courts, Church discipline has occurred.

The accused is to be presumed innocent until the alleged misconduct is proven or confessed, and all those involved are entitled to pastoral care.[96] In the case of child sexual abuse or abuse of other vulnerable people, the incident "must be reported to the appropriate authorities as required by law." Any proceedings under the ACC policy will not commence until after the civil authorities have completed their investigation; during an investigation, however, a person subject to such an allegation may be—but not necessarily—suspended with pay from his or her duties.[97]

Where the complainant is a child or vulnerable adult, the matter is reported to the appropriate civil authority (e.g., the Children's Aid Society) and "the officers of the General Synod will co-operate" with the completion of the investigation by the respective civil authority. Again, "no investigation or mediation will be commenced or continued under this Policy while an investigation is being made by an external [civil] authority." Further, the policy instructs that pastoral and other therapeutic support will be offered "to a child or vulnerable person, and to their family during any investigation by an external authority."[98]

The policy advises that before making a complaint, "anyone who believes they have been a victim of sexual misconduct by an employee or volunteer *should* inform the person responsible for the misconduct that it is unacceptable and must stop" (emphasis mine); however, this is not a prerequisite to filing a complaint, and is likely a further example of the policy's implicit emphasis on adult complainants.[99] Further, it is required that complainants from an identified vulnerable group will be connected to the appropriate civil authority and the complaint will be processed primarily through that system.[100]

When a complainant requests an informal process, the person receiving the complaint shall "promptly provide assistance and, if no formal complaint is made, shall endeavour to resolve the matter between the complainant and the" accused and "shall make a written report of the factual circumstances of the complaint, of the action taken and the result of such action" and deliver the report to the general secretary.[101]

In the case of a formal procedure, the complainant must submit "a formal written complaint giving particulars of the alleged sexual misconduct and requesting an investigation" to the general secretary; if the complaint is against the general secretary, it is delivered to the primate, and if it is against the primate, to the senior provincial metropolitan, "who shall carry out the responsibilities hereafter assigned to the General Secretary."[102]

In addition to the national-level policy, as has been stated, each diocese develops its own policy, which may or may not be consistent with the national-level policy. The policies of the Diocese of Huron are discussed below, followed by a briefer discussion of the Kootenay diocesan approach to the general issue of policy and current and historic sexual abuse complaints. These policy examples will continue to be traced in later sections of this chapter.

The Diocese of Huron covers much of southwestern Ontario, including the counties of Essex, Kent, Elgin, Middlesex, Lambton, Perth, Huron, Oxford, Waterloo, Bruce, Grey, Norfolk, and Brant. This diocese is geographically diverse, and includes the cities of London, Windsor, and Kitchener-Waterloo-Cambridge, as well as many small towns, villages, farming and cottage communities. As of May 2006, the diocese was composed of 220 parishes, and reported 48,039 people on the rolls of its congregations.[103] The diocese has 3,208 pupils in its Sunday Schools, taught by 835 teachers.[104]

It is the policy of the Diocese of Huron that sexual abuse (defined to include sexual harassment, sexual exploitation, sexual misconduct, and sexual assault) by any person of the Diocese of Huron (volunteer, paid, lay, or ordained) will not be tolerated, regardless of the jurisdiction in which a person carries out his or her work or ministry.[105] The responsibility for implementing Huron's protocol initially resided with a Sexual Abuse Response Team (SART) and later what was called the Safe Church Committee.

SART was formed in 1996 with responsibilities related to the diocesan policy on sexual abuse/harassment and issues of sexual misconduct.[106] The work of this team was to revise the existing policy; to improve procedural matters and ensure accuracy; to serve as a resource for the implementation of preventative measures within diocesan parishes; to provide for the ongoing education of all ACC members in the diocese; and to work with congregations when sexual misconduct was found or alleged.[107] Up until 2003, when SART was merged with the Screening in Faith Committee to form the Safe Church Committee, it had made only minor revisions to the original policy.[108] When the committees merged, so too did their policies.

The subsequent Safe Church Committee consisted of one overarching committee with three subcommittees: the Crisis Response Working Group, the Education Committee, and the Sexual Misconduct Response Team.[109] The Crisis Response Working Group compiled a "resource list of people who would be available to assist in the event of a parish crisis," noting that such a crisis need not be related to sexual misconduct, but could be a more general crisis in the wider community, such as a natural disaster.[110] The Education Committee was to provide information to individual parishes regarding the Safe Church initiative and assist with its implementation (see the "Screening Policies" section below).[111] The Sexual Misconduct Response Team was to assist "where allegations of abuse are made" and work on "procedures surrounding complaints and the investigation process."[112]

Detailed response procedures for the diocesan bishop and the Sexual Misconduct Response Team (SMRT) are provided in the *Safe Church Policy*. The policy is designed to assist in the discovery of "the truth and to protect the vulnerable, stop any abuse, and to promote restoration and healing." The policy also attempts to strike a balance between supporting the investigation of complaints and providing pastoral care for both the complainant and the accused.

Under this policy, complaints against members of the Diocese of Huron are addressed within the diocese. However, complaints against the senior diocesan bishop are received either by the metropolitan of the EPO or, if the senior diocesan bishop is also the metropolitan, the primate of the ACC adjudicates the complaint.[113]

Although "ultimate responsibility and authority" rest with the diocesan bishop, "subject to applicable criminal and civil law," the bishop may request the SMRT to be involved by

- meeting with the complainant and other persons who may have relevant information,
- recommending actions that may determine the truth of the allegations,
- enlisting additional professional people to assist,
- as a result of investigation, making recommendations about discipline and pastoral care,
- recommending appropriate long-term follow-up.

In addition to short-term investigative work, the SMRT is also available to respond to questions and provide support to clergy, lay workers, and volunteers.[114]

Other dioceses of the ACC have enacted policies similar to the Diocese of Huron. The Diocese of Kootenay, which covers the southeastern section of British Columbia, enacted its current policy in 1998. The policy provides for the appointment of a Diocesan Response Team to: investigate allegations "to a point beyond which it is the scope of criminal or child welfare or human rights investigations; ... recommend appropriate courses of action; ... offer support and help to victim and offender by encouraging and assisting in arranging pastoral and therapeutic care ...; [and] offer support education and information" to the diocese.[115]

In the case of allegations related to sexual misconduct and adult victims, a written complaint will be requested and a meeting between the Diocesan Response Team and the complainant arranged (Part D). The policy does not address directly complaints of historical child sexual abuse. Depending on the results of the meeting with the complainant and alleged perpetrator, the team will make recommendations to the diocesan bishop (Part S).

Investigative Procedures Regarding Complaints

The national *Sexual Misconduct Policy* (2005) details an investigative procedure regarding formal complaints. First, the "General Secretary shall provide a copy of the complaint to the person against whom it is made and shall either (a) refer the complaint to mediation or (b) direct the Human Resources Coordinator or/ and independent investigator or investigators to investigate the complaint and report within two week or such further time as the General Secretary allows."[116] The policy does not outline specific qualifications for investigators. Investigators are to carry out interviews with the accused, the complainant, and other people, and summarize and report on:

- the alleged misconduct
- the response of the person against whom the complaint was made
- admitted and established facts
- unestablished allegations
- a finding as to whether or not the alleged misconduct occurred
- make recommendations the investigators consider appropriate[117]

Under this 2005 policy, upon completion of the investigation it is the responsibility of the general secretary to "provide copies of the report to the complainant and the person against whom the complaint was made ..., determine if the complaint has been substantiated or not or may, if the parties agree, refer it to mediation." If, however, the general secretary determines that the complaint is substantiated, she or he may initiate "appropriate disciplinary and remedial actions," and if the matter amounts to sexual assault, refer it to "the appropriate police authority for criminal investigation." If criminal charges have been laid, in respect to a matter "about which a compliant has been made under this Policy, no proceeding under the Policy shall be commenced or continued until the criminal charges have been finally disposed of."[118]

At the time of the writing of this book, some dioceses have followed this policy, while others have developed their own processes, usually similar, and others have yet to develop either a policy or an investigative piece. All dioceses are committed to not interfering with civil investigations. The relevant sections of the Huron and Kootenay Diocesan policies, respectively, will provide illustrative examples of diocesan approaches to the investigation of child sexual abuse complaints.

The primary investigation process is to allow the legal investigation of the police or Children's Aid Society to take place unobstructed, and to make use of their findings. After the legal investigation is complete, the diocesan bishop may also choose to investigate the case.[119]

No general guidelines for investigations by the Diocese of Huron are outlined. However, there is a confidential reporting form and a complaint follow-up form that are to be completed by the SMRT.[120] Form B asks general questions about the nature of the alleged abuse, the victim, the time and location in which it is to have taken place, and the actions taken. Form D is a checklist of actions, including the notification of diocesan officials and the presentation of the complaint to the accused.

In the case of a complaint of ongoing child sexual abuse, the diocesan procedures make use of the *Child and Family Services Act (Ontario)* in conformity with Ontario civil law. Suspected cases of current child sexual abuse are reported directly to the Children's Aid Society (CAS).[121] As per the regulations made under the *Child and Family Services Act (Ontario)*, diocesan members are to permit the Children's Aid Society and the police to conduct their investigation unhindered. Pastoral care may still be offered to the complainant, his or her family, and the respondent.[122] In all cases, the bishop will assist with the police and/or CAS investigation(s) when asked, and "will normally consult with the SMRT about future actions," including meeting with the affected congregation once the police and/or CAS investigation is completed.[123]

In cases of allegations of sexual misconduct toward an adult where criminal charges are involved, the bishop also "will normally consult with the SMRT about future actions." If criminal charges are not involved and there is no police investigation, "The Bishop will ordinarily involve the SMRT ... [and] provide [them with] the initial information about the allegations." Usually the SMRT will then meet with the complainant to obtain a written complaint and written permission to present the complaint to the accused. The bishop will present the complaint to the accused "in the presence of representation from the SMRT in the course of an interview."[124] If, as a result of the investigation, the allegations are proven, "every effort needs to be made to hear, believe and empower victims and to enable them to be vindicated, to be set free form the power of the violation in their lives."[125]

Similarly, the Diocese of Kootenay's policy affirms that the diocese will co-operate with all civil investigations and requires suspected cases of current child sexual abuse be reported to civil authorities.[126] In all investigations, the diocese pledges to co-operate with civil authorities.[127]

Complaints Regarding People Who Are Not Church Personnel and Complaints Regarding People Who Are Church Officials and/or Employees

The policies described above make no distinction between those who are employees (clergy or lay), volunteers, or people who hold a particular office in the Church (e.g., a church warden), except in terms of the potential conse-quences to the respondent if the complaint is found to have substance. In the case of current child sexual abuse, the legal requirement to report compels any person with reasonable suspicion of abuse to make a report to the appropriate civil authority. In such cases, the diocesan policies examined provide for the pos-sibility of pursuing such complaints within the Church courts upon completion of the civil process. The bishop is able to use the diocesan Sexual Abuse Response Team (e.g., the Diocese of Huron's SMRT) or the diocesan Crisis Response Team, should either exist. This would also apply to complaints of historic child sexual abuse. The response teams could assist in providing pastoral care after such events have occurred, regardless of whether or not Church court proceedings are undertaken in response to a complaint.

Third-Party Complaints

Most policies do not make explicit mention of third-party complaints aside from the legal obligation to report suspicion of child abuse. Huron's policy states that "any complaint of sexual abuse of a child by any person" should be reported and acted upon.[128] Third-party complaints are not explicitly provided for regard-ing adult-to-adult cases. The language regarding appeals and the launching of complaints under *Canon XVIII: Discipline* is somewhat vague, suggesting that anyone who has launched a complaint may seek an appeal. Again, there is within this a suggestion that anyone, including third parties, may launch a complaint.

Responses to Involved People

The responses to involved people vary according to diocese and the findings of the complaint. In the case of the Diocese of Huron, if the respondent is a clergy member, staff person, or volunteer, she or he may be asked to voluntarily relin-quish duties or "be placed on a leave of absence, at the Bishop's discretion," with the understanding that "such leave is [paid and] without prejudice" during the course of any civil procedures.[129] Again, as with both the Roman Catholic and United Churches, the assumption that it is morally most appropriate to leave open the possibility of continuing one's duties during an investigation—either civil or Church—must be questioned. Not only is there the possibility that a respondent might continue to do harm within the Church if he or she is indeed guilty, but gossip and judgment perhaps are even more encouraged by such a subjective policy.

If the allegations are proven through a civil investigation, "offenders will be called to rediscover their own humanity for their own well-being and for the well-being of the community" through pastoral care.[130] Pastoral care is also to be offered to the victim, the victim's family, the parish family, colleagues, and the wider Church; a process for handling the trauma, debriefing, and healing necessary in the parish community is outlined in the diocesan policy.[131]

Disciplinary proceedings may be launched against those found guilty using the procedure outlined in *Canon XVIII: Discipline*. Further, staff members or volunteers "found guilty of a criminal sexual offence involving a child or vulnerable person may be dismissed from employment or removed as a volunteer."[132] Significantly, it is not necessarily the case that they will be "dismissed ... or removed." It would be constructive for the possible reasons for re-entry to be identified, otherwise it is easy to imagine a very questionable rationale that fails to prioritize the protection of the vulnerable.

Church penalties for conviction of sexual misconduct, either in civil courts or by ecclesiastical officials/courts, are arrived at through the application of *Canon XVIII: Discipline*. There are few other canons of General Synod that have such wide-reaching applicability as the canons dealing with discipline/ ecclesiastical offences and the licensing of clergy. Defining ecclesiastical offences and discipline resulting from an ecclesiastical conviction is a power of General Synod, and is codified in *Canon XVIII*. The licensing of clergy and the discipline of clergy and members is a historic power of the bishops.

Canon XVIII may be applied by a diocesan bishop to bishops (assistant, coadjutor, suffragan), priests, deacons, and lay members of the ACC under her or his jurisdiction; a diocesan bishop is similarly under the jurisdiction of a metropolitan, who is under the authority of the primate.[133] Some individual dioceses have created discipline canons building upon *Canon XVIII*, ceding precedence to the national canon.

Ecclesiastical offences are defined as

1 Conviction of an indictable offence;
2 Immorality;
3 Disobedience to the bishop to whom such person has sworn canonical obedience;
4 Violation of any lawful Constitution or Canon of the Church, whether of a Diocese, province or the General Synod by which the person is bound;
5 Willful or habitual neglect of the exercise of the ministry of the person without cause;
6 Willful or habitual neglect of the duties of any office or position of trust to which the person has been appointed or elected;

7   Teaching or advocating doctrines contrary to those accepted by the Anglican Church of Canada; and

8   Contemptuous or disrespectful conduct towards the bishop of the diocese in matters.[134]

Any ACC member convicted criminally of sexual misconduct could also come under ecclesiastical discipline. Even if the accused is not found criminally guilty of sexual misconduct, the complaint nonetheless could be investigated in the ACC as a matter of immorality.

There are four possible penalties that can be imposed as consequences for the conviction of an ecclesiastical offence: "(i) admonition, (ii) suspension from the exercise of ministry or office; (iii) deprivation of office or ministry; [or] (iv) deposition from the exercise of ministry if the person is ordained."[135] The diocesan bishop may deliver admonition, either publicly or privately, as he or she determines.[136]

Suspension is for a fixed duration and may include additional conditions.[137] This penalty can be imposed by a bishop or by an ACC court.[138] A person who is under suspension "shall not exercise the function of his or her ministry anywhere in Canada" and if found violating this or any other condition, a penalty of deprivation may also be imposed "after a further hearing." While under suspension, "the bishop may deprive the suspended person of the whole or part of any stipend, income or emoluments associated with the ministry or office from which the person stands suspended."[139]

Deprivation results in a severing of the relationship between the disciplined person and the "parish, mission, congregation, diocese or office." A person so disciplined "shall be incapable of holding any office or performing any function in any diocese in The Anglican Church of Canada" until he or she has been "restored by the bishop of the diocese in which the office from which the person was deprived is located."[140]

Deposition is the most severe penalty for a clergyperson and means that the clergyperson is assessed as having abandoned her or his ministry.[141] Abandonment "removes from the priest or deacon the right to exercise the office, including the spiritual authority, of a minister of Word and Sacraments conferred in ordination."[142] Notice of the person's abandonment of ministry is to be given to "all metropolitans and diocesan bishops."[143] A person so disciplined may seek restoration to his or her former status, and may also appeal both the charge of abandonment and a refusal of reinstatement.[144] The provisions of this section apply equally to bishops with appropriate modifications.[145]

Regarding the appeal process, a person convicted in an ecclesiastical court may ask the respective court to review both the determination of the offence and the penalty that has been imposed.[146] When reviewing whether or not an ecclesiastical offence has occurred, the court is to conduct the review "as if it were an original trial held in the court"; when reviewing the appropriateness of a penalty, the only evidence to be presented is that which is relevant to the review.[147]

An appeal process is also provided for the person or persons who made the original allegation. The complainant, or other person who made the original allegation, may petition the Executive Council of the diocese for a review of her or his decision on the matter of the offence and the penalty imposed.[148] A review may also be initiated by motion of the Executive Council.

Canon XVIII outlines specific procedures for all courts. In carrying out their work, all courts are to act in accordance with the principles of natural justice.[149] Notices of decisions of an ecclesiastical court are to be distributed to all clergy of the applicable diocese and all bishops of the ACC when the penalty is suspension; in the case of deprivation or deposition, notice of the decision is given to all metropolitans.[150]

There is provision to appeal a decision of a lower court to a higher court. "Any judgement or order of a diocesan court of the president thereof" may be appealed to the court of the ecclesiastical province of which the diocese is a member.[151] Further appeal may be made to the Supreme Court of the ACC, a national body under the responsibility of the General Synod.[152]

Case Examples. The former Diocese of the Caribou operated St. George's Indian Residential School (IRS) in Lytton, British Columbia.[153] "Mr. [Derek] Clarke had no training in child care" and had been asked to leave the position he held previously at another Anglican school "because he was unqualified." He was then hired as the dormitory supervisor at the Lytton school, where he was suspected of sexually assaulting several children and subsequently fired. The police, the Department of Indian Affairs, and the boys' parents were not informed of the suspected abuse. Justice Janice Dillon found the Diocese of the Caribou guilty by vicarious liability and awarded restitution.[154] With mounting expenses from this and other cases, this relatively poor diocese eventually declared bankruptcy.[155]

The case of Richard James Schenck is illustrative of diocesan sexual misconduct procedures applied to a lay worker. Schenck was responsible for training servers during the celebration of the Eucharist at an Etobicoke ACC church.[156] As a result of his ecclesial conviction, Schenck "was relieved of his duties at the church." He was also criminally charged.[157]

The case of Archdeacon Thomas Corston illustrates the application of diocesan policy in a case in which it was determined that there were no grounds for criminal charges. A complaint was made against the archdeacon and investigated by Sudbury Regional Police, who "found no basis for criminal charges." Subsequently, Archdeacon Corston was relieved of his duties as priest at Church of the Epiphany, Sudbury, and as archdeacon of the Sudbury-Manitoulin archdeaconry pending the results of a diocesan investigation. In this case, a charge of immorality was laid by the diocesan bishop against Archdeacon Corston, and the matter referred to an elected diocesan court for trial.[158] The ecclesiastical court process found Archdeacon Corston not guilty of the charge of immorality: "The ecclesiastical … court ruled on June 27 that the complainant was 'a totally unbelievable witness' and that the allegations were 'malicious and constitute a clumsy attempt to extort money from the diocese of Algoma.'" The archdeacon was awarded $50,000 by the diocese to cover court costs, and was reinstated.[159]

Similar to the above is a case from the Diocese of Nova Scotia and Prince Edward Island. A man made allegations of historic childhood sexual abuse against two priests serving in Nova Scotia. One priest, Rev. Wayne Lynch, pleaded guilty to the charges; at the time of his plea it was stated that "the church will decide what discipline it will impose ... [and] it is widely anticipated that Fr. Lynch will be asked to relinquish his priesthood. The other priest, Rev. Michael Boyd, pleaded not guilty and went to trial.[160] At the time the charge was laid against Rev. Boyd, the diocesan bishop, Arthur Peters, placed Boyd on paid leave, and stated that all contact between Mr. Boyd and Archbishop Peters "must end until the matter was cleared up."[161] After pursing the case, Crown prosecutors dropped the charges "for lack of evidence." A subsequent ecclesiastical investigation found Boyd not guilty of "inappropriate behaviour" under the immorality clause.[162] After the ecclesiastical investigation, Mr. Boyd was cleared and reinstated.[163]

Lastly, the case of John Gallienne, described by media reports as "a predatory paedophile who exploited his position of trust and authority as choir master and organist at St. George's Cathedral in Kingston [Ontario]," is a case worthy of a longer review. Gallienne pleaded guilty to twenty charges of child sexual abuse, mostly related to his work in Kingston.[164]

At the time of his release from prison, then bishop of Ontario, Peter Mason, placed three restrictions upon Gallienne, barring him from playing instruments during worship or concert events at any diocesan parish, leading or organizing singing groups for worship or concerts in the diocese, and leading or actively participating in "any church-related organisation which exists for the benefit of young people, or includes substantial numbers of them in its membership"; these restrictions were also adopted by the neighbouring Diocese of Ottawa.[165] Gallienne was banned "for life from setting foot in or near St. George's" as Bishop Mason considered the "pain and damage upon present and former members of St. George's Cathedral" to be so severe that his mere presence would be "unwelcome and offensive and destabilizing." Gallienne would, however, be able to join another Anglican parish "in order that he and his family may worship and receive pastoral care and enter into the life of a Christian community." Bishop Mason sent copies of this statement to all ACC dioceses.[166] Making his position clear, Bishop Mason told a reporter "Sexual abuse is wrong, it's evil and it's sinful and there will be zero tolerance for it in the church body."[167]

The abuses for which Gallienne was convicted first came to light in the 1970s. In 1977 then rector of St. George's Cathedral, Rev. David Sinclair, became aware of two cases of sexual abuse committed by Gallienne, one because of an admission by the perpetrator. Sinclair then spoke to other Church officials, including the diocesan chancellor (lawyer) and the bishop; "after a flurry of meetings, the church acted internally," telling Gallienne "not to be alone with choirboys," and warned that repeating his offence would mean immediate termination. After Sinclair left the cathedral a year later, the restrictions were abandoned.[168] Sinclair also noted that Gallienne had close personal ties with many members of the congregation who helped to shield him from suspicion.[169]

In the aftermath of the criminal proceedings, the Diocese of Ontario took several actions. In 1993, the clergy of the diocese were brought together for a study day on issues of sexual abuse focused on the "diocesan protocol on Sexual Misconduct."[170] This policy, now *Canon 35C*, was created largely in response to the Gallienne cases. As mentioned previously, the diocese also encourages all parishes to make use of the *Screening in Faith* workbook in order to create a safer environment.[171]

Since his release, Gallienne moved to Ottawa, where he volunteered with adult musicians at St. John the Evangelist Anglican Church. When asked about the situation, the priest in charge at St. John's stated that the restrictions were "very sad" and a "terrible infringement of human rights."[172] The priest also stated that most members of the congregation were aware of Gallienne's past, that Gallienne was a member in St. John's Circle of Support and Accountability ministry "that helps high-risk sex offenders re-integrate into the community," and that the Church has exercised "due diligence" in ensuring the safety of Church members who are minors. The current bishop of Ontario has "expressed his concerns to Bishop Peter Coffin of Ottawa," who at the time said he was considering what to do about the matter, but acknowledged that the guidelines previously adopted had been breached.[173]

These few cases help to illustrate the types of scenarios that emerge in religious institutions and the general responses of the ACC. The cases as discussed do not demonstrate in any detail how protocols are applied; rather, they demonstrate that child sexual abuse does occur in the Church and that the ACC responds through diocesan protocols.

Screening Policies and/or Mandatory Education for Church Volunteers, Employees, and/or Officials (in Positions of Responsibility Regarding Children and Youth)

Among those dioceses that have screening policies, a major "cluster" has chosen to use the same policy, which was developed largely by the Diocese of Algoma. This cluster includes the seven dioceses that make up the Ecclesiastical Province of Ontario (EPO) as well as the Dioceses of Nova Scotia and Prince Edward Island. EPO was one of the faith partners involved in the development of the *Screening in Faith* document, discussed below, and supported by the Ontario Ministry of Citizenship. The EPO is composed of the dioceses of Algoma, Huron,

Moosonee, Niagara, Ontario, Ottawa, and Toronto. The following discussion will focus on the Diocese of Huron's policy as an example representative of the EPO dioceses that share one screening policy.

The basis for the screening policies of the EPO cluster is the 1999 document *Screening in Faith*. As identified in earlier chapters, *Screening in Faith* was an outcome of work funded by the Ontario Minister of Citizenship, Culture, and Recreation, and undertaken by Volunteer Canada under the auspices of the Ontario Screening Initiative. The Synod of the Ecclesiastical Province of Ontario was one of the "faith" consortium partners. Other faith partners included the Ontario Conference of Catholic Bishops, the United Church of Canada, and the Canadian Unitarian Council; each organization sent one member to the consortium.[174]

At the 156th Session of the Diocesan Synod, in 2000, *Screening in Faith* was adopted without debate. The motion read as follows: "Resolved that this Synod of the Diocese of Huron endorses and implements the process of screening as proposed in the 'Screening in Faith' Manual. This process is for use in every congregation in the Diocese and all its ministries in order to honour our Christian responsibility to protect the vulnerable among us, thereby creating the safest possible environment for all in the Church."[175] Thus, the Huron screening policy was named *Screening in Faith*. Huron's decision to adopt *Screening in Faith* was significant because although the EPO had also adopted the policy, it was binding only on EPO events (e.g., a youth event at an EPO Synod) unless the individual diocese also expressly adopted the policy, in which case the policy applied to all diocesan events as well.

At the 157th Synod in 2001, the Screening in Faith Committee of the diocese provided a brief report outlining its progress from the previous year. It noted that "300 clergy and laity from across the Diocese were present when trainers from Volunteer Canada" led workshops regarding the "principles and purposes of screening."[176] The 2005 policy requires police record checks (PRCs) for those working in "areas that are deemed to be of highest risk" such as some Sunday Schools, youth groups, or seniors groups. Additionally, all were required to "be screened in a manner appropriate to the ministry or job being undertaken."[177]

The same year, the Synod passed a motion calling for "[e]very congregation to utilize resources available from the Screening in Faith Committee and our Synod office to implement a program of screening and report on the completion of this work to their Territorial Archdeacon by December 31, 2001."[178]

The relevance of context to the development of effective policy grew in recognition as the ACC progressed in their screening policy work. For example, in the 2002 *District of Huron, Journal of Proceedings* the importance of physical space design was stated: "Screening in Faith includes changing/revising physical layouts in order to protect the vulnerable." Recognizing the relevance of the wider social context, attention was directed to the development of a resource more applicable to the rural parishes of the diocese.[179]

In 2004, the Screening in Faith Committee joined with the Sexual Abuse Response Team (SART) to form the Safe Church Committee. As one of its first tasks, the committee surveyed the status of screening in the diocesan parishes.[180] In 2006, 50 percent of parishes had reported and of these reporting parishes, 80 percent had implemented the screening procedures.[181] Implementation of the screening policy is encouraged by the Safe Church Committee and the diocesan bishops. In 2005 the Safe Church Committee reported that "if a parish does not put in place screening appropriate to their needs, their liability insurance may not cover any costs arising from a claim within the parish" and it will be solely responsible for paying such a claim.[182]

The EPO's screening policy—*Safe Church: Our Sacred Trust* (2005)— explains the rationale for screening and provides necessary forms, as well as procedures, for responding to allegations of sexual misconduct. The document is informed by a primarily relational sexual ethic.[183] Sexuality is considered to be a gift of God, but when the gift is misused, it has "enormous potential to alienate people from God, one another, and even themselves." Further, "the church has a responsibility to understand and to be clear about the relationship between sexuality and power, and to acknowledge that where an imbalance of power exists in a relationship, genuine consent to sexual expression cannot exist."[184] Thus, the diocese recognized "that clergy, diocesan staff, parish staff, and volunteers serve in situations where sexual misconduct, harassment, or other abuse has the potential to occur" and therefore screening and ongoing management are necessary to maintain safety.[185]

The section on screening procedures uses the *Screening in Faith* workbook, but translates the material into a form more applicable to the particularities of the Diocese of Huron. Every position within the parish "shall be assessed for the amount of risk inherent to it, and assigned a rating of low, medium or high." This assessment is to be based on:

- The age and vulnerability of the people being ministered to;
- The size of group typically being ministered to (Group vs. 1-on 1 Activity);
- The location and visibility of ministry (Church Hall vs. Private Home);
- The type of activity involved in ministry (Morning Bible Study vs Camping Weekend);
- The level of supervision and monitoring that takes place;
- The degree of authority associated with the position ([Church]Warden vs.
- Chalice Bearers); and
- Other significant attributes of the position.[186]

For example, all clergy positions, "positions where one on one meetings or counselling occur in closed settings," and "all positions involving residential programs with children, youth, or vulnerable adults" are deemed high risk. Positions "involving children, youth, or vulnerable adults in a non-residential setting" are deemed either high-risk or medium-risk positions.

Typical screening procedures for use when evaluating applicants for volunteer or paid positions within the parish include "meeting with clergy or another direct supervisor to discuss the duties and responsibilities of the position and the candidate's suitability," requiring application forms and/or resumés from candidates, conducting reference checks, and obtaining PRCs with vulnerable position screening.[187] PRCs with vulnerable position screening are required for all clergy positions and "residential programs involving children, youth, or vulnerable adults."[188]

Screening records are to be kept for ten years after the death of the individual to whom they pertain.[189] Standardized and sample screening forms are included in the policy's appendices.

Due in part to the initiatives of the Ecclesiastical Province of Ontario, and the emergence of a high-profile abuse case, the Diocese of Ontario (centred in Kingston and covering a major portion of central-eastern Ontario) encourages all parishes to use the *Screening in Faith* document described above.[190] Similarly, the dioceses of Algoma, Ottawa, and Nova Scotia and Prince Edward Island have used the *Screening in Faith* document to create and implement screening policies for their parishes.[191]

Chapter Summary

The ACC's earlier work on marriage, divorce, and contraception helped to bring other issues related to human sexuality into the open. Historically, the wider Christian Church has tended to equate sexuality with sin and silence any broader conversation regarding sexuality as taboo. This taboo around human sexuality and the illusion of the moral purity of both family and Church needed to be challenged before child sexual abuse could be addressed.

The second wave feminist movement helped generate deeper engagement with "women's issues" within the ACC. As with the Roman Catholic and United Churches, work on gender preceded explicit and in-depth work on child sexual abuse.

Child sexual abuse was first seen as something terrible that happened outside of the Church family or at least was not perpetrated by trusted Church leaders. Thus, it was important that the ACC acknowledged its complicity in violence against women before it could look more diligently at its participation in violence against an even more vulnerable group—children. As with other institutions examined in this book, a growing awareness of the sexual abuse that occurred in residential schools also assisted in bringing the ACC's participation in and responsibility for child sexual abuse to the fore. This ability to confess and understand their participation in this violence was necessary for the ACC to create a policy that responded to internal complaints of child sexual abuse; in other words, preceding policy must be acknowledgement that child sexual abuse can and does happen in the Anglican Church. Further, fear of litigation and liability requirements have been powerful motivators for all of the religious institutions examined in this book.

Determined to take responsibility and address this abuse, in 1990 the House of Bishops requested that the primate "appoint a task force to establish sexual abuse policies and guidelines for use" across the Church. This call was strengthened in 1992, when the General Synod referred a resolution on the "Sexual Molestation and Abuse of Children" to the National Executive Council (NEC) and, momentously, moved to "recognize that sexual molestation and abuse of young persons by some church personnel while administering church programs has occurred and deeply regrets that the pastoral needs of some victims and their families have not been met."[192]

The ACC's diocesan structure has made the creation and adoption of sexual abuse policies very complex and not always consistent. Further, the degree of transparency varies with the diocese. In 1992 the ACC National Executive Council adopted its first *Sexual Assault and Harassment Policy*, which most recently was revised in 2005 as the *Sexual Misconduct Policy*. This policy addresses complaints of sexual abuse (including current and historic child sexual abuse) by national-level staff and volunteers; however, it can only be suggested as a resource for the individual dioceses. As with the RCC, at the diocesan level there are a variety of policies and there are some dioceses without any policies at all. These dioceses may opt to follow the national policy.[193] There is substantial overlap among diocesan policies, particularly concerning volunteer screening and the use of the *Screening in Faith* document, either as is or adapted to a particular diocese.

Penalties for conviction of sexual misconduct (including child sexual abuse), either in civil courts or by ecclesiastical officials/courts, are addressed under *Canon XVIII: Discipline*, resulting in a need to read all sexual misconduct policies in light of the disciplinary procedures of the national Church canons. Some within the ACC have questioned the wisdom of not including a policy on sexual abuse complaints in the canons of the national Church, as has been done regarding discipline. Similarly to the Roman Catholic Church in Canada, one must wonder how much of the reasoning behind this commitment to diocesan autonomy has to do with regional differences and the importance of diocesan autonomy, and how much is motivated by fear of litigation. Any such analysis must address possible consequences of choosing a decentralized diocesan policy approach and weigh it carefully in the light of the religious institution's faith convictions.

Chapter 5

The Mennonite Church in Canada

THE MENNONITES HAVE PRODUCED groundbreaking resources regarding sexual abuse in the Church and how to recognize and respond to it pastorally. Although initially not as strong in terms of concrete policy development pertaining to the lodging and processing of complaints, this varied Christian religious tradition has created some of the most radical social justice resources in the subject area. For this reason, a snapshot view of child sexual abuse policies and religious institutions must include at least parts of the Mennonite Churches' work.[1]

As is the case with other religious institutions examined in this book, legal action and subsequent insurance requirements have been significant motivators for the Mennonite Churches in addition to a theological commitment to protecting the vulnerable and safeguarding right relationship; as acknowledged in a 1996 polity document designed for the then anticipated merging of the Mennonite Church and the General Conference Mennonite Church, "lawsuits against conferences, ministers, and other church leaders are on the increase."[2]

Church Structure and Description of the Context

What follows is a very brief and incomplete background introduction to the complex Mennonite Church structure. The Mennonite Church emerged from the Protestant Reformation of sixteenth-century Europe, beginning in 1525.[3] Mennonites derive from the Anabaptist tradition, a wide-ranging group who generally sought reformation of what was experienced as clerical and Church elitism. Further, sacraments were rejected as theologically incorrect and elitist (e.g., from a Mennonite perspective, a sacrament "somehow effects an internal change or ... gives to the person greater worth"); instead baptism, ordination, and the Lord's Supper, for example, were understood as *rites* of the Church, although engagement with these rites continues to be debated within some Mennonite communities.[4] Since its inception, Mennonite Churches have been committed to a ministry of all believers, with the recognition that each is called to a particular form of ministry with no one being better or more worthy than another.[5]

The name "Mennonite" was adopted from the name of a Dutch priest, Menno Simons, "a church leader who rallied a scattered people and led them through a time of great tribulation."[6] The Mennonites have survived a history of persecution and suspicion largely owing to their marginal status: "Because they were not part of the state churches (Catholic, Lutheran, or Reformed), Mennonites were considered dangerous and were severely persecuted for the first several generations."[7]

There are two significant and most populous Mennonite denominations or traditions coexisting in the Canadian context: the Mennonite Church Canada (formed in 1999 by the merging of the Mennonite Church and the General Conference Mennonite Church) and the Canadian Conference of Mennonite Brethren Churches (CCMB). There are additional smaller Mennonite streams in Canada, including the Evangelical Mennonite Conference (Canada), Brethren in Christ General Conference (North America), and the Evangelical Mennonite Mission Conference. While the CCMB in particular has produced some relevant policies, this chapter focuses on the Mennonite Church Canada whose policies are very visible.

The separation of the Brethren Churches from the other Mennonites occurred in 1860, when a group of Mennonites in South Russia (the Ukraine) wrote "a letter of secession that explained their differences with the mother church. The letter affirmed their agreement with the teaching of Menno Simons and addressed abuses they saw in baptism, the Lord's Supper, church discipline, pastoral leadership and lifestyle."[8] The Brethren are overall the more theologically conservative of these two denominations; however, there are some very theologically traditional churches in the diverse Mennonite Church Canada.

The agrarian and rural roots of the Mennonite community remain strong, as 16 percent of Mennonites are classified as being among the farm population, the highest of any religious group.[9] For comparison purposes, 4.8 percent of the United Church of Canada, 1.7 percent of Roman Catholic, and 1.8 percent of Anglican affiliates are classified as part of the farm population. This statistic reflects the Mennonite theological and traditional commitment to the land.

The 2001 Canadian census counted 191,465 Mennonites in total, a decline of 7.9 percent from ten years earlier.[10] In 2009, the Mennonite Church Canada (MCCanada) put its membership at "33,000 baptized believers, plus over 24,000 children and youth in 225 congregations and 5 area conferences."[11] The balance of Mennonite members either belong to one of the other Mennonite traditions or identify themselves as Mennonite, but do not affiliate with a congregation. Before its merger with the Mennonite Church in the year 2000, the *Mennonite Directory* indicates that in 1999 the Conference of Mennonites in Canada (i.e., an organization of Canadian churches that related to the General Conference Mennonite Church) had a membership of 35,246.[12]

The present MCCanada was formed in the 2000 subsequent to a 1999 joint delegate session at which a new joint structure was approved by two Mennonite Church denominations, the Mennonite Church (MC) and the

General Conference Mennonite Church (GCMC), after years of discussion and negotiation. The two denominations had a long history, extending back to the 1940s, of working together on various projects, including the Mennonite Central Committee and two joint hymnals (i.e., *The Mennonite Hymnal* in 1969 and *Hymnal a Worshipbook* in 1992). Both denominations had congregations across Canada and the United States. MCCanada arose in 2000, followed in 2002 by the inauguration of the Mennonite Church United States of America (MCUSA); the first meetings of the MCCanada occurred in 2000.[13]

For governance purposes, MCCanada is divided into five conferences: Eastern Canada (MCEC), Manitoba (MCM), Saskatchewan (MCSask), Alberta (MCA), and British Columbia (MCBC). It is a representative structure with churches and conferences electing members to a Delegate Assembly. The Delegate Assembly has "the authority to act on behalf of MCCanada."[14] The Delegate Assembly meets annually to make decisions on spiritual matters and administrative business such as budgeting and bylaws.[15]

A General Board and three councils (i.e., Christian Formation, Christian Witness, and Support Services) "attend to the ministry of MCCanada."[16] The General Board, consisting of elected officers and representatives from the five conferences, is called to "act on behalf of MCCanada between delegate assemblies," and is accountable to the Delegate Assembly.[17] The board appoints a general secretary to "coordinate the total program of MCCanada."[18] A moderator is appointed to "(a) preside at all delegate assemblies; (b) chair all meetings of the General Board and Executive Committee; and (c) act as the official representative and spokesperson for MCCanada."[19] An Executive Committee fulfils the role of the General Board between meetings of the board.[20]

Operating internationally is the Mennonite World Council (MWC), a collegial body linking Mennonites from around the world, including the MCCanada. The MWC is governed by a General Council consisting of delegates from member churches proportionate to the number of people affiliated with each. "This group of church leaders meets every three years to shape the mandate of MWC, share concerns and insights, and worship together." Within this council there is an executive, consisting of two delegates per continent, that meets annually. Further, the council has a Faith and Life Commission and a Peace Commission, which foster collegial discussion to encourage and strengthen the MWC member churches.[21]

Another important structural component of Mennonite life is the joint Canada–United States Mennonite Central Committee (MCC), which the Canadian Mennonites joined in 1963. With both national and provincial levels in Canada, the MCC is a Mennonite agency "developed to be (and is to this day) the relief, development and peace committee of the Mennonite and Brethren in Christ Churches in Canada and the United States."[22] Its mission is "to demonstrate God's love by working among people suffering from poverty, conflict, oppression, and natural disaster."[23]

In general, despite the overarching co-operative organizations such as the MCC and MCCanada, the polity of the Mennonite churches is more that of associational congregationalism, which makes it different from Anglican, Roman Catholic, and United Church traditions.[24] Traditionally, Mennonites "have defined the church strictly in communal terms. The church consists of congregations organized for personal communion."[25] Mennonite bodies are "composed of autonomous local congregations" with varying degrees and systems of congregational oversight.[26] Thus, congregations within the overarching co-operative organizations can often choose to what degree to follow or how to interpret policies and guidelines offered regarding abuse complaints. Further, the conferences have some similar freedom regarding many policy issues. For example, MCEC appears to have developed its sexual abuse policy before MCCanada promulgated a policy. Additionally, MCCanada's bylaws govern how the national body shall function, and not how individual churches and conferences shall function; it is a polity document for the national Church only.[27] To join the national body, a congregation is required to accept the "Confession of Faith in a Mennonite Perspective" and support the "Vision and Purpose Statements," neither of which dictate local church or conference polity.

The resource *Leadership and Accountability in Mennonite Church Canada* provides a window into these dynamics regarding independence and centralization in the Canadian context. Historically, congregations were highly independent. However, the 1963 Confession of the Mennonite Church stated that

> in order to maintain the unity of the church it is Scriptural and profitable for congregational representatives to meet together in conferences. The concern for the welfare of the whole church calls for Spirit-led conferences to assist local congregations in maintaining Biblical standards of faith, conduct, stewardship, and missions. The decision of such conferences should be respected by individual congregations and members.[28]

In ethos, the constituent parts and predecessors of the MCCanada have tended to emphasize "the congregation as the primary unit" of the Church, with mutual accountability characterizing the relationship between congregations and conferences.[29] This emphasis arises more out of the General Conference Mennonite Church tradition than the Mennonite Church strand of the MCCanada.[30]

The 1995 *Confession of Faith in a Mennonite Perspective* further defined relationships between members and the Church in its section on discipline. This document was written jointly by the General Conference Mennonite Church and the Mennonite Church, and "provided the foundation" for both the later created MCCanada and MCUSA.[31] Members of the Church are said to "commit themselves to give and receive counsel within the faith community on important matters of doctrine and conduct" with the understanding that "corrective discipline in the church should be exercised in a redemptive manner."[32] At the level of the congregation or particular special ministry, "decisions made at larger assemblies and conferences are confirmed by constituent groups" when advice has been sought; "authority and responsibility are delegated by common and voluntary agreement, so that the churches hold each other accountable to Christ and to one another on all levels of church life."[33]

As made clear at ordination, pastors are accountable to the Church through the congregation, conference, and wider Church.[34] Importantly, although congregations have the authority to decide to ordain, the credentialing and licensing of ministers is at the provincial level (e.g., Mennonite Church Eastern Canada). Thus, complaints against ministers must be dealt with at the provincial level.

Approach to Child Sexual Abuse, Including Relevant Statements, Policies, and Practices: 1960–80

Women who became designated as missionaries in the General Conference Mennonite Church were eligible for ordination in 1945. In 1974 an official statement entitled "Understanding Ordination" was accepted by the General Conference Mennonite Church. This document made clear that women were not to be discriminated against for ordination, and that divorced pastors could remain in ordained ministry. These were significant moves for this denomination.[35]

The Mennonite Church, in its early history, included women in leadership roles. Since then, men have occupied those roles until the mid-1980s, when a Women in Leadership Ministries Committee was appointed "to encourage area conferences to include women in pastoral leadership ministries through ordination." A result was the 1986 Waterford "Statement of Convergence," which reads in part:

> A majority of participants in the Waterford consultation favoured equal eligibility of men and women for all ministries of the church. There was some dissent, however, from inclusion of women in ministries usually confirmed by ordination.

Final decisions about the ordination of women rest with the individual district conferences.[36]

It was not until the late 1990s into the 2000s that the Mennonites began to wrestle deeply with sexual orientation issues.

Approach to Child Sexual Abuse, Including Relevant Statements, Policies, and Practices: 1981–91

In 1986, at the triennial session of the GCMC meeting in Saskatoon, Saskatchewan, a *Resolution on Human Sexuality* was drafted. This document framed sexuality in a positive light, opening with affirmations:

> We affirm that sexuality is a good and beautiful gift of God, a gift of identity and a way of being in the world as male and female.
> We affirm that we can feel positive about our bodies and our sexuality because we know our Creator.
> We affirm that sexual drives are a real part of our lives, but that the satisfaction of those drives is not the chief good in life.
> We affirm both the goodness of singleness and the goodness of marriage and family in the Lord.

Included in the document are confessions regarding: participation in sexism, fear of discussing the body and sexuality, the rejection of different sexual orientations, and of "permissiveness which too often leads to premarital and extramarital sexual relationships."[37]

Next are a series of commitments, or covenants, for the Church to follow. The first focuses on the Bible and sexuality, encouraging further study. This first covenant includes the assertion that the Bible teaches "that sexual intercourse is reserved for a man and a woman united in marriage … this teaching also precludes premarital, extramarital and homosexual sexual activity. We further understand the Bible to teach the sanctity of the marriage covenant and that any violation of this covenant, including spouse abuse, is sin."[38] The second covenant calls for understanding and forgiveness. The third commitment was to begin discussing sexuality openly, using the Bible and the book *Human Sexuality in the Christian Life: A Working Document for Study and Dialogue*. The final covenant appeals to God for help in discernment. In 1987, in Indiana, the MC released its own version of the resolution, entitled *A Call to Affirmation, Confession, and Covenant Regarding Human Sexuality*. This document is very similar to the aforementioned resolution, containing only minor variations.[39]

In 1990 the MCC published a resource entitled *The Purple Packet: Domestic Violence Resources for Pastoring Persons—Wife Assault*. The packet was prepared under the auspices of the MCC Domestic Violence Taskforce with the purpose "to break the silence surrounding one form of domestic violence, namely wife abuse." The hope was that it would assist pastors "to clarify … [their] role in responding to families who are suffering from wife abuse."[40]

In 1991 what would become a foundational book in the Canadian Mennonite community, *Assault on God's Image* by Isaac Block, was published. Block presented evidence that there is indeed domestic abuse among Mennonites in Winnipeg, and that "Mennonite pastors in Winnipeg appear ready to deal in a serious way with the issue of abuse in and around their congregations." Further, regarding domestic abuse, pastors "hear reports and do not hesitate to deal with the issue."[41] He recommended that the willingness to help was evident, and more internal work was needed: "while ... [the Mennonites] put forth a concerted effort to provide services for disadvantaged communities and people around the world, they must also turn inward and put considerably more effort into dealing with the issue of abuse within their congregations."[42]

Block made four general recommendations for Mennonite churches, including a recommendation that the pastoral theology used by pastors should be based in experience and attend to the experiences of the abused. "When this happens, the traditional theological issues are dealt with from the point of view of the person in the abusive situation. Victims are given a voice so that theological questions get asked by victims rather than by professionals."[43] Further, he strongly critiqued the traditional theological claim that suffering is good; he wrote "in the survey of Mennonite pastors in Winnipeg, 46% of the pastors reported that they held this view." The glorification of suffering as a redemptive end in itself encourages abuse. He stated "the church's task must be to confront abusers with the reality that violence destroys relationships. Pastors must be more assertive in counselling victims to leave the abuser. The victims' safety and sense of personal worth are at stake."[44]

Block recommended increased networking and institutional leadership regarding professional conduct. The Church must realize its limitations and therefore network intentionally with the wider secular community regarding abuse and resources: "The church could benefit by the realism of the secular agencies and the secular agencies could benefit by the hope of the church."[45]

In 1991 the MCC produced *Crossing the Boundary: Sexual Abuse by Professionals*. (This resource would be re-released in 2000.) The first section is comprised of personal narratives of abuse experienced from Church counsellors and a reflection by the relative of a perpetrator of abuse. Next is a series of articles from people working in the field of sexual abuse, including "An Introduction to Professional Abuse" by Shirley B. Souder and excerpts from *Sex in the Forbidden Zone* by psychologist Peter Rutter. Following these resources is material on sexual harassment, general sexual misconduct, and sexual misconduct by clergy. A limitation of this otherwise valuable resource is that it is informed only by US law; the authors indicate that "guidelines are similar in Canada although each province has its own legislation," but no specific instruction or information is provided for Canadian churches.

Worthy of mention are two resource sheets included in this packet that address the process of reporting sexual abuse. The first, "Reporting Professional Sexual Abuse," advises a complainant to find a "'friendly' person to whom to make your initial disclosure of abuse," to know the options for formal reporting, and to "clarify your own needs and interests in making a report."[46] Further, this resource sheet advises that the "abuse of minors generally carries mandatory reporting requirement to civil child protection authorities, as outlined in state or provincial codes. If minors are involved, seek special counsel on these legally-mandated reporting processes."[47]

The second resource sheet is "A Checklist for Church Response to Professional and Pastoral Sexual Abuse." Churches are advised to have clear policies, and those policies should include "clear mechanisms[s] for reporting the abuse including to whom and where." When responding to victims of child abuse, the "local Family and Children Services" agency should be notified. It is important to remember that this resource packet is a resource for the various Mennonite churches and denominations and is not official policy; local congregations were free to choose whether or not they followed any recommendations.

It was also in 1991 that the MCC first released a resource packet that addressed child sexual abuse by clergy. Participants in Canada and the United States jointly compiled the packet *Broken Boundaries: Resources for Pastoring People—Child Sexual Abuse.*[48] In the opening section it is explained that "when children are used to meet the emotional and sexual needs of the adults in the family, exploitation and violation of personal and role boundaries are clearly the result." The role of the Church in healing and justice seeking is explored, as is the role of other professionals in this work. The packet addresses child abuse within Church communities, child abuse in families, and adults who were victims of historic child abuse.

Approach to Child Sexual Abuse, Including Relevant Statements, Policies, and Practices: 1992–2009

A Resolution on Male Violence against Women was adopted at the Mennonite Church General Assembly on July 31, 1993. The resolution acknowledged violence against women and children both inside and outside the Church. It refuted the argument that it is the natural order for man to rule woman, stating instead that such domination resulted from sin: "The fall into sin has shattered God's intended mutuality of women and men, distorting personal relationships and resulting in dominance and violence of men against women." It is only through the life, death, and resurrection of Jesus that "this curse has been lifted" and women and men can live as the equals that God intended. However, as long as we resist this grace we will continue to "live in a society whose structures imply men's power and superiority over women." Moreover, the document confesses the Church's complicity in this violence: "Within that system too many Mennonite fathers, husbands, employers and even church leaders have used their power in oppressive and violent ways. They have excluded women from opportunities, silenced their ideas and protests, sexually harassed them and violently abused them."

Eight actions were recommended in the resolution. First, the Church as a whole must confess that abuse exists within the Mennonite community. Second, the Church needs "to listen to, believe and feel the pain of women who have been violently abused or sexually harassed by men." Third, marital abuse must not be tolerated. Fourth, abusers must be called to account and repentance, with help and healing from the Church community. Fifth, survivors must be protected by the Church. Sixth, "church agencies … [must be held] accountable for dealing appropriately with abuse that occurs within their organizations." Seventh, in a proactive vein, Church mission must include outreach "to model, within our congregations, alternative and counter-cultural ways of being male and female; [and] to practice parenting skills that help families learn how to share power and resolve conflict peacefully." Finally, the last resolution called for congregational level proactive work and suggested that a series of resources to assist in such work be prepared by the MCC.[49]

In the mid-1990s, the MCC released two training manuals. The *Advocacy Training Manual: Advocating for Survivors of Sexual Abuse by a Church Leader or Caregiver* (by Heather Block, 1996) is intended for those responding pastorally to victims/survivors of clergy abuse and, later, *Expanding the Circle of Caring: Ministering to the Family Members of Survivors and Perpetrators of Sexual Abuse* (by the MCC) was written primarily for those caring for family members of survivors. These documents do not propose policy or procedure, but provide educational material directed primarily at Mennonite Church members.

Parts of the Mennonite communities did additional work in the more general area of human sexuality and ethics in the later 1990s. For example, the document *A Mennonite Polity for Ministerial Leadership*, which created a governance structure for authorizing ministerial credentials for the anticipated Mennonite Church Canada (2000), includes a brief discussion of sexuality in the "Ethics in Ministry" section, which reads in part: "Our deepest longings for God are related to our needs for intimacy with other human beings. Spiritual yearnings are related to our sexuality.... Sometimes, however, relationships develop which are not appropriate. Because ministers are accorded authority and power in the church, such inappropriate relationships result in great pain and grief for the victim."[50]

Additionally, in 2000 sexual orientation issues became explosive in MCCanada. For example, the Mennonite Church Alberta conference saw "several" congregations withdraw from the denomination over "congregational acceptance of homosexual members."[51]

In December 2000, the MCC, in conjunction with the US and Canadian Women's Concerns offices, re-released *Crossing the Boundary: Sexual Abuse by Professionals* (1991), with updated resources. This is a collection of resources and articles put together to educate others regarding the meaning of professional abuse and how to address it. The packet "is heavily focused on pastoral abuse. This is done not in an effort to diminish other types of professional abuse, but to reveal our specific concern as a church agency."[52]

The next section defines professional abuse and describes how it can happen in the Church. Articles by Marie Fortune, a pioneer in the field of abuse and professional ethics, and feminist theologians Susan Brooks Thistlethwaite and Pamela Cooper-White are included. Cooper-White is quoted regarding the abusive nature of sexual relationships between pastors and parishioners: "a pastor's sexual or romantic involvement with a parishioner is not primarily a matter of sex or sexuality but of power and control."

The appended articles address related issues, including how to work with victims in recovery, "the reasons why people are afraid to disclose having been sexually abused by their pastor,"[53] and ministry with the offenders as well as with the congregation in which the abuse took place.

A collection of preventative measures is provided in the third section. Appropriate behaviour in a pastoral counselling relationship is discussed. Included are articles directed toward clergy to assist them in identifying warning signs. The packet also suggests proactive measures for congregations, including: having clear guidelines, finding "ways to promote and support health of individual clergy persons," educating everyone regarding sexuality and abuse, and training regarding ministry among the abused.[54] The final section consists of resources to help develop sexual abuse complaint policies, including guidance on how to receive complaints and conduct investigations.

In 2002 the MCUSA and Canada's Women's Concerns Committee released another educational resource entitled *Making Your Sanctuary Safe: Resources for Developing Congregational Abuse Prevention Policies.* "The focus of this packet is [to] offer resources on how to prevent abuse from occurring in your church."[55] The first part of the packet emphasizes that "the main objective is to provide a safe and secure environment for the children who are entrusted to your church. In seeking to accomplish this objective, you will be accomplishing another very important objective—reducing legal risk and liability."[56] Moral and legal issues are identified, as well as sample anonymous cases and resources for abuse prevention within the congregation (see "Screening Policies" section later in the chapter).

At the time of the writing of this book, policies and procedures for filing child sexual abuse complaints were available in each Canadian conference. Further, each provincial MCC offers investigative and usually educational services to each of its Mennonite conferences. Although policy and procedures are thus offered to all Mennonite churches, as a congregational religious institution, each church is not required to embrace these procedures. However, as is the case for other decentralized religions, such as the Unitarians, Islam in Canada, and the diocesan churches, much pressure is brought to bear by insurance companies requiring such a policy to be in place. For the sake of brevity and as a means of providing one example, I will consider the Mennonite Church Eastern Canada (MCEC) conference.

Complaints of Child Sexual Abuse and Complaints by Adults of Historical Childhood Sexual Abuse

Broken Boundaries—Child Sexual Abuse (1991) provides guidance for responding pastorally to complaints of historic and current child sexual abuse; however, it focuses on family sexual abuse and not so much on sexual abuse within the Church, including clergy misconduct.

When hearing a complaint, the pastor is reminded to "avoid blaming, judging or minimizing what has happened" and to "know about support or self-help groups" in the local area that can help the victim/survivor deal with the memories of his or her experience.[57] The resource sheet does not discuss the procedure involved in making a complaint; rather, the emphasis is on pastoral care.

A person receiving a complaint from a child is to "assume that the child is telling the truth ... assure the child that he/she is not to blame ... and remain with the child until" civil authorities arrive. If a family member has abused the child, the parents or legal guardians of the child are not to be contacted; if the child has been the victim of abuse by someone outside the family, the parents or legal guardians are to be contacted.

The MCEC's later policy, *A Plan to Protect Our Children, Youth & Leaders,* includes procedures for investigating complaints of ongoing child sexual abuse; it does not overtly address complaints of historic child sexual abuse, although it appears that the same procedures could be used.

Investigative Procedures Regarding Complaints

A Plan to Protect Our Children, Youth & Leaders outlines how to conduct an appropriate investigation. This investigation, if assessed as warranted, is to be carried out by the Sexual Misconduct and Abuse Response, Resource Team (SMARRT) offered by the Mennonite Central Committee Ontario (MCCO). The SMARRT is supported financially by all of Ontario's Conferences, including the MCEC, the Brethren in Christ, and the Mennonite Brethren Conference. Members from each of the conferences are included on the SMARRT. According to the official MCCO website, the "SMARRT provides resourcing and recommendations to Mennonite and Brethren In Christ churches as well as responding to allegations of boundary crossing and sexual misconduct by leadership within these churches."[58]

In all cases, civil procedures must not be interfered with: "no person shall conduct any investigation or question any individuals regarding suspected child abuse unless otherwise authorized by the appropriate [civil] authorities."[59] Also, "any MCEC volunteer or employee having reasonable suspicion of abuse of a child attending a conference sponsored event must report the suspicion to the local Family & Children's Services or the police immediately."[60]

When there is suspicion of child abuse, it is appropriate for the observer to "ask a child how an observed symptom appeared, [but] it is never appropriate to ask any leading questions which might suggest to a child that s/he has been abused or suggest names, place or methods of abuse." Further, anyone involved in the Church complaint process is to "refrain from attempting to convince a parent that the alleged abuse happened or did not happen." Similarly, *Broken Boundaries—Child Sexual Abuse* (1991) cautions Church investigators that when responding to the accused, they must remember that "abusers seldom tell the truth about their behaviour ... [and] seldom express remorse or a sense of wrongdoing."[61]

Anyone who observes possible symptoms of abuse is to document his or her observations in a specific report form included in the policy. This report form gathers:

1   specific signs of observed symptoms;
2   any report of abuse made by the child or others, and/or any witnessed event that raised the suspicion; as well as
3   the date and time relating to any of the above; and
4   any response the child made to any of the above.

Any witnesses to the abuse are to be given support and "should also be instructed on how to respond if the child, parents, or other interested parties contact him/her." At all times civil processes, including investigations, are to be respected: "[no] statement made by the child [is to be shared] with anyone other than the authorities until the authorities have determined whether or not the child needs to be protected from contact with the person in question."[62]

Responses to Involved People

The MCEC policy emphasizes the need "to ensure that the victim of abuse and other children at the event or events are kept safe during the ongoing investigation by authorities."

This *may* mean the suspension of an accused employee or volunteer, "pending the outcome of the [secular] investigation" with full pay and without prejudice or interference with any investigation.[63]

In the case of a criminal conviction, "the abuser will not be restored to his/her previous position or duty within the conference," and "reinstatement will be done only if it is deemed safe and proper to do so" in consultation with the civil authorities and other experts.[64] If an ordained person is found culpable by the Church and/or secular authorities, discipline and/or removal of credentials is the "responsibility of the area conference ministerial committee in consultation with the congregation and denomination." An appeal can be made through the denomination. If a pastor is found culpable, ordination could be revoked through the removal of credentials or silencing.[65]

The MCEC policy underscores the importance of care in the Church's response: "Plans for pastoral and possible clinical support of all parties involved will be developed as soon as the investigation is under way."[66] The resource *Broken Boundaries—Child Sexual Abuse* is particularly helpful regarding the provision of pastoral care to the involved parties. For example, potential caregivers are advised that an abuser's disclosure to a person in authority in the Church "may be a cry for help to change," in which case the abuser should be helped to find treatment and encouraged to self-report to the appropriate child welfare agency.

Following the MCEC and MCCO policy and procedures, Listowel Mennonite Church (LMC) (Listowel, Ontario) developed a congregational policy, *Safe Church Policy: A Plan to Protect Children, Youth, and Adults* in 2003. LMC is a member of MCEC and, as such, has followed the MCEC policy with some additions and contextual adjustments.

The response section of the Listowel Mennonite Church (Ontario) policy is much shorter than its MCEC counterpart. Again, there is the admonition that "suspicion of abuse must be taken seriously," and that the person who receives the complaint or who has the suspicion must not taint a civil investigation.[67] It is repeated that under Ontario law, suspicions of child abuse must be reported to civil authorities, and also should "be reported to the senior pastor and/or any committee that LMC has put in place for the purposes of responding to such concerns" if the allegation "involves personnel or program under the auspices of LMC." Upon receiving a complaint, the senior pastor and, if established, the committee are to follow specific procedures. An "Abuse Incident Report form" must be completed, and "the alleged offender [ought to be suspended] from duties, pending [the] outcome of the investigation." Although suspension is not mandatory, the policy clearly leans in favour of that option during an investigation. There is also a provision to "contact LMC's insurer to satisfy the statutory conditions of our liability policy and to avoid jeopardizing any available coverage response."[68] Again, liability issues are a priority.

The MCCO's restorative justice portfolio includes the SMARRT, as well as "Circles of Support and Accountability," which are described as "small 'circles' of volunteers and MCCO staff [who] become new communities for men whose crimes have marginalized them from society."[69] The Mennonites' work in restorative justice is significant; in many ways they are on the leading edge of justice and healing work for offenders. For the most part, little is done in either faith communities or wider society to facilitate the rehabilitation or reintegration of offenders. Restorative justice approaches this healing work as part of the broader work of justice, so the victims are not forgotten. A restorative rather than a purely punitive understanding shapes offender work and care.

Screening Policies and/or Mandatory Education for Church Volunteers, Employees, and/or Officials (in Positions of Responsibility Regarding Children and Youth)

Materials to assist in the implementation of a screening policy are in the second part of the resource packet, *Making Your Sanctuary Safe: Resources for Developing Congregational Abuse Prevention Policies*. This part opens with a checklist for congregations to conduct a self-assessment that asks questions pertaining to screening, training, policy, and insurance coverage. It establishes some basic procedures for ministries involving children and youth. One of the major preventative measures is the avoidance of private meetings since "abusers thrive on secrecy, isolation, and their ability to manipulate victims. When abusers know they will never have a chance to be alone with potential victims they quickly lose interest in 'working' with children."[70] Accordingly, it is suggested that churches involve multiple supervisors for all youth programs and ministries, have an open-door policy when counselling, and have windows on all the doors. Further, supervisors must be at least eighteen years old and there must be at least a five-year age difference between supervisors and participants.

Appropriate questions for screening interviews are also provided. The interviewer is encouraged to watch for signs of anxiety. Regarding the relevance of personal background in screening for a position, "volunteers are not excluded because of an abusive childhood or highly dysfunctional family history, but it is important to assess that those issues do not interfere with their ability to help others." Also, direct questions about abuse and molestation ought to be asked. People with a history of having been abused themselves, however, are not automatically excluded as "adults-abused-as-children can be wonderful volunteers if they have resolved their issues with help from therapy, family, support systems, or other kinds of healing."[71]

The final section encourages groups within each congregation to proceed with safety audits.[72] Three sample policies are provided; these are developed from sources in the United States. These recommend full screening of all volunteers and employees, practical methods for prevention, as well as investigative and reporting procedures. Regarding the latter, these procedures vary from mandating immediate reporting to civil authorities to encouraging an internal discussion among leaders and lawyers before reporting.

In 2005 the MCEC released a policy on child abuse and volunteer screening called *A Plan to Protect Our Children, Youth & Leaders*, building on *Screening in Faith*. It must be emphasized that this policy is binding only on MCEC as a conference-level structure and not on its member congregations, although congregations are to take such matters under advisement as part of the covenant of mutual accountability. The plan states clearly the need for proactive policies to protect the vulnerable in Church communities:

to grow as communities of grace, joy and peace, MCEC events must provide an environment in which children and youth can grow physically emotionally and spiritually. We recognize that this requires providing an environment in which the risk of physical, sexual or emotional abuse in absolutely minimized through policies that outline expectations of positive expectations of positive relational boundaries between MCEC staff and/or volunteers and the children or youth at MCEC events. There will be no tolerance for abuse, harassment or neglect by staff and/or volunteers working with children and youth at MCEC events.[73] MCEC advised that at all "sponsored events involving children and/or youth, a team approach will be employed to ensure that there are always two or more adults present."[74]

The policy's screening procedures are mandatory for MCEC events and recommended to the particular churches in the conference. The level of risk or responsibility for each event is assessed as low, medium, or high. A low-risk or responsibility event is defined as one in which "children and youth do not attend." A high-risk or responsibility event is "any event [involving children and/or youth] with an overnight component." Medium-risk or responsibility events are more ambiguous; generally they are events that involve youth or children, but do not have an overnight component. Medium-risk event screening involves two steps: "a) targeted recruitment, [and] b) volunteer registration." High-responsibility positions have five requirements: "a) targeted recruitment, b) volunteer registration, c) background reference checks, d) [a] minimum waiting period, [and] e) police records check." In the case of a police records check, "a record involving any abuse of children or youth will, in all cases, disqualify the individual from working with children and/or youth."[75]

When adults accompany children or youth from their home congregation, the congregation is responsible for screening these adults, otherwise the conference is responsible for screening conference-level positions and assessing conference-level events.[76]

The stated purpose of the LMC policy is "to ensure that LMC is a safe place for all people" and the intent of the policy and its procedures "is to protect children and youth from harm and abuse, adults who work with them from false allegations, and the church from unnecessary litigation."[77] The policy has a number of risk-minimization protocols, including a prohibition against "vehicle transportation by workers alone with unrelated youth" and the use of "a sign-in/out sheet" for the church's nursery program.[78] Again, liability issues are a significant concern.

The LMC policy includes a section outlining the requirements for screening. The congregation is committed to "screen all children's and youth ministry workers to a degree that is appropriate with their interaction with children." People new to the congregation must wait six months before they can be involved with these ministries, and once the waiting period has ended, they must agree to background checks, which involve consulting former pastors or supervisors of the potential volunteer. High-risk positions include "pastors, elders, youth group sponsors, children's club leaders [and] nursery helpers." Medium-risk positions include "Sunday School superintendents, Vacation Bible School directors, Christian Education committee member [and] music directors for children's programming." No person "with a child abuse conviction [may] serve in any capacity where s/he could be involved with children or youth."[79]

In 2007 Mennonite Church Canada released the *Volunteer Screening Policy and Procedures Manual*. This document acknowledges the *A Plan to Protect Our Children, Youth & Leaders*, as well as an earlier document by the national Church that was designed to help local congregations, *The Volunteer Screening Guide*. In describing the rationale for the creation of *The Volunteer Screening Guide*, MCCanada identifies the relevance of legal reprisals, but underscores the importance of protecting the vulnerable as the primary motivation:

> In Ontario and B.C., many churches have already experienced the reality of having a portion of their liability insurance threatened or removed due to the absence of adequate volunteer screening policies. This is because insurance companies and the legal courts are considering the lack of such policies to be a sign of negligent behaviour.... Although liability insurance is or will be a concern for all churches in the near future, we want to acknowledge first and foremost that it is the church's responsibility to provide a safe place for all people, and that its most vulnerable members must be protected to the utmost of our capabilities.[80]
> Additionally, MCCanada states that volunteers are greatly appreciated and it is the responsibility of the Church to support them.

MCCanada recommends that "every church should have written volunteer screening policies tailored to meet its own needs." In creating screening policies, individual churches are advised to consult the *Screening in Faith* document, available from Volunteer Canada or the denominational Resource Centre, consult with a local volunteer centre, and obtain a copy of *Reducing the Risk of Child Sexual Abuse in the Church*, from either the Resource Centre or *Church Law Today*.[81]

The MCCanada document *Volunteer Screening Policy and Procedures Manual* is organized under the following headings: "Our Responsibilities," "Developing Your Screening Policies and Procedures," and "Incidents: Reporting and Responding." The first section provides a discussion on the possibility of abuse in the Church, the role of power in abuse, and the Church's duty of care to those participating in its programs.[82] Readers are reminded that "the person with more [power] is accountable for the proper use of resources and abstinence from abusing those with less."[83]

The section entitled "Developing Your Screening" leads readers through the process of policy development. It is recommended that a group of four or five "members of your church write these policies, with further review done by qualified legal counsel."[84] Participants are advised that effective screening will require written volunteer job descriptions, assessment of risk factors, the determination of "what screens are available to ... answer questions about the risk associated with that category" of job, volunteer recruitment, and the orientation, supervision, and covenant with volunteers.[85]

The final section, "Incidents," addresses how one should respond to a complaint or observation of abuse. Readers are advised that "it is the law in Canada for all adults to immediately report suspected child abuse to the appropriate authorities," and are told not to attempt to investigate the incident themselves. The guide also advises that "your local child and family services agency" may be able to provide advice, should one be unsure as to whether to report a situation."[86]

Recognizing that Church communities will have emotional responses and questions or concerns regarding civil investigations of alleged abuse incidents, each church is advised that "a task force of three to five impartial members should be struck to process the issues surrounding the investigation and after the investigation." Also provided are suggestions regarding how best to communicate with Church leaders, area conferences, or the national office regarding complaints or incidents of abuse.[87]

Nationally, in 2007 MCCanada adopted the *Volunteer Screening Policy and Procedures Manual*, building upon the previously discussed *Volunteer Screening Guide* and the policy of the MCEC. [88] Again, this policy is applicable only to events undertaken under the auspices of MCCanada and is not binding on local congregations. This is not a significantly different policy; the reliance upon the previous documents is easy to discern; large sections, such as those regarding power and the possibility of abuse are almost identical.[89]

The policy describes the process for MCCanada to determine the appropriate screening approach for leaders who will be working with children and youth. The greater the responsibility, the greater the level of screening required. For example, at an event where children and youth will not be present or where MCCanada has only an administrative responsibility, leaders will have a "low responsibility," so volunteer registration may or may not be required. Should the event include children and youth and have an overnight component, it will be considered "high responsibility" and a full slate of screening tools, including PRCs and additional background checks, will be employed.[90] However, the screening of volunteers and staff from area conferences and the screening of adults who accompany the children or youth to an event (e.g., "adult sponsors") are the responsibilities of the respective area conference or the congregation.[91] A table, at the conclusion of this section of the policy, provides a list of event types, the level of responsibility for each event, and who is responsible for the screening of volunteers.

The MCCanada policy also includes a number of operating procedures to ensure a safe space. These include: an "open-door policy" and preference for facilities where this can best be achieved (e.g., those with windows in doors); ongoing, random monitoring of space during an event; restrictions on building entry (e.g., only one door is to be open or unlocked for access from outside the facility); and an overall team approach.[92] Also included in this section are the first responses to allegations of abuse with an emphasis on the legal requirement to contact the appropriate civil authorities.[93] The policy concludes with appendices containing relevant and useful model forms for participant registration, volunteer screening, and a volunteer behavioural covenant.

The MCCanada has also made information regarding child sexual abuse and other forms of abuse readily available. On its official website is a section called "Abuse: Response and Prevention," which provides resource materials designed for "survivors: people suffering from abuse at home, school, church or work, ... those unsure if the treatment they are receiving ... is really abuse, ... pastors or others seeking to support an abused person, ... [and] congregational leaders seeking resources for people in their community."[94] The website includes subsections on sexual abuse, child sexual abuse, domestic violence, and senior abuse, among other relevant topics. Resources include a network of adult survivors, articles, and a section entitled "Faith Teachings and Abuse" that provides exegeses of selected biblical passages and discusses how some have been misused to support abusive behaviour. Similar material is provided in printed form in the booklet "Abuse: Response and Prevention," published by the MCCanada in 2008. Much of the information is available in both printed and electronic form, and builds upon the resource packets discussed earlier in this chapter.

MCCO also has developed a policy entitled *Children, Youth & Vulnerable Adults Protection Policy* (policy 2.14), amended on April 7, 2008. This policy is brief and states the minimal requirements for screening volunteers and staff, "operational procedures," physical space requirements, training, and responding to allegations. For example, a PRC, reference checks, and an interview are required of all applicants. At least two such adults must be "available" when working with children and/or youth. Doors "in activity rooms [must] have windows." And all staff and volunteers must be trained and made aware of this policy.[95]

In the Mennonite organizations discussed in this chapter, the emphasis has been on supporting civil procedures for addressing child sexual abuse complaints, generating proactive measures within the Church, including screening policies and relevant educational material, and assuring that procedures and policies are available to congregations for responding to abuse complaints.

Chapter Summary

Obtaining information regarding policies of the Mennonite communities proved difficult. Not only is this religion divided into several streams or traditions, but the congregational nature of Mennonite polity means there are no overarching policies applicable to all congregations. However, umbrella Mennonite organizations have taken a proactive stance on issues of domestic violence and child abuse, and within the confines of their polity have attempted to educate their constituents on these matters and provide suggested policies. The policies of the MCEC and LMC for dealing with screening of staff and volunteers and complaints of child sexual abuse are excellent examples of congregational work that follow on the heels of resources developed by the MCC, MCCO, and MCCanada.

The Mennonites have placed a strong focus on restorative and educational efforts on behalf of umbrella organizations, especially the MCC and the provincial MCCs, regarding their response to child sexual abuse. They have been committed to breaking the silence around this abuse and taking proactive measures, particularly in terms of screening, distributing educational materials, and making available "Circles of Support and Accountability" for offenders.

As with the other religious institutions, legal and insurance requirements have been significant motivators behind the development of policies to address complaints and to provide effective screening. A theological rationale is also clear, but, as is the case with all of these institutions, one must wonder which carries the greater weight.

Chapter 6

Islam in Canada

ASIDE FROM THE PRIMARY sources cited in this chapter, there were no other publicly available written sources regarding child sexual abuse policy and Islam in the Canadian context. As a result, much of the research for this chapter was conducted through telephone and email interviews. In total, thirty-five mosques or other Islamic leaders were contacted; of these, twelve responded and provided very helpful information.

Institutional Structure and Description of the Context

The first mosque in Canada was built in Edmonton in 1938. According to the 2001 census, between 1991 and 2001 the percentage of the Canadian population self-identifying as Muslim increased by 128.9 percent, Jewish by 3.7 percent, Buddhist by 83.8 percent, Hindu by 89.3 percent, Sikh by 88.8 percent, and Roman Catholic by 4.8 percent, while Protestant Christians declined by 8.2 percent. Of the approximately 580,000 Muslims in Canada,[1] it is estimated that between one-half[2] and three-quarters are foreign-born.[3] Most Muslims live in Ontario (352,530), followed by Quebec (108,620).

Creating a home in a country such as Canada, which values diversity in principle, but often not in reality, can be challenging. There are differences in values between dominant Canadian culture and the Islamic faith: "Living in a non-Muslim society and struggling to maintain our Muslim identity and values and to further instill them in our children requires spiritual and communal support."[4] Further, for some Muslims it is an issue that Canadian laws often contradict the shariah, the Islamic holy law. Unlike the shariah, Canadian law does not prohibit mixed marriages or premarital sex.[5] Others are equally concerned that the shariah has been interpreted by some in ways that contravene women's rights and, therefore, strongly support Canadian law above the shariah.[6] A concern for some is that Canadian-born Islamic children will lose their traditional values while growing up in a culture that espouses some different values and that often does not support, and sometimes discriminates against, Muslims.

Of particular interest to concerns regarding child abuse is the Muslim cultural tendency to be physically demonstrative. Adults often show affection publicly for their children and grandchildren, just as adult Muslim male friends have tended to hold hands in public. Much of these habits have been curtailed in Canada due to a dominant North American culture that is suspicious of such expressions.[7]

Mohamed Elmasry, president of the Canadian Islamic Congress, addresses the topic of cultural and religious differences for Muslims in Canada. In a paper entitled "Towards Smart Integration: The Choice of Canadian Muslims," he argues against assimilation and isolation as the two patterns that tend to be followed most by Muslims in Canada. Instead, he proposes "smart integration," a model that encourages both the preservation of one's culture and faith claims, and participation in Canadian society.[8]

The problem of how to live in a place that is sometimes at odds with and even hostile to one's religious beliefs is very relevant to threatening issues such as child sexual abuse; a felt need to protect the community and the faith may well mitigate against a willingness to bring any "dirty laundry" into the open.

The Islamic religion is structurally decentralized. Each mosque in Canada is a separate incorporation (as religious charitable organizations) and is run by a board of directors. An imam, who may range from being paid full-time to unpaid part-time, leads the mosque community. Further, each mosque establishes its own set of bylaws, which are in accordance with both the law of the land and the Quran.[9]

The board of directors makes the policy decisions for each mosque. The imam is an ex-officio member of the board and, therefore, does not have voting power, but can have significant power of influence, particularly in matters of faith. Policies specific to complaints of child sexual abuse would have to be developed and approved by the board of directors of individual mosques; there is no recommended policy or protocol aside from compliance with secular law.

Although each mosque is autonomous, there are national Islamic organizations that provide services for Muslims in Canada, including the following: the Canadian Council of Muslim Women, the Canadian Islamic Congress— the Canadian Islamic Congress is "Canada's largest national non-profit and wholly independent Islamic organization"[10]—and the Islamic Social Services Association of Canada.

Approach to Child Sexual Abuse, Including Relevant Statements, Policies, and Practices: 1960–2009

The early 1980s saw the beginning of organized internal efforts to support the rights and well-being of Muslim women in Canada, including the formation of the Canadian Council of Muslim Women in 1982. Similar to the other religious institutions examined in this book, during the 1980s, the council's focus was more internal as the organization needed to be built and awareness of women's issues raised. By the mid-1990s "it started its aggressive outreach to women."[11] This organization has developed several chapters across Canada and "believes Muslim women must develop their Muslim identity, make significant contributions to Canadian society, and provide positive role models for Muslim youth."[12] Further, the organization's proponents "are guided by the Qur'anic message of God's mercy and justice, and of the equality of all persons, and [the conviction] that each person is directly answerable to God."[13] One of their main purposes is "to attain and maintain equality, equity, and empowerment for all Canadian Muslim women."[14]

The first national study in North America regarding the prevalence of physical abuse among Muslims was conducted in 1993; the study found that 10 percent of Muslims in the United States were experiencing physical abuse, which is consistent with the general population and other faith groups.[15]

According to a phone interview with Shahina Siddiqui, the president of Islamic Social Services Association of Canada, the Muslim community focused on self-identity and establishing themselves in Canada.[16]

Further, as Elmasry has pointed out, since 9/11, resources have been directed primarily at issues and concerns arising from the popular misperception that Islam and its followers are linked to terrorism: "Prejudice against Canadian Muslims today is compounded by media stereotyping that has built an image colouring them all as terrorists, potential terrorists, or terrorist sympathizers."[17]

Moreover, since "9/11, domestic violence has been on the rise in the American Muslim community, according to social-services agencies nationwide."[18] The tragedy of 9/11 and the resulting increased suspicion of Muslims, especially Muslim men, seem to have contributed to male rage within Muslim communities and an increased hesitancy among Muslim women to report abuse for fear that the authorities would, in turn, abuse their male partners. Further compounding the problem, seeking refuge at a shelter is even less attractive to Muslim women than many other women since many Muslim women feel misunderstood and not accommodated by community social service agencies regarding their religion and culture. Added to this is the reality that "Islam has a long history of associating runaway women with immorality…. Shame and the difficulty of adhering to religious customs in a shelter means many women eventually return to the socially appropriate, albeit abusive, place beside their husbands."[19]

Related to this concern regarding shelters and abused Muslim women is concern for the availability of resources for abused Muslim children. In 1999 an article was published on the Canadian Islamic Congress's website regarding Muslim foster homes in Canada. In it is a statement acknowledging the existence of child abuse in some Muslim families: in some families "parents through emotional and financial neglect and ignorance tend to apply excessive physical and verbal discipline…. In anger we as parents forget the examples set by our own Prophet Muhammad and the Qur'anic teachings…. Under certain conditions that are considered unsafe for the child such as physical abuse, sexual abuse, neglect, etc., the children are removed from their own home." The fact that there are very few Muslim foster families is a serious problem for Muslim children who need to be removed from their families due to abuse allegations;[20] "usually, Muslim victims do not want to go to non-Muslim shelters or foster homes and this is sometimes a barrier in seeking help."[21] When there are no adequately safe options perceived for these children, sometimes the abusive status quo is judged least harmful.

A booklet entitled "Women Friendly Mosques and Community Centers: Working Together to Reclaim Our Heritage," was produced in 2005 by the Islamic Social Services Associations Inc. (both in Canada and the US) and Women in Islam Inc. (US). This publication is significant as it calls individual mosques in North America to be more faithful to the Quran by arguing that "when we empower women, we will empower future generations of Muslims and fortify their Muslim identity."[22] Further, leaders "must honor and promote the right of female servants of Allah to assume full inclusion in affairs of the community and to worship in peace and dignity … without fear and anger."[23] These arguments were grounded by references to the Quran and to the 2001 *Report from the Mosque Study Project*. The study project, which was co-sponsored by the Council of American Islamic Relations, the Islamic Society of North America, and others, surveyed and interviewed mosques and Muslim women, finding that women have been both underrepresented in mosques as members and leaders, and discriminated against.[24]

Efforts to support women and to encourage them to find their voices are relatively new but underway in North American Muslim communities. With the emergence of these voices, more attention is being called to the limited resources, such as social services for victimized Muslim women and children. The roots of this lack, which go beyond limited financial resources to include systemic prejudice and misunderstandings of the Islamic faith, are being gradually brought into the open.

Policies

This study found no formal child sexual abuse policies internal to Islamic communities before 2009 in Canada. If an incident of child sexual abuse was reported to a mosque member, most mosque representatives stated that the complaint would usually then be communicated to someone in the mosque's office or to a board member.[25] Generally, each board of directors would talk with both the complainant and the person accused to determine if the complaint could be resolved informally or if it needed to be reported to the police or appropriate child protection agency in the case of suspected child abuse.[26]

The only internal process available in case of a criminal conviction is termination of employment.[27]

Representatives from the Muslim community with whom the researchers spoke indicated that according to Islamic teachings, sexual abuse is a sin; the perpetrator has a moral and religious obligation to "apologize and repent."[28] Further, "The Muslim child has a number of Allah given rights; these include the right to be born through a legitimate union, to know fully one's parentage, to be suckled, and to be reared with kindness and respect."[29] Other relevant teachings include the Prophet Muhammad's advice that children of a certain age (six is advised) have separate beds, and the Quranic directive for children and adults to dress modestly.[30]

There is a strong reliance on Islamic faith teachings, by some, to address social issues, including child sexual abuse; other secular resources or policies are not used as often. Some of the people contacted within Muslim communities indicated that because of their faith teachings, they did not require such policies. For example, Dr. Ahmad Al-Hashimi, of the Ihsan Muslim Heritage Society, indicated that if Muslims follow the strict values and traditions, which they should, including a regard for the permanence of heterosexual marriage outside of which no sexual expression is to occur, then nothing else, including a policy to respond to child sexual abuse complaints, is needed.[31]

There is a general reluctance to acknowledge that child sexual abuse may be perpetrated by Muslim leaders:

> There is an unhealthy denial within our community that sexual abuse does not exist. The fact is that it is more common than we think.... The lack of resources and services within the community ... may result in low reporting.... In addition, the cultural taboo of talking about sexual matters makes disclosure of sexual abuse particularly difficult.... [Further, a tendency] to blame Western societies for this ill ... result[s] in Muslim communities hindering the victim's family from accessing help. In some cases, immigrant families ship the victim (especially girls) to the family's country of origin for a quick marriage to cover up the situation.[32]

Also, the Islamic emphasis on modesty can discourage open dialogue regarding sexuality due to feelings of discomfort and immodesty.[33]

Canadian secular law is upheld by Muslim communities as the main resource for addressing complaints of child sexual abuse. The Canadian Council of Muslim Women states: "as Canadians we abide by the Charter of Rights and Freedoms and the law of Canada."[34] Most people with whom we spoke were clear that the law is the appropriate authority when dealing with child sexual abuse complaints.

Screening Policies and/or Mandatory Education for Volunteers, Employees, and/or
Officials (in Positions of Responsibility Regarding Children and Youth)

Research for this book revealed no screening policies in Canadian mosques, at least until 2007. Mohammad Darr, member of the board of directors at the Cambridge (Ontario) Islamic Centre, reported that their board tried to implement a police record check screening policy for all volunteers and staff, but members were reluctant to be screened. As a result, the number of volunteers diminished and the screening requirement was abandoned.[35] In 2007, Bader Siddiqi, president of the Ottawa Muslim Association, reported that their board was discussing the implementation of a screening policy. They recognized the need for screening as one mechanism through which to safeguard vulnerable people, including youth and children. The teams from Siddiqi's mosque who visit people in hospital undergo police record screening in accordance with hospital policy. This mosque hopes to implement a similar screening process in the near future for their staff and volunteers.[36] Some Muslims, such as Darr, have indicated that references are checked for anyone who is placed in a position of trust with vulnerable people, including children. In terms of other safeguards, some point to the Muslim rule against one-to-one counselling with the opposite sex and the general tendency to separate males and females in vulnerable settings (for example, in at least half the mosques in Canada, only women teach girls and only men, boys).[37] As the Badgely Report indicated, most child abuse is perpetrated by men against girls, so this tendency to separate the sexes may help to safeguard some children from sexual abuse, but not all. Again, there seems to be a great deal of reliance on Islamic teachings for safeguarding against abuse rather than maintaining theological convictions *and* working toward policies to address such complaints.

Educational Work

Educational work is underway within various Canadian Islamic communities regarding abuse. By 1999, these Muslim communities were becoming more aware of social service supports and were identifying areas of need more clearly.[38] A critical part of this educational work is directed at women and children; the voices of women and children in Islam are needed to raise awareness regarding such issues as abuse.

A series of booklets have been published by the Islamic Social Services Associations in both Canada and the US. Of those related in any way to child abuse, the first was published in 2002 and is entitled "Muslim Culture and Faith—a Guide for Social Service Providers." It has a small section on child abuse that reads, in part:

Islamic parenting emphasizes mercy, gentleness and respect when dealing with children. The duty of parenting is seen as one of the most important roles in society. Physical, emotional and sexual abuse of children has zero tolerance in Islamic law and Muslim communities....

Sexual abuse is … unacceptable in Islam. Sexual intimacy is solely reserved for a marital relationship.... The current increase in child pornography and the exploitation of young children by the advertising industry is disturbing to Muslims.

The cycle of abuse against children, in many cases by parents or guardians who were themselves abused as children is one that needs to be broken with sensitivity and support. Muslim survivors and Muslim perpetrators of child abuse are often not able to discuss their situation with others. In Muslim culture it is a taboo topic.[39]

At this time, child sexual abuse was not commonly discussed, and possible sexual abuse of children by people in positions of trust in mosques was even more taboo.

Booklets regarding "domestic abuse" and "sexual abuse" were published in 2005 and 2006 respectively. The first addresses wife abuse, acknowledging that "thousands of Muslim women are victims of abuse every year around the world by their husbands and other family members, usually in-laws,"[40] and "[d]omestic violence accounts for 50% of murdered women in Canada."[41] Wife abuse is against both the shariah and Canadian law.[42] This booklet is in its second printing and more than one thousand copies have been requested and distributed in Canada and the US.

Shahina Siddiqui, the primary author of "Sexual Abuse Prevention and Intervention," was the president of the Canadian Islamic Social Services Association. "Islamic Social Services Association (ISSA) has produced this pamphlet in response to the growing number of documented cases of sexual abuse in Muslim communities. These incidents clearly indicate a critical problem that must be addressed immediately by imams, parents and community leaders."[43] The booklet discusses the sexual abuse of adults, particularly women, and the sexual abuse of children, offering information, including signs of sexual abuse, barriers to addressing this abuse effectively, how best to care for victims, and available resources. ISSA also offers, in the booklet, to arrange workshops on the topic for anyone interested.

Distribution of this sexual abuse booklet began in November 2006 and data regarding the number distributed were not available at the time of this book's writing. No mosque representatives of those successfully contacted as part of the research for this chapter reported any knowledge of this resource.

Chapter Summary

The decentralized structure of Muslim communities means that there have been no overarching policies. Further, representatives of the mosques contacted for this research suggested that individual mosque policies, apart from following Canadian law, are yet to be established. The reasons for this are multiple.

As with the other religious institutions examined in this study, the emergence of women's voices and the identification of violence against women have preceded the establishment of policies that address child sexual abuse. On an organized level, women's voices emerged later than in other religious institutions examined, likely in part due to the relative newness of Islam in Canada. As women and children gain more voice, issues of sexual abuse are being discussed increasingly.

Another factor is the Muslim taboo around sexuality and related issues. Until sex can be discussed and reflected upon in the faith community context, it is difficult, if not impossible, to get child sexual abuse on the agenda. Part of the reason for this is the shame that accompanies sexual abuse, which is exacerbated by a communal tendency to view sexual abuse as shameful for not only the perpetrator but the victim. Shame is related to issues of voice and silencing.

A significant factor is the wider context; there is much prejudice and/or misunderstanding in North America regarding Islam and Muslim practices. Until this ignorance and prejudice are more fully challenged and transformed, it will be very difficult to break the silence regarding child sexual abuse in Muslim communities. Partly due to these wider systemic issues, there are very limited acceptable social resources for Muslims experiencing abuse. Further, discrimination usually causes groups to be more self-protective; external persecution is a real threat and most do not want to risk adding to this threat. These wider contextual issues contribute to the resistance within some Muslim communities to engage in strong self-critique; some own that child sexual abuse occurs not only within some Muslim families, but also within some mosques and by some mosque leaders, including imams, while others are not yet prepared to admit this possibility.

Most Muslims, consistent with the teachings of sacred texts, are committed to cultivating a safe and nurturing environment, especially for the most vulnerable. The teachings of the Prophet are central to the Islamic faith and provide excellent impetus for work to end violence. There are important educational steps being made in many Canadian Muslim communities.

Chapter 7

The Canadian Unitarian Council/The Unitarian Universalist Association

THE CANADIAN UNITARIAN COUNCIL/the Unitarian Universalist Association (CUC/UUA) paid most attention to education and the establishment of effective screening measures before turning their attention to policies for receiving and responding to complaints. While policies addressing complaints of sexual abuse by volunteers or employees other than "religious professionals" are to be established and implemented by each congregation individually, complaints against "religious professionals" must all be addressed under the CUC/UUA's ministerial misconduct policy administered out of the United States' UUA head office.[1]

Church Structure and Description of the Context

The Canadian Unitarian Council emerged from the Unitarian Universalist Association of the United States as an independent organization in 2001. After the formation of the CUC, the UUA retained the responsibility for both the CUC and UUA for setting ordination standards for clergy and responding to formal clergy misconduct complaints. The CUC took on the particular responsibilities of providing administrative and educational guidance to Canadian congregations regarding preventative measures and reporting formal complaints to the UUA. Further, the CUC responds to informal concerns or complaints before they are substantiated. In all matters of child sexual abuse, as with the other religious institutions, Canadian law is followed.

CUC and UUA congregations function autonomously. This chapter offers a brief summary of relevant UUA activity from 1960 to 2000 and then shifts to reporting in more detail on responses to the need for creating preventative congregational "safe space" from 2001 to 2006.[2] Similar to the approach of the Mennonite Church Canada, the Unitarians have tended to focus most on preventative education and screening efforts; policies for responding to complaints of child sexual abuse had been administered exclusively out of the UUA office of the director of congregational services until 2008, when a detailed complaint policy was first released. Now formal complaints (e.g., those judged to be of substance) continue to be received by the United States office, but are handled by the UUA consultant in the Office for Ethics in Congregational Life.[3]

The Unitarian and Universalist denominations first formed congregations in Canada in the mid-1800s. The Canadian congregations forged working relationships with those in the United States, eventually joining either the American Unitarian Association or the Universalist Church of America. These two organizations merged in 1961 to form the Unitarian Universalist Association (UUA), with headquarters in Boston, Massachusetts. As both organizations were governed by congregational polities, the merger resulted in only minimal changes at the local level. Many congregations retained their historical name, so some are known as Unitarian, others Universalist, with the majority adopting the Unitarian Universalist name.

The Canadian Unitarian Universalist congregations continued as members of the UUA. In 2001, the Canadian Unitarian Council (CUC) formally incorporated to provide services for the Unitarian Universalist congregations in Canada, with the exception of ministerial support and oversight, and the maintenance of some broader-based programs. Most notably, the UUA retained sole responsibility for the education, ordination, and oversight of clergy, as well as continental youth and young adult programs and services, and religious educators.[4]

The CUC is divided into four regions, and the UUA is divided into twenty districts. Each region and district has a president or moderator and a board of directors. Every congregation, within the region or district, is autonomous and voluntarily joins the CUC/UUA, contributing funds each year to the denomination as a member congregation.

The CUC/UUA and member congregations uphold seven "Principles of Faith." These principles describe how UUs choose to be in the world; the UUs' faith and theologies are more oriented toward how one lives in the world than in a transcendent faith. The "Principles" were adopted by the UUA General Assembly in 1985 and are:

- the inherent worth and dignity of every person;
- justice, equity, and compassion in human relations;
- acceptance of one another and encouragement to spiritual growth in our congregations;
- a free and responsible search for truth and meaning;
- the right of conscience and the use of the democratic process within our congregations and in society at large;
- the goal of world community with peace, liberty, and justice for all;
- respect for the interdependent web of all existence of which we are a part.[5]

Unitarian Universalists consider their faith to be a "living tradition" that draws from many sources of authority, including possible individual experiences of transcendent mystery, words and deeds of prophetic women and men, wisdom and teachings of the world's religions, humanist teachings, and the teachings of the Earth-centred traditions.

According to Phillip Hewitt's *Unitarians in Canada*, "Unitarians have never been the religion of more than a tiny segment of the Canadian people. The 1991 census recorded no more than 16,535 in the whole country."[6] Statistics Canada records show marginal growth between 1991 and 2001; the 2001 census tabulated 17,480 people affiliated with the UU.[7]

Since each congregation is autonomous, the president of the CUC is the leader of the council, but not of the local congregations. The UU's congregationalism means that each congregation has "full authority to order its own affairs."[8] Thus, the CUC offers guidance and may suggest policies for congregational use, but cannot require compliance.

The importance of independent communities is reflected in the CUC mission statement:

> The Canadian Unitarian Council is an organization of Unitarian and Unitarian Universalist member congregations and individual members acting to enhance, nurture, and promote Unitarian and Unitarian Universalist religion in Canada. The CUC provides tangible support for religious exploration, spiritual growth and social responsibility. It represents our faith in the larger social and religious environments which can be summarized as: Growing Vital Religious Communities in Canada.[9]

Although congregations are independent, the belief in the seven "Principles of Faith," with an emphasis on the importance of religious freedom, is shared by all.

As autonomous congregations, membership requirements are determined at the local level. However, all congregations in the CUC/UUA agree that membership in a congregation will not be dependent upon agreement with a statement of faith or creed. Individuals are free to choose whatever spiritual path they desire (e.g., derivatives of humanism, Hinduism, Buddhism, Christianity, Paganism, etc.). Accordingly, members will not be excommunicated for their beliefs—when to leave a congregation for reasons of belief is each individual's decision. Each congregation develops its own policies regarding excommunication for other reasons, such as behaviour that may be dangerous to others. Thus, congregations are diverse in their spiritual pursuits, while unified in their beliefs regarding the inherent dignity and worth of every individual.

Each local congregation determines the religious education curricula for its children and youth. The CUC/UUA offers curricula to the local congregations that are age-appropriate and seeks to fulfill the need to educate without indoctrinating.[10] Since 1985, there has been shift in emphasis to teach more about what it means to be a Unitarian Universalist and a shift from mostly secular to more religious content.[11]

These shifts in foci are also evident in educational material regarding human sexuality. For example, the 1999 child and youth sexuality curriculum, entitled *Our Whole Lives*, teaches "not only facts about anatomy and human development, but [seeks] to help clarify values, build interpersonal skills, and to create an understanding of the spiritual, emotional, and social aspects of sexuality." This human sexuality curriculum addresses five age-group levels, and covers topics such as "sexual abuse, exploitation, and harassment." The CUC/UUA approach to human sexuality reflects a belief in the inherent dignity and worth of every individual. Again, each congregation selects its own curriculum, with many choosing to use the suggested one. According to Ross, "as of 2000, more than three hundred congregations had already trained teachers in the new curriculum."[12] Sylvia Bass West, CUC director of lifespan learning in 2007, reported that out of forty-five member congregations, about half are using the *Our Whole Lives* material.[13]

Approach to Child Sexual Abuse, Including Relevant Statements, Policies, and Practices: 1960–2009

In April 2008, the first highly visible and detailed policy for receiving internal complaints of sexual abuse, including child sexual abuse, was released by the Unitarian Universalists Association. This policy is entitled, *Process for Handling Complaints of Misconduct*. Previous to this policy, policy response to ministerial misconduct had been evolving: "In May of 2000 an Ad Hock Task Force on Ethics and Congregational Life was convened by UUA Executive Vice President Kay Montgomery to recommend clarifying changes in the UUA process for responding to complaints of ministerial misconduct. In March 2001 the Task Force concluded its work, presenting recommendations for improvement. In July 2002, as a part of the restructuring of UUA staff, those recommendations were used to guide changes in the process for handling complaints of misconduct."[14] Since 2002, the policy has been further scrutinized and developed in greater detail. Additionally, previous to April 2008 the policy was difficult to access; much of the information had to be gleaned through telephone and email interviews. Since then the policy, as established in April 2008, has been posted on the official UUA website.

Complaints of Child Sexual Abuse and Complaints by Adults of Historical Childhood Sexual Abuse

In cases of alleged abuse of a minor, the complaint is to be reported to the state or province in accordance with secular law. If a complaint is also filed with the UUA, possibly simultaneous investigations will take place.[15]

Generally, misconduct incidents occurring "more than six years prior to the date of the complaint" will not be pursued; the exception to this is in cases involving "abuse of children or particularly egregious behaviour or repetitive actionable behaviour."[16]

Investigative Procedures Regarding Complaints

Under the process used prior to April 2008, if the complaint was contested by the respondent, the director of congregational services contacted the complainant and asked the person to be as forthcoming as possible with information to aid in determining the next steps.

If it was decided that the complaint warranted adjudication by the ministerial fellowship committee (MFC), a request was made to put the complaint in writing. The director of congregational services in 2007, Tracey Robinson-Harris, also noted that if the case warranted, in the face of significant information, the MFC could initiate an inquiry in the manner of a third-party complaint.

Once all information was gathered (the UUA holds primary responsibility for gathering information), the director of congregational services would meet with the UUA executive vice president and director for ministry and professional leadership to make one of three determinations:

a   The complaint is sufficient;
b   Additional information is needed. In this case the Director of Congregational Services is charged with the responsibility for follow-up investigation; or
c   The case is of such a nature that a significant amount of additional information is needed. At this point, the Director of Congregational Services would appoint a volunteer investigator.

If it was determined that the complaint is sufficient and thus required adjudication by the MFC, the director of congregational services presented the case to the committee.[17]

The 2008 policy builds on this process. In order to provide a "safer" place to lodge complaints, complaints are made directly to the UUA consultant, Office for Ethics in Congregational Life; previously they had been made to the director of congregational services. The UUA consultant will then manage the process and will:

10. receive and investigate complaints
   - coordinate support services to affected individuals and congregations
   - present cases for adjudication by the Ministerial Fellowship Committee
   - involve a corps of volunteer investigators and volunteer liaisons, the latter providing both pastoral support and process information/advice to the complainant
   - involve, when needed, a crisis response team, to provide support to congregational staff and leaders
   - include an education and training component for congregational leaders.

The UUA consultant initiates the process by listening to the complainant, and then explains the steps of the policy and answers initial questions. At this stage "the UUA Consultant has the discretion to refer matters not suitable for adjudication by the Ministerial Fellowship Committee (MFC), to other resources such as District Staff."

In all instances where a complaint is presented for adjudication by the MFC, the consultant will ask to receive it in writing. The consultant will then assign one or more volunteers to initiate a "fact-finding investigation," the result of which will be a report submitted to the consultant. At this point, the consultant will "define the scope of the case to be presented to the MFC" in preparation for presenting the case to the MFC at a later date. Throughout the process one person will be designated to act as a liaison with the complainant.

Upon receipt of the written complaint, the accused minister "may be invited to meet with the executive committee of the MFC, who will then determine subsequent actions." The executive committee

- may determine that no further action is warranted,
- may propose to the full Committee a mutually agreed upon course of redress,
- or may determine that further investigation and a full Committee Fellowship Review is warranted.[18]

In cases where it is determined that the next step should be a "full Committee Fellowship Review," the executive will "charge the Executive Secretary to determine the type and scope of the investigation and appoint an investigation team in consultation with the MFC Chairperson."[19]

Once completed, the investigator(s) will file a report, containing all collected materials, with the executive secretary and the report will be reviewed for completeness by both the executive secretary and the MFC chairperson. If it is determined that additional information is required, it will be collected.[20] Once the report is judged complete, it is presented to the executive committee to determine if "there is sufficient concern to believe the minister has engaged in unprofessional/unbecoming conduct."[21]

In cases where the executive committee determines there is insufficient reason to proceed, it will notify the parties of its decision. Should the complainant disagree with the findings, the executive's findings and decision can be appealed to the MFC committee.[22]

In situations where criminal proceedings are being undertaken, the executive committee "may suspend all or part of the investigation until" criminal proceedings are completed; at that time it may resume its process, making use of court transcripts as part of the investigation.[23]

In cases where the executive committee determines there is sufficient reason to proceed, all parties will be notified and a review scheduled and undertaken according to the rules of the MFC.[24] The rules provide for a written response from the respondent, and ask that the response and any other materials be submitted to the MFC at least fourteen days prior to the review.[25]

If the complaint is against a candidate for admission into fellowship (i.e., one working toward becoming a minister), the MFC process is modified. The complaint is directed to the ministerial development director (MDD), who notifies the candidate of the written complaint. Consistent with general procedure, the candidate respondent has fourteen days in which to provide a written response. It is then the responsibility of the MDD to determine if there is sufficient evidence to warrant further action; during this time, the MDD ensures that the complainant is informed of the proceedings.[26] Where it is decided that the complaint warrants further action, the ministerial credentialing director (MCD) is responsible for undertaking an investigation. "If the complaint involves either a candidate or complaint from a traditional marginalized community, the UUA Identity Based Ministries Staff Group will also be consulted." The MCD writes a report of the findings and recommendations in consultation with the MDD, which is then presented to the executive committee of the MFC.[27]

Complaints Regarding People Who Are Not Church Personnel and Complaints Regarding People Who Are Church Officials and/or Employees

The version of the policy, effective July 2002–April 2008, entitled "Process for Handling Complaints of Misconduct," underwent several revisions. In 2007, according to Robinson-Harris, then director of congregational services, a Canadian congregation would contact her department with any complaint of sexual misconduct by a religious professional. "Religious professional" was understood to include ministers and religious educators who are members of the LREDA, as well as those who are or who may be seeking credentialing with the UUA.

As stated earlier, when a complaint is received, the religious professional involved is notified of the complaint. If the allegations are not contested, the religious professional may negotiate for a voluntary resolution without an investigation. The UUA holds all responsibility for investigating clergy misconduct.

Individual congregations are responsible for developing and implementing policies and procedures regarding alleged misconduct of staff and volunteers. In detailing its process for the handling of complaints of professional misconduct, the association notes that "[u]nlike many other religious bodies, the UUA is an association of member individual and independent congregations. The role of the UUA is to provide support to its member congregations. It does not govern them."[28] It is the tradition and polity of the CUC/UUA that each congregation has complete independence to hire, discipline, and dismiss all staff, including clergy, and to set its own policies and procedures in all areas of practice. Nonetheless, due to its power and responsibility for the credentialing of ministers and religious educators, a UUA process is in place to respond to complaints specifically against these people.

Third-Party Complaints

"In some cases, a third party submission will be acceptable, for example a congregation's Board of Trustees could file a formal complaint," according to Robinson-Harris in 2007. She noted that "I would review third party complaints on a case by case basis." For her to accept a third-party complaint, the complaint would need "the permission/agreement of the victim to file" and also more than "hearsay information … [but] in many instances a third party complaint would, at the least, prompt an investigation."[29]

Under the 2008 policy, this continued to be the practice. When a complaint is presented to the MFC for adjudication, the MFC rules state that "[c]omplaints should be from a person or persons with first-hand knowledge of the circumstances, the congregational, institutional, or agency board with whom the minister works, or the UUA Ministry and Professional Leadership Staff Group."[30] When the case is one "involving children or dependent adults," the director of congregational services may choose to advance the complaint himself or herself if there is any suspicion, regardless of the alleged victim's willingness to file a complaint.[31]

Responses to Involved People

Regarding ministerial misconduct, while the case is in the adjudication phase, the complainant will be appointed a liaison within the UUA. The liaison helps the complainant through the process and is the point person to contact with any queries. The liaison is not intended to function as a spiritual care provider.

The congregation receives support and guidance throughout this process by the regional staff of the denomination (CUC). Of note, the policy states that all "participants in any complaint process will be informed that confidentiality may be breached to protect against harm."[32]

If the UUA finds the complaint to have substance, the complainant will have to endure going through the process of adjudication, which is usually very difficult. For religious professionals, "the most serious consequences would be loss of position, loss of credential and/or legal action."[33]

When, as a result of the proceedings, the executive committee of the MFC decides that the minister's fellowship is to be terminated, the executive committee of the MFC "shall inform all ministers and congregations, by letter" and publish the notice of termination in the UUA's official magazine, *Unitarian Universalist World*.[34] Should the minister in question, at a future date, seek readmission to fellowship, the executive committee of the MFC will notify parties to the complaint, and seek their comments on the matter.[35] Possible consequences in addition to termination include but are "not limited to, a letter of reprimand, suspension, counseling, return to aspirant status or removal from candidate status."[36]

Regarding candidates for admission into fellowship, where the MCD's recommendation is that candidate status be removed, the executive committee makes the recommendation to the full committee, which will meet to consider the matter. If the full committee decides to remove candidate status, he or she may reapply for candidate status, through the executive committee, "upon furnishing appropriate evidence that the concern no longer exists."[37]

When the person against whom the complaint has been brought is an aspirant (the stage before becoming a candidate), the "Ministerial Credentialing Director will conduct an investigation and may consider a range of resolutions, including, but not limited to, a letter of reprimand, suspension, counseling, or removal of aspirant status." Additionally, the MCD writes a letter detailing the complaint and resolution "to the administrator of the Regional Sub-Committee on Candidacy where the aspirant is expected to interview," with a copy placed in the aspirant's permanent file.[38]

Screening Policies and/or Mandatory Education for Church Volunteers, Employees, and/or Officials (in Positions of Responsibility Regarding Children and Youth)

As part of the consultation group who developed and published *Screening in Faith* in 1999, the Unitarians have recommended the use of this tool to its Canadian congregations.[39] As explored in previous chapters, this resource offers details on how to implement screening as part of hiring practices and ongoing evaluation. As the booklet states, "The aim of *Screening in Faith* is to provide each faith community with tools to create and maintain a safe environment, to protect those who are to be cared for and to prevent sexual, physical and emotional misconduct from occurring in places of ministry."[40] Included in this resource are exercises to assist an organization in creating policies and procedures, job applications, and screening tools.

The CUC initiated several projects following their involvement with the *Screening in Faith* consortium. A web page, "Safe Congregations/Screening in Faith,"[41] was developed to aid congregations in implementing a screening policy. Information available on this web page includes: the aim of the program; how to assess risks; steps to develop and implement a program; a list of resources, legal implications; a director's liability paper; and the CUC's recommendation that each "congregation … actively work toward prevention of sexual misconduct and deal with every allegation or accusation promptly, seriously, and systematically, in co-operation with the proper authorities, where appropriate."[42]

Several congregations volunteered to champion this program and were involved from its inception in 1999. They attended a "train the trainer" workshop in 2002 to better assist other congregations in developing and implementing screening programs. Congregations participating as "screening champions" included, but were not limited to, Toronto, London, Hamilton, and South Peel.[43]

Sylvia Bass West, director of lifespan learning, conducted "Screening in Faith" workshops at the CUC annual meetings in Calgary in 2000 and in Montreal in 2001. Additionally, workshops were held at the regional fall gatherings in 2002 and in congregational clusters. Bass West and congregations that have implemented the screening program continued to be available to coach congregations through the process of implementing a screening program.

To inform congregations about the need for screening, the CUC published and distributed a "Screening in Faith" brochure. These brochures have been available to congregations upon request.

To assist youth in understanding the meaning of "safe space," the CUC board developed, approved, and ratified Youth Program Rules in 2001–2.[44] Amended in February 2005, the rules state:

- No drugs or alcohol
- Adults must remain in the role of advisor at all times
- All conferees/parents must sign the medical release
- No weapons, violence or threats of violence
- No leaving the site except as part of an activity
- All participants must follow site rules
- No drop-ins
- Code of ethics must be signed
- No violating the policy on sexual behavior
- Must be between 14 to 20 years of age
- No sharing of sleeping bags
- Nudity in CUC youth con community is not permitted
- Participants must have a completed registration form submitted before the weekend begins

Breach of the above rules may result in participants being disallowed to participate in the remainder of the conference.[45]

The 2005 amendments included the deletion of a requirement that one "adult will remain awake at all times during the conference." Added was the rule that "[n]udity in CUC youth con community is not permitted."

Data are not available regarding the number of congregations that have implemented screening protocols for volunteers and staff. Seventeen Ontario congregations were contacted and four responded. At the time of these interviews, in 2007, all four congregations had policies and procedures in place regarding "safe communities." Two of the four used the *Our Whole Lives* curriculum in their religious education programs.

Don Heights Unitarian Congregation submitted a working draft of their *Worth and Dignity Policy 2005–2006*, which was adopted in 2007. This policy was based on the seven principles and states: "We are committed to creating a safe and welcoming environment for all, free of harassment and abuse as defined by this policy." Section 4.3 of the policy defines child abuse as "physical, sexual, or emotional abuse or neglect of a minor." To further define sexual abuse, the policy states: "1) unwelcome physical touch or exposure with sexually suggestive overtones or 2) sexual involvement with a minor or 3) sexual involvement with any person unable to give informed consent."[46]

Another congregational policy was obtained from the Kingston Unitarian Fellowship, which first developed a *Screening in Faith Policy*, approved by the board on May 9, 2005, and amended in June and August 2005. This policy states: "We are aware of the occurrence of sexual abuse, interpersonal violence, harassment, and criminal acts in human society, and that it crosses gender, racial, age, sexual orientation, and socio-economic lines.... We recognize that the maintenance of a safe environment must be proactive, not reactive, and as such, we must take steps to make all persons safe while they are participating in Kingston Unitarian Fellowship gatherings."[47]

This Kingston (Ontario) policy establishes screening as part of the volunteer selection process by: determining risk (both congregants and candidate risk), having application forms that include contact information and references, doing police checks, and conducting personal interviews. The policy states that screening is an ongoing process and is to be incorporated into orientation and training sessions. Appendices to this policy include: a position description template, a list of positions, a harassment policy (complaint process), guidelines for working with children, a child-care policy, and a child abuse prevention and response policy.[48]

This congregation also developed a *Field Trip Policy*,[49] which was approved by the board in August 2006. This policy establishes the requirement for permission slips, emergency medical information, and a minimum ratio of adult to youths on overnight trips.[50]

Chapter Summary

The CUC/UUA has done significant policy work regarding ministerial misconduct with the inception of the 2002 "Process for Handling Complaints of Misconduct." A revised version, released on April 4, 2008, is significantly more detailed, attends more to the safety of the complainant, and is posted on the institution's official website.

Given the relatively small size of this religious institution, their misconduct policy was created quickly—only ten years after the three large institutions examined in this book created theirs.

The focus of the policy is on professional misconduct in ministry. Responsibility for addressing abuse complaints against other CUC leaders, including volunteers and any staff besides "religious professionals," is left in the hands of each individual congregation. Child sexual abuse complaints against religious professionals are understood within the conceptual framework of "misconduct," which appears to soften the alternative framework provided by "abuse." However, in recent years clergy or ministerial misconduct has become conflated to a significant degree with abuse and, particularly, sexual abuse. As the title of the CUC/UUA policy indicates, the policy is meant to address complaints from adults, youth, and children. There is no separate policy for complaints of child sexual abuse; the only religious institution to provide a policy dedicated to child complainants or complainants of historic child sexual abuse is the Roman Catholic Church.

Due to the structure of the CUC/UUA, all religious professionals endorsed and employed by the institution are bound by one misconduct policy. This places the CUC/UUA in a position, most similar—of the institutions examined here—to the United Church of Canada.

Most CUC congregations have demonstrated a commitment to screening programs and several have developed such policies in some detail, as made clear through the examples provided.

Chapter 8

Gathering the Pieces

WRITING THIS BOOK HAS been very difficult and at times disheartening, but also sustaining and hopeful. Images of damaged souls and destroyed relationships move between the lines of these chapters. Awareness that this violence is persistent and pervasive can make it challenging to engage the subject; it has occurred over centuries and seemingly will continue. Yet, at the same time, doing this research has given me profound hope. Although the causes and motives underlying policy creation are ambivalent, a hope for greater justice emerged with the 1992 construction of policies by the most populated Canadian religious institutions. The creation of policy has required the admission that some religious leaders have and do abuse their positions, power, authority, and their faiths by sexually abusing children. The creation of policy has signalled that this abuse is recognized and that the respective religious institutions are responding seriously to complaints.

Several common causal factors led these religious institutions—the Roman Catholic Church in Canada, the Anglican Church in Canada, the United Church of Canada, the Mennonite Church of Canada, the followers of Islam in Canada, and the Canadian Unitarians—to address child sexual abuse through the development of policy. These commonalities include factors in wider society as well as internal movements and shifts that preceded policy creation.

Themes and Historical Shifts

Every one of the religious institutions examined in this study first recognized women's voices and violence against women before addressing child sexual abuse in any depth, with the exception of the Roman Catholic Church, which recognized both at about the same time. The Roman Catholic Church began producing literature on woman abuse (for example, in 1989 the Quebec Assembly of Bishops produced a booklet regarding "conjugal violence" and pastoral care)[1] and child abuse (including the first child sexual abuse protocols) in the late 1980s. However, in the global context, liberation theology, including feminist theology, was generated primarily by Roman Catholic theologians in the 1970s. Several feminist theologians from the Roman Catholic Church, including Elizabeth Schüssler Fiorenza and Rosemary Radford Ruether, were writing extensively at this time regarding sexism and the Church.

The Anglican Church's official records throughout the 1960s, 1970s, and 1980s include much attention to the changing roles of women in Church and society, as do the records of the United Church. For example, the Anglican General Synod of 1986 received the report of the Taskforce on Violence against Women, *Violence against Women: Abuse in Society and Church and Proposals for Change*.[2] Further, the Anglican Church first ordained women as priests in 1975.

The United Church created its first task groups and committees dedicated to "women's concerns" in the 1970s. Pornography was discussed in depth during the late 1970s. In addition to pornography, sexual harassment was identified by the mid-1980s as a form of sexual abuse to which the Church had a responsibility to respond. In 1986, as a result of this increasing concern, General Council approved a policy statement on sexual harassment as proposed by the Women in Ministry Committee (WIM) in consultation with the Standing Committee on Sexism. This was their first policy statement regarding any form of sexual abuse. Further, sexism was the first systemic form of violence in which the United Church officially confessed its complicity.[3]

The Mennonite Central Committee's first educational packet on a form of sexual abuse was *The Purple Packet: Domestic Violence Resources for Pastoring Persons—Wife Assault*, published in 1990. Shortly thereafter, in 1991 a parallel resource was produced regarding child sexual abuse: *Broken Boundaries: Resources for Pastoring People—Child Sexual Abuse*.

Although the Islamic communities in Canada produced educational material regarding sexual abuse later than did the other religious institutions examined, women's issues related to sexism and abuse were explored in advance of child sexual abuse.

Lastly, the Unitarians' founding principles are built on a belief in the inherent dignity of every person and a belief in the equality of the sexes. These convictions undergird their current policy regarding sexual abuse complaints.

Throughout the late 1970s and 1980s second wave feminist movements proliferated in Canada and raised, through advocacy work and education, issues of child abuse and woman abuse.[4] Spurred on by secular women's movements, similar groups began to emerge on a structural level in the mainline Churches.

One of the first issues for which these movements agitated was the legalization and availability of birth control.[5] In 1973, the first Canadian rape crisis centre opened in Vancouver.[6] Twenty-one crisis centres had come into being by 1978 and by 1982 this number had increased to forty-eight.[7] In the mid to late 1970s, feminist groups in Canada paid particular attention to physical and sexual violence against women. Pornography was also an important issue to these groups in the late 1970s. Child abuse was raised in conjunction with these concerns and soon gained a place in the public domain.

Liberation theologies, including feminist theologies, emerged in the late 1960s and 1970s. Marginalized voices were claiming their right to speak and to challenge dominant societal normative presumptions. As these marginalized voices, particularly of women and the poor, gained volume through organized grassroots and institutional means, previously silenced experiences, including sexual abuse, were heard. As stories were told and demands made for greater equity and justice, women educated both society and religious institutions regarding the effects of systemic oppression, including widespread exploitation and violence. These stories then led to increased awareness of other narratives of violence experienced by marginalized groups, including children.

An additional precursor common to the different religious traditions examined was experience addressing sexuality within the religious community. Taboo and silence have surrounded sexuality in religion. Before child sexual abuse can be understood not as aberrant sexual acts, but as a terrible abuse of power and sexuality, sexuality in general has to be understood as more than a series of good or bad acts with sex within heterosexual marriage defined as "good" and all sexual acts outside of marriage defined as "bad." This requires open discussion of sexuality and the awareness that sex is not sin as has often been presupposed historically within many religious traditions. Rather, the relationship within which sexuality is expressed determines the moral character of these expressions. If the relationship is characterized by a power differential that prevents authentic consent, then there is nothing mutual or life-giving in such sexual expression. Such expression is soul destroying. It is abuse. It is sin.

Systemic oppression has meant that vulnerable groups of people have been and continue to be exploited. A capacity to understand sin in terms of systemic injustice and in primarily relational terms is necessary to the recognition of the systemic nature of child sexual abuse and, therefore, to the reality that religious institutions are not immune from this evil. This willingness to be self-critical and admit that child sexual abuse can and does happen within one's religious community has been necessary to the creation of relevant policies and protocols. As religious institutions recognize the existence of systemic power imbalances, they become better able to recognize and address their complicity in abuse.

For the United, Anglican, Roman Catholic, and Mennonite Churches, this awareness did not begin to occur significantly until the 1980s, and the most responsive congregations have often been those who have first-hand knowledge of the destructiveness and reality of such abuse.

It has been more difficult for Islam to attend systematically to the issue of child sexual abuse. The reason behind this delay includes the reality that, unlike the others with the possible exception of some Mennonite traditions, Muslims experience widespread systemic prejudice themselves, which has been exacerbated in the wake of 9/11. The Unitarians and Mennonites also were slower to develop policies, although they now have comprehensive ones. This is likely due at least partially to their relatively small memberships and consequently fewer complaints and resources with which to develop and implement policies.

Before child sexual abuse policies could be developed, each religion had to be confronted by evidence that this does happen in their faith group and is perpetrated by some religious leaders. The illusions of morally pure religions and religious leaders have been powerful factors in delaying the creation of policies. The recognition of woman abuse and the awareness of complicity in sexism helped to establish that sexual abuse was not restricted to the "unfaithful"; belonging to a faith group or even devoting one's life to religious leadership does not necessarily elevate one morally or spiritually.[8] This construction of clergy as automatically morally superior has been challenged by media revelations since the mid-1980s, thereby creating possibilities for addressing this abuse of power, particularly through responsive (complaint policies) and proactive (screening and educational measures) policy development.

There were other notable factors precipitating policy creation. First, the Badgely Commission's findings, released in 1984, garnered much attention, which was increased with the later media exposure of the Mount Cashel abuses and particularly those of Father Hickey. Revelations of Anglican organist and choir director John Gallienne's abuses generated awareness that not only Roman Catholic priests sexually abuse children. The revelation of years of abuse in Canadian residential schools and consequent court proceedings caused the Anglican, United, and Roman Catholic Churches in particular to examine their participation in and responses to child sexual abuse.

The media and lawsuits have been very effective in generating popular pressure and financial duress. Connected to the lawsuits is insurance providers' subsequent requirement that religious institutions have a sexual abuse policy; this requirement has been very persuasive and cannot be overstated as a causal factor.

One further factor has been children's increasing awareness that they are valuable and worthy of respect and love; such regard is shared in principle by the religious traditions examined here and was reinforced by the *United Nations Conventions on the Rights of the Child*, ratified by the Canadian federal government in 1991.

These factors have led the most publicly culpable and largest religious institutions examined in this study to develop the earliest policies. A pivotal year was 1992, when the UCC established its first sexual abuse policy, which included child sexual abuse; the RCC published *From Pain to Hope* (some dioceses had policies preceding *From Pain to Hope* beginning in 1987); the ACC National Executive Council adopted its first *Sexual Assault and Harassment Policy*, which was later revised in 2005 and named the *Sexual Misconduct Policy*.

The Mennonite Central Committee released its study packet on child sexual abuse in 1991. Detailed internal policies for addressing complaints, aside from supporting the Canadian legal processes and providing pastoral care, emerged after 2000. In 2001, the MCC published *Making Your Sanctuary Safe: Resources for Developing Congregational Abuse Prevention Policies.* Shortly thereafter the provincial MCCs produced policies and created investigative teams collaboratively with the relevant conferences. The MCC's educational resource emerged around the same time, as did the policies of the three larger religious institutions.

The Unitarians' policy involves the organization's United States officials if the complaint is against a religious professional and is serious enough to warrant investigation. This religious institution is the only one of the smaller three examined that has developed *one* comprehensive policy to address complaints against its religious professionals.

All of the religions examined, with the exception of Islam, have implemented and/or strongly advised the use of screening resources. A consortium of faith communities (UCC, Catholic, Anglican, and Unitarian) developed and published a workbook entitled *Screening in Faith* in 1999. This resource has proven formative for all the involved faith groups. Mennonite Churches have been directed to develop their own policies using the guidance provided by the MCC.

Relevant Differences between the Identified Religious Institutions

Structure has been significant to the development and implementation of child sexual abuse policies. Because of the United Church's conciliar structure, it has been possible for one overarching and binding policy to be implemented. The other religions examined are much more decentralized in terms of their institutional structures, so there is no one binding policy for any of those religions, with the partial exception of the Unitarians, who have a binding policy for complaints against "religious professionals." In addition to this structural particularity concerning against whom the complaint can be made, one of the main differences between the CUC/UUA and the UCC policies is that the former is administered by the institution's US-based head office, not by the individual congregations. Also the ACC has a more limited binding policy that applies only to their General Synod and national office employees and volunteers. The Roman Catholics and Anglicans are organized by dioceses and archdioceses. The Mennonites are comprised of some quite theologically disparate traditions and each church functions with a significant degree of autonomy. In Islam each mosque is run by an independent board of directors and although there are some important national Islamic organizations, similar to the Mennonites and Unitarians, none has the power to dictate policy for individual mosques. The Unitarian congregations function independently with guidance from head offices, except regarding its clergy and trained religious educators (e.g., religious professionals).

The main stated reason why the Roman Catholic and Anglican Churches do not choose to dictate a universally binding child sexual abuse policy is that there are sufficient regional and diocesan differences that a binding policy would be impractical. However, there have been patterns of institutional cover-up and avoidance of responsibility, particularly in the RCC, that cause one to question the persuasiveness of these reasons. Clearly, by limiting responsibility to the individual dioceses and archdioceses, the Churches have limited their institutional liability. While this may be what saves these Churches from financial disaster, the cost may bear out more in terms of people's trust and regard. Of course this quandary must prompt these Churches and other religious institutions to ponder their own intrinsic meaning and the larger theological issues of ecclesiology. Does there come a point at which the preservation of the present incarnation of the Church is outweighed by other needs?

The respective size of the different religious institutions has also proven to be a significant factor influencing the development of child sexual abuse policies. Three institutions—Roman Catholic (43.2 percent of Canadians), United Church (9.6 percent), and Anglican (6.9 percent)—are much larger than the other three—Mennonite (under 1 percent), Islam (2 percent), and Unitarian (under 1 percent). Because of their relatively large memberships, the first three have more financial and human resources with which to facilitate policy development within Canada. Also, the larger the organization, the more likely that there will be a higher incidence of child sexual abuse simply due to its numbers.

Although the numbers of Mennonites are relatively low, they have produced, largely through their international body, the Mennonite Central Committee, significant and early educational resources. Their emphasis on education and restorative justice is distinct among the institutions examined.

The Islamic communities do not have policies at this point and the Islamic Social Services Association has recently produced an educational booklet on sexual abuse that addresses child sexual abuse; their work on the subject is relatively new.

Other differences among the religious institutions include varied foci within the existing policies. The Roman Catholic Church is the only religious institution examined that has a policy dedicated only to child sexual abuse; the policies of other religious institutions are applicable to sexual abuse of children and adults. The RCC policies focus on children as potential victims and priests as potential perpetrators, whereas the ACC and UCC focus on adult women, often implicitly, as potential victims and clergy as potential perpetrators, but with more attention to other officials and volunteers. The Mennonite and Unitarian complaint and screening policies are not focused on religious leaders, but do include them. Muslims, to date, have focused more on family members as potential abusers, with incest being emphasized when sexual abuse is discussed in printed material.

In terms of policy particularities, only the United Church had a policy at any point that explicitly excluded third-party complaints. This changed in July 2007. The reason for excluding third-party complaints was empowerment of those victimized; out of a commitment to empower the complainant and not further victimize him or her, the United Church policy was complainant-driven. Concerns about a wider duty of care prompted the UCC to change this approach in favour of one that may call more abusers to account.

The Roman Catholic Church has particularities that distinguish it further from other religious institutions. The first is the seal or confidentiality of the confessional. As discussed, the Roman Catholic canon law that forbids breaking this confidentiality can potentially place a priest in conflict, both morally and legally, regarding a confession of child sexual abuse. On the other hand, the safety afforded by the confessional may allow some to disclose abuse that they are experiencing.

The second is the requirement of celibacy for most priests.[9] The RCC has devoted much attention to sexuality and the training of candidates for the priesthood. However, it has been, and in many dioceses continues to be, taboo to even talk about priests' sexualities. It can be easier for sexual abuse to go undetected in a religious community when the community's leaders find it difficult to discuss sexuality. If this silence is to be broken further, more work needs to be done. Further, if a healthy sexual theology is not developed or is underdeveloped, a prevailing tendency to perceive the body and spirit as binaries reinforces a systemic devaluing of the body and sexualities.

Probably related to this concern are several studies in the past few decades, which have found a significant level of emotional and sexual immaturity among Roman Catholic priests. As Kathleen M. Sands has observed, "as a celibate institution, [the priesthood] ... attracts a number of men who are immature or conflicted about sexuality."[10] For example, a 1972 study by Eugene Kennedy and Victor Heckler, commissioned by the National Conference of Catholic Bishops of the United States, concluded that of the Roman Catholic priests in the United States at that time, 7 percent were "psychologically and emotionally developed," 18 percent were "developing," 66 percent were "underdeveloped," and 8 percent were "maldeveloped."[11] As Thomas P. Doyle well argues, these findings raise questions regarding the relationship of the wider Roman Catholic Church's "internal structural dynamics" and sexual abuse by priests.[12]

Third, only men can be priests owing largely to a particular interpretation of apostolic succession. This has reinforced the idea that men are more God-like than are women or children and therefore are to be valued more highly. The relationship of this claim to the image and nature of God has been explored and critiqued, particularly by feminist theologians in the 1980s and later. This theology and ecclesiology can have the consequence of silencing the more marginal voices of women and children. Thus, an all-male priesthood remains a challenge to the wholeness of the Roman Catholic Church.

The differences among the religious institutions examined in this book can serve as resources for faith groups in deciding how to proceed in future regarding child sexual abuse policy. To do this more effectively, more networking and gathering of information is necessary.

Future Directions

There is much work yet to be done if we are to better understand the dynamics behind the creation of child sexual abuse policies and further the efforts toward justice and healing that have begun in religious institutions.

An ongoing question concerns motivation. Have fears of court costs and liability issues (with insurers' concomitant requirement that religious institutions have a sexual abuse policy) been the most important motivations for the development of child sexual abuse policies and educational resources in religious communities, or has this work been more morally and theologically motivated? Judging by the many factors behind the emergence of child sexual abuse as a concrete issue on the agenda, albeit to varying degrees, of religious institutions in Canada, it would be reasonable to conclude that fear of liability is one very significant factor, but not the only one.

Another question that could be investigated is the degree to which policies regarding screening and the processing of complaints have been implemented and their effectiveness assessed in the individual faith communities. A policy's existence indicates neither how well it is used nor its degree of effectiveness as experienced by the involved parties.

Regarding policies, there will always be more work to be done as experience is accumulated and insights gained. For example, the United Church will need to assess the costs and benefits of a third-party complaint system. Such an assessment could also be useful to other religious institutions. Further, there are many grey areas that need to be considered when revising policies. For example, how would a religious institution respond if a seventeen-year-old youth leader became romantically involved with a fifteen-year-old youth member?

Although there are many policies at this point, there can still be a reluctance to talk openly about child sexual abuse during worship or at other religious gatherings. This issue must be engaged more publicly.

The care of religious communities after abuse is an ongoing issue. Many religious communities are split apart for years following complaints of child sexual abuse against a religious leader. The Mennonites have contributed most significantly, perhaps, to this healing dimension through restorative justice work, which has included the creation of Circles of Support and Accountability for offenders. The assumption undergirding this work is that caring for those who have victimized others will break the cycle of violence and lead to the end of abuse.

Even with the emergence of good policies for responding to sexual abuse complaints, there remains deep devastation. Further, no matter how good the policy may be in theory, the process will not always be, and indeed has not been, healing for many complainants and others involved.

As stated in Chapter 1, similar research needs to be done regarding numerous other religious institutions to deepen both the comparative value of this study and the knowledge of each individual institution. Several very important religious traditions and new religious movements were not examined in this study. This book is a beginning; additional religions must be researched and this research put into dialogue with this work.

Finally, more integrative work is needed. Analysis of policies and analysis of the dynamics of child abuse are related; these connections will be important to examine. Broad theological issues will need to be analyzed in relation to this discussion, including ecclesiology and the future of religious institutions.

Child sexual abuse was long perceived as an aberration outside of moral religious institutions. Religious institutions in Canada are now addressing child sexual abuse. Most have developed policies under which internal complaints can be received. Overall, there is a commitment to the well-being of children as particularly vulnerable people within any community, including those of religious institutions. Although there many miles yet to walk, there is reason to hope.

Summary Table

Issues	Roman Catholic Church in Canada	United Church of Canada	Anglican Church in Canada
1 Institutional structure	• diocesan • 71 dioceses • each diocese/archdiocese has its own governance and policies regarding most matters • 43.2 percent of Canadians self-identify as RC	• conciliar • generally one policy applies to all congregations and members • 9.6 percent of Canadians self-identify as UCC; the UCC is the second largest religious institution in Canada	• diocesan • 30 dioceses • each diocese/archdiocese has its own governance and policies regarding most matters • 6.9 percent of Canadians self-identify as Anglican
2 Women's roles	• all-male priesthood • RC theologians generated liberation theology in the 1970s; feminist theologies arose out of this movement in the late 1970s and 1980s • in 1989 the Assembly of Quebec Bishops produced a booklet on "conjugal violence"	• ordained women beginning in 1936 • women's groups and gender task groups emerged in the late 1970s and 1980s • a sexual harassment policy (1986) was the first UCC policy regarding sexual abuse	• ordained women beginning in 1975 • through the 1980s there were efforts made to increase the number of women in senior church positions • 1981 a task force on Violence against Women was created; report of the task force released in 1987 acknowledging the Church's complicity
3 Approach to human sexuality	• sexuality is a gift from God in whose image we are created • priests must be celibate • sexual abuse became a prominent issue with the exposure of child sexual abuse at Mount Cashel orphanage in the late 1980s; the Winter Commission (1990) made recommendations regarding the priesthood and complaints of sexual abuse • sexual abuse in residential schools raised awareness in the late 1980s and 1990s	• sexuality is a gift from God in whose image we are created • addressed human sexuality in depth through the 1980s • moved from a primarily act-centred sexual ethic to a primarily relational sexual ethic since 1960 • sexual abuse in residential schools raised awareness in the late 1980s and 1990s • officially supports same-sex marriage and ordains people regardless of sexual orientation	• sexuality is a gift from God in whose image we are created • beginning in the late 1970s, sexual orientation was studied and debated • moved from a primarily act-centred sexual ethic to a primarily relational sexual ethic since 1960 • sexual abuse in residential schools raised awareness in the late 1980s and 1990s • from the late 1980s to the 1990s the case of John Gallienne raised awareness of sexual abuse by Church leaders other than clergy
4 Emergence of policies regarding complaints of child sexual abuse	• in 1987 the Canadian bishops produced the first guidelines and Canada's first RC diocesan child abuse protocols emerged • in 1992 *From Pain to Hope* was released as the first set of nationally recommended procedures • in 2005 a review of *FPtH* was released	• in 1992 the *Sexual Abuse: Harassment, Exploitation, Misconduct, Assault, and Child Abuse* was produced and presented • it has been revised in 1997, 2001, and 2007 with minor revisions in later years	• in 1992 the *Sexual Assault and Harassment Policy* was released as the first nationally recommended guide • in November 2005 it was revised as *Sexual Misconduct Policy Applicable to National Staff and Volunteers*

Summary Table, continued

Issues	Roman Catholic Church in Canada	United Church of Canada	Anglican Church in Canada
5 Investigative procedures	• generally there are separate meetings with the complainant and suspected aggressor to determine if the appropriate child protection agency should be notified • other interviews may be conducted	• detailed procedure was implemented July 2007; previously included a "fact-finding" piece—later renamed a "response" step—through discussion with the complainant and respondent	• diocesan bishop may choose to investigate complaint after the legal investigation is complete • the national policy outlines a specific investigative procedure
6 From whom and against whom complaints may be received and made	• generally from anyone, including a third party, who has reason to suspect someone in a position of trust in the RC Church of child sexual abuse	• from anyone who has reason to suspect someone in a position of trust in the UC of child sexual abuse • 2007: third-party complaints process was implemented	• generally from anyone, including a third party, who has reason to suspect someone in a position of trust in the ACC of child sexual abuse
7 Historical and/or current complaints of child sexual abuse	• complaints of historical abuse are received and can be investigated depending upon diocesan policy • complaints judged to be of substance of current child sexual abuse must be reported to the authorities	• complaints of historical abuse are received and can be investigated • complaints judged to be of substance of current child sexual abuse must be reported to the authorities	• complaints of historical abuse are received and can be investigated depending upon diocesan policy • complaints judged to be of substance of current child sexual abuse must be reported to the authorities
8 Responses to involved people	• pastoral care for all involved parties is encouraged • financial support is encouraged for those who claim to have been abused • is compliant with legal proceedings • if accused is a paid employee, including priests, leave with pay and benefits may be required during proceedings • reappointment of an offending priest is very unlikely under the 2005 revised policy • RC Church could find the accused guilty regardless of legal verdict • discipline may include therapy, termination of employment, restrictions, voluntary laicization, retirement, canonical penal proceedings, or financial compensation	• pastoral care for all involved parties is required • financial support is available for those who claim to have been abused • is compliant with legal proceedings • if accused is a paid employee, including ordained ministers, leave with pay and benefits may be required during proceedings • reappointment of an offender is very unlikely and requires letters of apology, repentance, restitution, supervision, and restriction of activities • the UCC could find the accused guilty regardless of legal verdict • discipline may include: therapy, termination of employment, restrictions, restitution, admonition, rebuke, suspension, deposition, discontinued service list, expulsion	• pastoral care for all involved parties is encouraged • financial support is encouraged for those who claim to have been abused • is compliant with legal proceedings • if accused is a paid employee, including priests, leave with pay and benefits may be required during proceedings • reappointment of an offender is very unlikely • if complaint is found to have grounds, proceedings under Canon XVIII: Discipline may be pursued • ecclesiastical discipline follows any criminal conviction • ecclesiastical discipline may occur regardless of legal verdict • discipline may include admonition, suspension, deprivation of office or ministry, or deposition

Summary Table, continued

Issues	Roman Catholic Church in Canada	United Church of Canada	Anglican Church in Canada
9 Screening policies and/or mandatory education	• most bishops require psychological assessment and training for priesthood candidates and require candidates to have a CPE unit • in 1999 the OCCB endorsed Volunteer Canada's *Screening in Faith*	• in 1999 the UCC endorsed Volunteer Canada's *Screening in Faith* • in 2000 *Faithful Footsteps* (built on *Screening in Faith*) was released as a required guide to screening those in positions of trust	• most bishops require a CPE unit before a candidate is ordained • in 1999 the ACC endorsed Volunteer Canada's *Screening in Faith* • some dioceses developed policies usually based on *Screening in Faith*
10 Issues particular to the religion	• seal of the confessional • celibacy of the priesthood	• third-party complaint procedures and in-depth investigative step implemented July 2007	

Issues	The Mennonite Church Canada	Islam in Canada	CUC/UUA
1 Institutional structure	• less than 1 percent of Canadians self-identify as Mennonite • structure is congregationalist: there are different traditions that function mostly autonomously with international Mennonite organizations (ex. Menno Central Committee [MCC]) providing links • each congregation functions mostly autonomously	• 2 percent of Canadians self-identify as Muslim • very decentralized structure; each mosque is autonomous and has its own policies • national Islamic organizations in Canada provide links	• less than 1 percent of Canadians self-identify as Unitarian • CUC emerged from the UUA as an independent organization in 2001 • all share seven principles of faith • congregations are autonomous
2 Women's roles	• in 1990 MCC produced *The Purple Packet: ... Wife Assault* • in 1993 the Mennonite Church General Assembly adopted *A Resolution on Male Violence against Women;* the Church recognized its complicity	• the 1980s saw the beginning of organized internal efforts to support Muslim women in Canada, including the 1982 formation of the Canadian Council of Muslim Women • in 2005 *Women Friendly Mosques* was produced	• CUC/UUA uphold the equal dignity and worth of all people both spiritually and institutionally
3 Approach to human sexuality	• Mennonite Church of Canada: in 1986 *Resolution on Human Sexuality* affirms sexuality as a gift from God • affirms sexual intercourse only in heterosexual marriage • spouse abuse is a sin	• other issues have taken precedence • understands sexual intimacy to belong only within heterosexual marriage	• belief in the dignity and worth of everyone and the goodness of human sexuality • welcomes all sexual orientations • is committed to educating members regarding appropriate sexual expression

Summary Table, continued

Issues	The Mennonite Church Canada	Islam in Canada	CUC/UUA
4 Emergence of policies and resources regarding complaints of child sexual abuse	• in 1990 the MCC published *Broken Boundaries: Resources for Pastoring People—Child Sexual Abuse* • in 1991 the MCC published *Crossing the Boundary: Sexual Abuse by Professionals*, which includes guidance for Mennonite Churches on how to receive complaints	• no policies yet • any complaints would be received following each mosque's approach to receiving a complaint regarding any matter • in 2005 and 2006 the Islamic Social Services Association produced resources on wife abuse and child abuse, respectively	• in 2002 the first policy emerged: *Process for Handling Complaints of Misconduct* • in 2008 the policy was revised and made more accessible • policy is recommended for use by all congregations
5 Investigative procedures	• in 1991 the MCC produced *Crossing the Boundary*, which includes resources for congregations to help establish investigative procedures, but there is no one recommended procedure aside from supporting legal proceedings	• are dealt with as other complaints would be addressed according to each mosque's tradition/policy	• all formal complaints of ministerial misconduct are investigated and reviewed by the UUA consultant, Office for Ethics in Congregational Life (located in the US); all other complaints are processed autonomously at a congregational level
6 From whom and against whom complaints may be received and made	• the MCC encourages those who have experienced abuse or have third-party knowledge to tell the Church	• has no official policy	• anyone in a position of trust can have a complaint made against him or her by anyone under the person's care
7 Historic and/or current complaints of child sexual abuse	• there is no universal Church policy in place to investigate complaints of historical abuse; • complaints judged to be of substance of current child sexual abuse must be reported to the authorities	• has no official policy	• complaints of historical abuse are received and can be investigated • complaints judged to be of substance of current child sexual abuse must be reported to the authorities
8 Responses to involved people	• pastoral care for all involved parties is encouraged • is compliant with legal proceedings • if accused is a paid employee, including pastors, leave with pay and benefits may be required during proceedings • if found guilty in a court of law, in the case of at least one conference, the abuser will never be reappointed	• most agree that spiritual care ought to be provided for all involved parties • a criminal conviction may lead to termination of the person's employment or volunteer position • Canadian law is the main resource; is compliant with legal proceedings	• spiritual care for all involved parties is encouraged • is compliant with legal proceedings • if accused is a paid employee, leave with pay and benefits may be required during proceedings • the membership of the accused may be withdrawn and/or other actions may result

Summary Table, continued

Issues	The Mennonite Church Canada	Islam in Canada	CUC/UUA
9 Screening policies and/or mandatory education	• in 2002 the MCC released *Making Your Sanctuary Safe*; many congregations have since developed similar policies	• has no recommended screening policies yet • general reliance on faith teachings to safeguard against sexual abuse	• in 1999 the CUC endorsed Volunteer Canada's *Screening in Faith*; many congregations have developed policies based on this resource

Notes

Notes to Introduction

1 Trevor Pritchard, "Cornwall Child Sex Abuse Inquiry: That's a Wrap," *Toronto Sun*, January 30, 2009, http://www.torontosun.com/news/canada/2009/01/30/8204911.html; Neco Cockburn, "Report by Cornwall Inquiry into Sex-Abuse Response Delayed Again," *Ottawa Citizen*, October 13, 2009, http://www.ottawacitizen.com/story_print.html.

2 Greg Peerenboom, "Minister to Meet Local Groups," *Cornwall Standard-Freeholder*, November 18, 2004, front page; "Judge Rules That Diocese Is a Public Institution," *Catholic Insight*, no. 1.7 (July–August 2006): 39; "Time Line," *Project Truth 2*, http://www.projecttruth2.com/timeline%20and%20the%20story.htm.

3 Terry O'Neill, "Insufficient Proof," *Alberta Reports* 28, no. 19, Canadian Periodicals Index Quarterly, Queen's University Library, http://library.queensu.ca; "Time Line," *Project Truth 2*.

4 O'Neill, "Insufficient Proof."

5 Pritchard, "Cornwall Child Sex Abuse."

6 Ibid.; The Canadian Press, "Victims to Testify at Project Truth Sex Abuse Inquiry," *cbcnews*, October 4, 2006, http://www.cbc.ca/canada/ottawa/story/2006/10/04/cp-project-truth.html.

7 Indrid Peritz and Richard Mackie, "Police Discount Cornwall Pedophile Ring: OPP Team Finds No Evidence of Organized Sexual Abuse after Four-Year Investigation," *Globe and Mail*, August 23, 2001, Canadian Periodicals Index Quarterly, Queen's University Library, http://library.queensu.ca.

8 "Time Line," *Project Truth 2*; Peerenboom, "Minister to Meet Local Groups."

9 Ibid.

10 Terry O'Neill, "A Catholic Priest Is Acquitted of Sex Charges after Accusing Other Priests of Pedophilia," *The Report Newsmagazine*, October 8, 2001, Canadian Periodicals Index Quarterly, Queen's University Library, http://library.queensu.ca.

11 Ibid.

12 Ibid.

13 Ontario Executive Council, Order in Council 558/2005, April 14, 2005, http://www.cornwallinquiry.ca/en/legal/index.html.

14 Ibid.

15 Ibid., section 3.

16 Ibid.

17 Ibid., section 8.

18 Ibid., section 7.

19 The four studies produced are:
    Joseph P. Hornick and Chelsey Morrice, for the Canadian Research Institute for Law
    and Family, *A Historical Review of the Evolution of Police Practices, Policies, and Training
    Regarding Child Sexual Abuse.*

    Simon N. Verdun Jones, Carla McLean, Valerie H. Gregory, and Lauren Freedman, *A
    Survey of Policies and Practices of Government Agencies Involved in the Administration
    of Youth Justice and Custodial Care with Respect to Complaints of Child Sexual Abuse
    and Complaints by Adults of Historical Child Sexual Abuse Who Were Provided with
    Government Services, Whether by Employees of the Government or by Volunteers.*

    Carol A. Stalker, Amanda Topham, Maxine Barbour, and Natalie Forde, *Policies and
    Practices of Child Welfare Agencies in Response to Complaints of Child Sexual Abuse
    1960–2006.*

    Tracy Trothen, *A Survey of Policies and Practices in Respect to Responses by Religious
    Institutions to Complaints of Child Sexual Abuse and Complaints by Adults of Historical
    Child Sexual Abuse, 1960–2006,* http://www.cornwallinquiry.ca/en/healing/research/
    index.html.
20 G. Normand Glaude, "Cornwall Public Inquiry: Statement of Commissioner G. Normand
    Glaude" (Ottawa: Ontario Provincial Government, December 15, 2009).
21 Ibid., 21–22.
22 Ibid., 4.
23 Ibid., 24.
24 Ibid., 34–35.
25 Ibid., 24.

Notes to Chapter 1

1   Shawn Pogatchnik, "Children Beaten, Raped at Irish Schools: Report," *Kingston Whig
    Standard,* May 21, 2009, p. 1.
2   Adele M. Banks, "Southern Baptists Face Sexual Abuse Crisis," *Christian Century,* May
    15, 2007, p. 10.
3   Religious News Service, "Canadian Churches Accept Ruling on Indian Sex-Abuse Claims,"
    Christian Century, November 15, 2005, p. 16.
4   CBC News, "Lahey Laptop Had Many Porn Files," October 16, 2009, http://www.cbc.ca.
5   The power imbalance between child and adult is very significant. Add to this the power
    of the religious leader as one perceived as being closer to God and morally exemplary.
    In the case of the Roman Catholic Church, for example, this is further complicated
    since the priest himself is consecrated as a sacrament: "It is the priest's touch that sanc-
    tifies and the priest's words that forgive. How vulnerable, then, are children when their
    own sexuality is touched by a priest and their own forgiveness promised?" Kathleen M.
    Sands, "Speaking Out—Clergy Sexual Abuse: Where Are the Women?" *Journal of Feminist
    Studies in Religion* 19, no. 2 (Fall 2003): 81. The abuse victim experiences intense shame
    and usually feels responsible; since the leader is so good, the child must be the bad one.
    Complicating this dynamic even further is the place of the wider religious institution;
    in the context of the psychological dynamic of traumatic bonding, Doyle reflects on the
    added shame perpetrated by the Church on victims:

    The traumatic bonding is affirmed by the Church's apparent sanction or
    approval of the priest's behavior. Approval is perceived to be the case when the
    victim senses shame or feels harm, yet the clergy perpetrator carries on with

his life with no one calling him on his abusive behavior.... Thomas P. Doyle, "Roman Catholic Clericalism, Religious Duress, and Clergy Sexual Abuse," *Pastoral Psychology* 51, no. 3 (January 2003): 224.

This shaming is compounded again by the link between the church or other religious institution and the Divine; surely God approves of the behavior of the abusing religious leader as well. Further, there is some indication that at least in the case of child sexual abuse by Roman Catholic priests, children are often chosen by their abusers in part because they exhibit avoidant personality characteristics which include shyness and hesitancy, making them less likely to confront or challenge. See Eric G. Mart, "Victims of Abuse by Priests: Some Preliminary Observations," *Pastoral Psychology* 52, no. 6 (July 2004): 467–68.

Complicating the devastation, studies have shown that a relationship with a "benevolent God" contributes to healing from sexual abuse; since the abuser was strongly associated with God, important resources for a healing process are compromised. As pastoral theologians Terry Lynn Gall et al. note in their literature review, "Even when God may be experienced as more distant, survivors still voice a need for spirituality in their healing and ability to make meaning of the trauma." Terry Lynn Gall, Viola Basque, Marizete Damasceno-Scott, and Gerard Vardy, "Spirituality and the Current Adjustment of Adult Survivors of Childhood Sexual Abuse," *Journal for the Scientific Study of Religion* 46, no. 1 (March 2007): 103. Although, as the authors of this study make clear, spirituality is not the same as an institutional religion, it can be much more difficult for those survivors who were abused by a religious leader to access and reconstruct healing spiritual resources as these too have usually been very tainted by the abuse. Other studies have findings consistent with this conclusion. For example, see Stephen J. Rossetti, "The Impact of Child Sexual Abuse on Attitudes toward God and the Catholic Church," *Child Abuse and Neglect* 19 (1995): 1469–81.

A 2004 study by forensic psychologist Eric G. Mart found that children sexually abused by Roman Catholic priests tended to exhibit avoidant personality traits, making them even more sensitive to "ridicule and/or shame" before the abuse occurred (Mart, "Victims of Abuse," 468). Mart examined the psychological assessments of twenty-five adult males who had been sexual abused as children by priests. After the abuse, the majority stayed away from all organized religion due to their traumatic associations. This further impeded their healing resources and exacerbated the spiritual crises they experienced connected to their abuse:

> Discussions with these subjects regarding their spiritual lives made it clear that they experienced particular distress and difficulty resolving the spiritual and religious issues raised by their experiences of abuse by priests.... These individuals have not made confession or otherwise taken the sacraments of the church for many years due to an aversion born of their victimization. As a result, a number of them expressed deep concerns about the status of their souls and their risk of going to hell when they die. However, they have no way to deal with these concerns outside the context of the Catholic Church, which they cannot bring themselves to attend. (Mart, "Victims of Abuse," 470)

Clearly, victims of child sexual abuse by religious leaders experience significant damage to their spiritual and religious selves in addition to the multiple layers of trauma that many noted psychologists and other mental health experts have studied and published. (The most noted such specialists include D. Finkelhor, E. Bass, and L. Davis. There are numerous others who have done very significant work, including some pastoral theologians and ethicists, such as Marie Fortune.)

6   Doyle, "Roman Catholic Clericalism," 190.

7   For example, included in the census statistics concerning religious affiliation is a category identified as "Other Protestants." People are not always sure what to call their faith and consequently may have marked this box when perhaps the faith community they attend or favour is also identified by one of the other more particular options. Further, some will identify as belonging to a certain faith group, but not be practising members. It is impossible to determine the numbers of those actively involved in a faith community through the census data. Thus, these numbers are best used as a guide.

8   The census data indicates that "other Christian" (i.e., Apostolic, Born-Again, Evangelical) comprise 2.6 percent, Baptist 2.5 percent, Lutheran 2.0 percent, Presbyterian 1.4 percent, and Pentecostal 1.2 percent. Statistics Canada, *2001 Census: Analysis Series: Religions in Canada*, May 13, 2003, http://www12.statcan.gc.ca/english/census01/products/analytic/companion/rel/contents.cfm.

9   All other identified faith groups, Christian and others, totalled less than 1.0 percent each. Statistics Canada, *2001 Census*.

10 While several other religious traditions could have been selected, one of my research assistants belonged to the Canadian Unitarian Council/the Unitarian Universalist Association and had excellent access to key people and resources. She also had significant interest in pursuing this particular research.

11 Nancy Adamson, Linda Briskin, and Margaret McPhail, *Feminists Organizing for Change: The Contemporary Women's Movement in Canada* (Toronto: Oxford University Press, 1988), 45; Corrinne Bjorge, "Porn, Obscenity, and the Supreme Court," *Kinesis: News about Women That's Not in the Dailies* (April 1992): 5.

12 The Church Council on Justice and Corrections and the Canadian Council on Social Development, *Family Violence in a Patriarchal Culture: A Challenge to Our Way of Living* (Ottawa: Keith Press, September 1988).

13 Doyle, "Roman Catholic Clericalism," 202.

14 Marie Fortune, *Sexual Violence—the Unmentionable Sin: An Ethical and Pastoral Perspective* (New York: Pilgrim Press, 1983).

15 Roberta Morris, *Ending Violence in Families: A Training Program for Pastoral Care Workers* (Toronto: United Church of Canada, 1988).

16 For example, see Gillian A. Walker, *Family Violence and the Women's Movement: The Conceptual Politics of Struggle* (Toronto: University of Toronto Press, 1990).

17 There are published sources that trace much of this history since the creation of the institutional Church. One of the best short surveys is Doyle, "Roman Catholic Clericalism," 192–97.

18 R. Brian Howe, "Implementing Children's Rights in a Federal State: The Case of Canada's Child Protection System," *The International Journal of Children's Rights*, no. 9 (2001): 363.

19 Carol A. Stalker and Amanda Topham for Cornwall Public Inquiry, Phase 1 Research, "Policies and Practices of Child Welfare Agencies in Response to Complaints of Child Sexual Abuse 1960–2006" (Ottawa: Ministry of the Attorney General for Ontario, 2007), 31–32.

20 Ibid., 36.

21 Howe, "Implementing Children's Rights," 367–71; Diane Walters, "Mandatory Reporting of Child Abuse: Legal, Ethical, and Clinical Implications within a Canadian Context," *Canadian Psychology* (August 1995), http://findarticles.com/p/articles/mi_qa3711/is_199508/ai_n8726833/.

22 Howe, "Implementing Children's Rights," 373.

23 Stalker and Topham, "Policies and Practices," 37.

24 Howe, "Implementing Children's Rights," 372.

25 Pamela Gough, "Ontario's Child Welfare System," *CECW* (Centre of Excellence for Child Welfare) *Information*, 2005, http://www.cecw-cepb.ca.

26 Throughout this book there are references to "religious institutions" generally and also to Churches in particular. Many of the references and examples used in this introductory chapter and the conclusion are from Christian Churches. This is largely because the preponderance of religious institutions examined in this book are Christian and the highest incidence of child sexual abuse resulting in media exposure and litigation in religious institutions has occurred in Churches.

Notes to Chapter 2

1 Special thanks to research assistant Tim Crouch for his work on this chapter. The Canadian Conference of Catholic Bishops' (CCCB) website and particular diocesan websites were investigated first. A number of these websites contain helpful information and are updated regularly. For example, the Diocese of London's sexual abuse policy is available on their website and updates on sexual abuse issues in the diocese are provided.

   Email messages were sent to all the dioceses and eparchies in Canada by research assistant Tim Crouch. Responses varied with the most common being no response. Some responses were mildly antagonistic while others were very forthcoming. A number of dioceses and archdioceses, such as London, Ottawa, Antigonish, and Edmonton, were very communicative over email. Representatives from the Diocese of Alexandria-Cornwall and the Archdiocese of Toronto—the archdiocesan lawyer, media relations director, and judicial vicar—met with Mr. Crouch formally. They also provided him with copies of the archdiocesan policies as they have evolved. In some cases there was a language barrier since emails were sent in English and some dioceses are French. The focus of this report is on dioceses with whom Crouch was able to communicate in English. Two requests for meetings and archival visits were responded to with offers of assistance. In another instance archival access was denied. Additional research was done using news articles, reputable websites, and reading relevant secondary sources.

2 G. Normand Glaude, commissioner for the Cornwall Inquiry, *Report of the Cornwall Inquiry*, vol. 1 (Ottawa: Ministry of the Attorrney General for Ontario, 2009), 861.

3 Statistics Canada, *2001 Census: Analysis* (see Ch. 1, n. 8).

4 Canadian Conference of Catholic Bishops, "CCCB Overview" (Canadian Conference of Catholic Bishops), http://www.cccb.ca/site/content/view/1895/987/lang,eng/.

5 Canon Law Society of America, on behalf of The Holy See, *Code of Canon Law* (Washington, DC: Canon Law Society of America, 1999), S. 349, http://www.vatican.va/archive/ENG1104/__P1.HTM.

6 Ibid., S. 351.2.

7 *Catechism of the Catholic Church* (Citta del Vaticano: Libreria Editrice Vaticana, 1993), S. 882, http://www.vatican.va/archive/ENG0015/_INDEX.HTM#fonte.

8 Roman Catholic Church, "The Roman Curia" (The Holy See), http://www.vatican.va/roman_curia/.

9 Roman Catholic Church, "Congregation for the Doctrine of Faith" (The Holy See), http://www.vatican.va/roman_curia/congregations/cfaith/documents/rc_con_cfaith_pro_14071997_en.html.

10 Pope John Paul II, Sacramentorum Sanctitatis Tutela, Apostolic Letter Given *Motu Proprio* AAS93 (2001), 737–39.

11 *Catechism of the Catholic Church*, S. 883.

12 Ibid., S. 886.

13 Richard McBrien, *Catholicism* (London: Geoffrey Chapman, 1994), 769.

14 A Latin copy of the text is referenced in the bibliography.
15 McBrien, *Catholicism*, 769–71.
16 Canadian Conference of Catholic Bishops, *Directory 2006* (Ottawa: Concacan, 2006), 7, http://www.cccb.ca/site/content/view/1218/1075/lang,eng/; Canadian Conference of Catholic Bishops, "CCCB Overview."
17 CCCB, *Directory 2006*, 7.
18 Hon. Gordon A. Winter et al., *The Report of the Archdiocesan Commission of Enquiry into the Sexual Abuse of Children by Members of the Clergy*, vol. 1 (St. John's: Archdiocese of St. John's, 1990), 65.
19 CCCB, "Statutes of the Canadian Conference of Catholic Bishops," October 19, 2007, Article 10; John Paul II, "Apostolos Suos," III.22, IV.21, http://www.cccb.ca/site/images/stories/pdf/statuts_cecc-statutes_cccb.pdf.
20 Glaude, *Report of the Cornwall Inquiry*, 846.
21 CCCB, "Statutes," 78.
22 Glaude, *Report of the Cornwall Inquiry*, 855.
23 Ibid., 856.
24 Francis G. Morrisey, "Introduction" in "Addressing the Issue of Clergy Abuse," *Studia Canonica* 35, vol. 2 (2001), http://proquest.umi.com/pqdlink?did=338270761&Fmt=3&clientld=14119&RQT=309&VName=PQD.
25 Ibid.
26 John Paul II, Apostolic Letter "Mulieris Dignitatem"—*On the Dignity and Vocation of Women* (Ottawa: Canadian Conference of Catholic Bishops, 1988).
27 Social Affairs Committee of the Assembly of Quebec Bishops, *A Heritage of Violence: A Pastoral Reflection on Conjugal Violence* (Montreal: L'Assemblée des évêques du Quebec, 1989).
28 Ibid., 7.
29 Ibid., 9.
30 Ibid., 10–11.
31 Ibid., 25, 26.
32 Diocese of London, "Progress Report," December 20, 2006, http://www.rcec.london.on.ca/Abuse/20061220_Progress_Report.htm.
33 Canadian Broadcasting Corporation, "Earlier Reports of Priest's Abuse Surface in Diocese Files," *CBC News*, December 21, 2006, http://www.cbc.ca/canada/toronto/story/2006/12/21/priest-victims.html.
34 Diocese of London, "Progress Report."
35 Marie Carter, "Our Former Bishop Reflects on Personal Experience of Church's Journey from Pain to Hope Regarding Sexual Abuse Scandals," http://www.rcec.london.on.ca/Abuse/Sherlock_reflects.htm.
36 CBC, "Earlier Reports."
37 Trevor Wilhelm, "Canadian Bishop Works to Regain Trust after Pedophile Priest," *Windsor Star*, November 2, 2006, http://www.snapnetwork.org/news/canada/canadian_bishop_works.htm.
38 CBC, "Earlier Reports."
39 Michael Harris, *Unholy Orders: Tragedy and Mount Cashel* (Markham: Viking, 1990), 4; Winter et al., *The Report of the Archdiocesan Commission*, 12.
40 Harris, *Unholy Orders*, xxiii–xxiv.
41 Ibid., 28.
42 Ibid., 35.
43 Ibid., 47.
44 Ibid., 132.

45 John Paul II, "Apostolic Constitution Sacrae Disciplinae Leges," The Holy See, January 25, 1983, http://www.vatican.va/archive/ENG1104/__P1.HTM.
46 Glaude, *Report of the Cornwall Inquiry*, 857.
47 Ibid., 858–59.
48 Winter et al., *The Report of the Archdiocesan Commission*, 13–15.
49 Stephen J. Rossetti, *A Tragic Grace* (Collegeville: Liturgical Press, 1996), 7; Winter et al., *The Report of the Archdiocesan Commission*, 15.
50 Winter et al., *The Report of the Archdiocesan Commission*, viii; Rossetti, *A Tragic Grace*, 15.
51 Winter et al., *The Report of the Archdiocesan Commission*, vii; Rossetti, *A Tragic Grace*, 8.
52 Harris, *Unholy Orders*, 17.
53 Gordon Winter to Monsignor Eugene P. LaRocque, October 30, 1989; Winter et al., *The Report of the Archdiocesan Commission*, 192–206.
54 Morrisey, "Addressing," S. 2.1; Winter et al., *The Report of the Archdiocesan Commission*, 152.
55 S. 3.2, as quoted in Rossetti, *A Tragic Grace*, 8.
56 Winter et al., *The Report of the Archdiocesan Commission*, 24, 138.
57 A.W. Richard Sipe, *Sipe Report: Preliminary Expert Report*, s.d., 2003, www.richardsipe.com.
58 Rossetti, *A Tragic Grace*, 5.
59 Ibid., 6.
60 Morrisey, "Addressing," S. 2.1.
61 Ibid.
62 Thomas P. Doyle, A.W. Richard Sipe, and Patrick J. Wall, *Sex, Priests, and Secret Codes: The Catholic Church's 2,000-Year Paper Trail of Sexual Abuse* (Los Angeles: Bonus Books, 2006), 88.
63 Ibid., 163.
64 Ibid.
65 Ibid., 168–69.
66 Ibid., 167–68.
67 Morrisey, "Addressing," S. 2.1.b
68 Francis G. Morrisey, "Proposed Procedure to Be Applied in Cases of Alleged Sexual Misconduct by a Cleric," quoted in Jerome E. Paulson, "The Clinical Considerations in Cases of Pedophilia: The Bishop's Role," *Studia Canonica* 22 (1988): 77–124.
69 Ibid., 122.
70 Ibid., 121.
71 Ibid., 122.
72 Ibid.
73 Francis G. Morrisey, "Procedures to Be Applied in Cases of Alleged Sexual Misconduct by a Priest," *Studia Canonica* 26 (1992): 56–57.
74 Morrisey, quoted in Paulson, "The Clinical Considerations," 123.
75 Ibid., 124.
76 Ibid., 123.
77 Father Brian Clough, Peter Lauwers, and Neil MacCarthy, interview by T. Crouch, Toronto, Ontario, February 27, 2007.
78 Archdiocese of Toronto, *Procedure to Be Followed in Cases of Alleged Misconduct* (Toronto: Archdiocese of Toronto, 1989), 5.
79 Clough, Lauwers, and MacCarthy interview.
80 Archdiocese of Toronto, *Procedure*, Commentary, 2.
81 Ibid., Commentary, 1.

82 Ibid., Commentary 2.
83 Ibid., S. 13.
84 Ibid., S. 6.1.
85 Ibid., S. 7.1.
86 Ibid., S. 22.
87 Ibid., S. 22.d and 23.d.
88 Clough, Lauwers, and MacCarthy interview.
89 Ibid.
90 Diocese of London, "What Has Been Done," http://www.rcec.london.on.ca/Abuse/ SexualAbuseHistory.htm); http://www.rcec.london.on.ca/08/about/safeenvironment .htm.
91 Father John Sharpe, email to T. Crouch, January 25, 2007.
92 Diocese of London, *Safe Environments* (London: Diocese of London, 2008), 18.
93 Phyllis Giroux, "Healing for All," December 1991, http://www. rcec.london.on.ca/ Abuse/199112_SAC.htm.
94 Diocese of London, "Diocese of London Committee Procedure Regarding Allegations of Sexual Impropriety," 1989, http://www.rcec.london.on.ca/, sec. 3.
95 Ibid., S. III.
96 Ibid., S. IV.
97 Father John Sharpe, email to T. Crouch, January 26, 2007.
98 "Diocese of London Committee Procedure Regarding Allegations of Sexual Impropriety," S. 6a, b,j.
99 Ibid., S. 6d-h.
100 Ibid., S. 6l-p.
101 Ibid., S. VI.0.
102 Ibid., S. VI.k and VI.h.
103 Ibid., S. VII.
104 Diocese of London, "What Has Been Done"; the Archdiocese of St. John's drafted a policy and procedures for responding to complaints in March 1990 shortly before the release of the Winter Commission Report (Winter et al., *The Report of the Archdiocesan Commission*, 66).
105 Canadian Conference of Catholic Bishops, *From Pain to Hope: Report of the CCCB Ad Hoc Committee on Child Sexual Abuse* (Ottawa: Canadian Conference of Catholic Bishops, 1992), 13.
106 Rossetti, *A Tragic Grace*, 8.
107 CCCB, *From Pain to Hope*, 14.
108 Ibid.
109 Rossetti, *A Tragic Grace*, 8–9.
110 CCCB, *From Pain to Hope*, 18.
111 Ibid., 26.
112 Ibid., 64.
113 Ibid., 45.
114 Ibid., 46–47.
115 Ibid., 72.
116 Ibid., 47.
117 Ibid., 48.
118 Ibid., 40, 48.
119 Ibid., 61.
120 Ibid., 62.

121 Archdiocese of Edmonton, *Archdiocese of Edmonton Guidelines for Dealing with Cases of Sexual Abuse* (Edmonton: Archdiocese of Edmonton, June 12, 2000).

122 Ibid., S. I.1a.

123 Ibid., S. I.4.

124 Ibid., S. II.9.

125 Ibid., S. II.10.

126 Ibid., S. II.11.

127 Archdiocese of Regina, *Guidelines for Dealing with Cases of Sexual Abuse* (Regina: Archdiocese of Regina, 2006). This policy was updated in June 2009.

128 Archdiocese of Ottawa, *Protocol Regarding Situations of Child Sexual Abuse* (Ottawa: Archdiocese of Ottawa, 2001), 2.

129 Ibid., S. 5d.

130 Ibid., S. 2.

131 Ontario Conference of Catholic Bishops, "Statement by the Ontario Conference of Catholic Bishops," 2002, http://www.occb.on.ca/english/abuse.html.

132 Diocese of Calgary, "Bishop's Message, May 2002: Addressing Sexual Abuse," May 2002, http://rcdiocese-calgary.ab.ca/bishop/bishop_articles/bishops-message-may-2002.htm.

133 Diocese of Antigonish, "Guidelines for Responding to Complaints of Sexual Misconduct," July 2002, http://www.antigonishdiocese.com/SexualMisconduct.htm.

134 Glaude, *Report of the Cornwall Inquiry*, 859–60.

135 Ibid., 860.

136 Ibid.

137 Canadian Conference of Catholic Bishops, "Report of the Special Taskforce for the Review of *From Pain to Hope*," September 2005, http://www.cccb.ca/site/Files/TaskForceGroup_A .pdf, 4.

138 Ibid., 5.

139 Ibid., 6.

140 Ibid., 7.

141 Ibid.

142 Ibid., 8.

143 Ibid., 14.

144 Ibid., 15.

145 Ibid.

146 Canadian Conference of Catholic Bishops, "Protocol of the Canadian Conference of Catholic Bishops for the Management and Prevention of Sexual Abuse of Minors in the Catholic Dioceses of Canada," 2005, 17.

147 Ibid., 21.

148 Ibid., 23–24.

149 Canadian Conference of Catholic Bishops, "Orientations Issued by the Canadian Conference of Catholic Bishops for Updating a Diocesan Protocol for the Prevention of the Sexual Abuse of Minors and the Pastoral Response to Complaints Regarding Abuse," October 2007, 3.

150 Ibid., 2–3, 11–12.

151 CCCB, "Report of the Special Taskforce," 12.

152 Ibid., 22.

153 Ibid., 3–4.

154 Ibid., 6–7.

155 Ibid., 4.

156 Archdiocese of Ottawa, *Protocol*, S. 2a.

157 Ibid., S. 11.

158 Archdiocese of Edmonton, *Guidelines*, S. III.18.

159 Ibid., S. III.25.

160 Ibid., S. III.31.

161 Ibid., S. III.23.

162 Ibid., S. III.32.

163 Ibid., S. III.20.

164 Ibid., S. III.17.

165 Ibid., S. III.41.

166 Ibid., S. III.43.

167 Clough, Lauwers, and MacCarthy interview.

168 Archdiocese of Edmonton, *Guidelines*, I.

169 Canon Law Society of America, on behalf of The Holy See, *Code of Canon Law* (Washington, DC: Canon Law Society of America, 1999).

170 Archdiocese of Edmonton, *Guidelines*, S. II.15.

171 Archdiocese of Regina, *Guidelines*, S. 1.2.

172 Roman Catholic Church, *Code of Canon Law*, S. 1388.

173 Clough, Lauwers, and MacCarthy interview.

174 Archdiocese of Edmonton, *Guidelines*, S. II.13.

175 Recommendations 10, 11, and 12 focus on the victims (CCCB, *From Pain to Hope*, 47).

176 CCCB, *From Pain to Hope*, 48.

177 Archdiocese of Edmonton, *Guidelines*, S. I.6.

178 Ibid., 47, 50.

179 Clough, Lauwers, and MacCarthy interview.

180 CCCB, *From Pain to Hope*, 59.

181 Archdiocese of Ottawa, *Protocol*, 2.

182 CCCB, *From Pain to Hope*, 52.

183 Ibid., 50, 59.

184 Diocese of London, "What Has Been Done."

185 Peter Geigen-Miller, "Canadian Diocese Lifts Gag Order," *The London Free Press* from *The SNAP Network*, March 3, 2005, http://www.snapnetwork.org/news/Canada/diocese_lifts _gag_order.htm.

186 CCCB, *From Pain to Hope*, 50–52.

187 Ibid., 31.

188 Ibid., 50.

189 Ibid., 60.

190 Janice Tibbetts, "Catholic Church in Canada Escapes Liability," *Calgary Herald* from *The SNAP Network*, March 26, 2004, http://snapnetwork.org/news/canada/church_escapes _liability.htm.

191 Canadian Conference of Catholic Bishops, *Factum of the Intervener* (Ottawa: Supreme Court of Canada, 2003), Part III.a.5.

192 CCCB, *From Pain to Hope*, 53.

193 Ibid., 57, 79.

194 Ibid., 55.

195 Ibid., 56.

196 Ibid., 54.

197 Ibid., 53–54.

198 Ibid., 58–59.

199 CCCB, "Report of the *Special Taskforce*," 23.

200 The Initiative's objectives were to:
   • raise awareness about screening;

- create leadership on screening within consortium members' organizational structures;
- provide training and support to community-based branch or organizational affiliates of the provincial consortium partners; and
- increase access to resources, materials, tools (i.e., Internet, public libraries). Volunteer Canada, "Screening: Provincial Initiatives—Ontario," http://www .volunteer.ca/volcan/eng/content/screening/ontario-init.php?display=4.

201 Brenda Gallagher, *Screening in Faith* (Ottawa: Volunteer Canada, 1999).

202 Diocese of Huron, *Journal of Proceedings of the Synod of the Diocese of Huron 158th Sess.* (2002): 2–79. Under the advisement of the faith consortium, and working through Volunteer Canada, author Brenda Gallagher produced *Screening in Faith*, based upon the workbook *Safe Steps: A Volunteer Screening Process for Recreation and Sport*, which had been previously developed with the support of the Solicitor General Canada, Department of Justice, Health Canada and Department of Canadian Heritage (Gallagher, *Screening in Faith*); Ontario Conference of Catholic Bishops, "The Ontario Screening Initiative," 2002, http://www.occb.on.ca/english/osi.html; Ministry of Citizenship and Immigration, "Ontario Screening Initiative: Protecting Children and Vulnerable Adults" (Government of Ontario, 2002); and http://www.citizenship.gov.on.ca/english/citdiv/voluntar.osi.htm.

203 OCCB, "Ontario Screening Initiative."

204 Diocese of Hearst, "Screening in Faith—Ten Steps," 2000, http://www.hearstdiocese .com/16scr/scrng05e.htm, S. 2.1.

205 Ibid.

206 Ibid., S. 2.5.

207 Ibid., S. 2.6.

208 Ibid., S. 2.7.

209 Ibid., S. 2.8.

210 Ibid., S. 2.9.

211 Diocese of Hearst, "Screening in Faith—Strategies for the Management of Risks," 2000, http://www.hearstdiocese.com/16scr/scrng06e.htm, sec. 1.

212 Ontario Conference of Catholic Bishops, "Provincial Guidelines" (Ottawa: Ontario Conference of Catholic Bishops, 2001).

213 Diocese of Thunder Bay, *Diocesan Policy on Screening* (Thunder Bay: Diocese of Thunder Bay, January 6, 2002), 7.

214 Archdiocese of Toronto, *Strengthening the Caring Community Parish Volunteer Screening Program* (Toronto: Archdiocese of Toronto, 2005), 18.

215 Ibid., 19.

216 Ibid., 20.

217 The archdiocese also provides procedures regarding the transfer of a volunteer to another parish. It calls for the screening process to be followed through in the new environment with a reference from the former pastor and a copy of the volunteer's file, if deemed necessary.

218 Diocese of Hamilton, *Volunteer Screening Initiative Information Booklet* (Hamilton: Diocese of Hamilton), 13.

219 Diocese of Prince Albert, *Policy for Persons Working with Children and Youth* (Prince Albert: Diocese of Prince Albert, March 5, 2005), 3.

220 Diocese of Calgary, *Model Code of Pastoral Conduct: For Priests, Deacons, and Religious Brothers* (Calgary: Diocese of Calgary, 2003). This was preceded by *Child Protection Protocol and Guidelines for Church Personnel and Volunteers* (Calgary: Diocese of Calgary), which was adopted in 1990.

221 Ibid., S. 4.5.
222 Ibid., S. 3.1.
223 Winter et al., *The Report of the Archdiocesan Commission*, 97.

Notes to Chapter 3

1   The research for this chapter was accessed primarily through the United Church Archives, located at Victoria University of the University of Toronto, Toronto, Ontario; consultations with the United Church legal counsel; consultations with former members of the national Church sexual abuse policy members; examination of my personal files as a former member of this national committee (1996–2004); the United Church's official *Records of Proceedings* of General Council meetings; and copies of the revised sexual abuse policy received through offices of the United Church. I had no difficulty accessing information, except for statistics regarding the number of complaints made.

2   United Church of Canada (UCC), "Governance—Congregations and Courts of the United Church of Canada," http://www.united-church.ca/organization/governance/structure.

3   UCC, "Organization Statistics," http://www.united-church.ca/organizations/statistics.

4   UCC, *Record of Proceedings of the 5th General Council*, 1932, 280.

5   Ibid., 277; UCC, *Record of Proceedings of the 7th General Council*, 1936, 326–27.

6   UCC, *Record of Proceedings of the 10th General Council*, 1942, 83.

7   Tracy J. Trothen, *Linking Sexuality & Gender—Naming Violence against Women in the United Church of Canada* (Waterloo: Wilfrid Laurier University Press, 2003), 27.

8   UCC, *Record of Proceedings of the 1st General Council*, 1925, 125.

9   UCC, *Record of Proceedings of the 4th General Council*, 1930, 109.

10 Mariana Valverde, *The Age of Light, Soap, and Water: Moral Reform in English Canada, 1885–1925* (Toronto: McClelland & Stewart Inc., 1991), 102–3.

11 UCC, *Record of Proceedings of the 18th General Council*, 1960, 157.

12 UCC, *Record of Proceedings of the 24th General Council*, 1972, 70.

13 Ibid., 70, 164–73.

14 UCC, *Contraception and Abortion* (Toronto: Division of Mission in Canada, UCC, 1982).

15 UCC, *Record of Proceedings of the 27th General Council*, 1977, 112–13.

16 UCC, *Record of Proceedings of the 10th General Council*, 312.

17 UCC, *Record of Proceedings of the 30th General Council*, 1982, 63.

18 Trothen, *Linking Sexuality & Gender*, 82.

19 UCC, *Gift, Dilemma, and Promise: A Report and Affirmations on Human Sexuality* (Toronto: United Church of Canada, 1984), 20–21.

20 UCC, *Record of Proceedings of the 28th General Council*, 1980, 756, 964.

21 UCC, *Pornography Kit* (Toronto: CANEC, 1985).

22 UCC, *Record of Proceedings of the 30th General Council*, 311.

23 Ibid., 313.

24 Ibid., 314.

25 UCC, *Record of Proceedings of the 29th General Council*, 1986, 683–84; UCC, *Record of Proceedings of the 32nd General Council*, 1988, 114, 731.

26 UCC, *Record of Proceedings of the 31st General Council*, 1986, 221.

27 Ibid., 206–8.

28 For example, UCC, *Record of Proceedings of the 28th General Council*, 167ff; UCC, *Record of Proceedings of the 29th General Council*, 166ff; UCC, *Record of Proceedings of the 31st General Council*, 547ff.

29 UCC, *Record of Proceedings of the 13th General Council*, 1948, 258.

30 Ibid., 645.

31 UCC, *Record of Proceedings of the 32nd General Council*, 1988, 513.

32 Ibid., 113.

33 Ibid., 114.

34 UCC, *Record of Proceedings of the 33rd General Council*, 1990, 182–83, 187.

35 Legacy of Hope Foundation, "Where Are the Children? Healing the Legacy of the Residential Schools," http://www.wherearethechildren.ca/en/exhibit/.

36 UCC, *Record of Proceedings of the 31st General Council*, 230–31.

37 UCC, *Record of Proceedings of the 32nd General Council*, 79.

38 UCC, "The Healing Fund," http://www.united-church.ca/funding/healing/.

39 UCC, "Update on the ADR Process" and "Aboriginal Solidarity Sharing Circle," http://www.united-church.ca/residentialschools/2006/04.shtm.

40 For an excellent analysis of the limits of this conceptual framework of "family violence," see Gillian A. Walker, *Family Violence and the Women's Movement: The Conceptual Politics of Struggle* (Toronto: University of Toronto Press, 1990).

41 UCC, *Record of Proceedings of the 34th General Council*, 1992, 327.

42 Ibid., 328.

43 Ibid., 329.

44 Ibid., 329–30.

45 Ibid., 442.

46 Global systemic analysis was a significant concern characterizing third wave feminism of the 1990s.

47 UCC, *Record of Proceedings of the 34th General Council*, 333–35.

48 Ibid., 338.

49 Ibid., 331.

50 Ibid., 137–38.

51 Ibid., 138.

52 Ibid., 331.

53 Ibid., 442.

54 It should be noted that the 1997 General Council passed a motion authorizing the General Council Executive to approve revisions recommended by the DMPE as necessary between General Councils (UCC, *Record of Proceedings of the 36th General Council*, 1997, 447).

55 Ibid., 408.

56 Division of Ministry Personnel and Education, Minutes of the Annual General Meeting, 1996, 15.

57 Ibid.

58 As defined in the *Sexual Abuse Policy and Procedures* booklet (as revised in 2007), the consultant is "a person appointed by the Conference Executive to act in a consultative capacity either to an individual(s) who comes forward with a complaint of sexual abuse or child abuse or to an individual who is accountable to the United Church and who has been accused of sexual or child abuse," 24.

59 UCC, *Record of Proceedings of the 36th General Council*, 411, 412.

60 UCC, *Record of Proceedings of the 34th General Council*, 446.

61 Ibid., 447.

62 Ibid., 446.

63 Ibid., 458.

64 Ibid., 446.

65 Ibid.

66 UCC, *Record of Proceedings of the 36th General Council*, 421.

67 UCC, *Sexual Abuse Policy*, 8.

68 UCC, *The Manual*, S. 364.

69 Cynthia Gunn, United Church legal/judicial counsel, interview by the author, Toronto, Ontario, January 11, 2007.

70 UCC, *Record of Proceedings of the 34th General Council*, 450.

71 UCC, *Record of Proceedings of the 34th General Council*, 450; UCC, *Sexual Abuse Policy*, 8.

72 UCC, *Sexual Abuse Policy*, 13.

73 UCC, *Record of Proceedings of the 34th General Council*, 450; UCC, *Sexual Abuse Policy*, 9.

74 UCC, *Sexual Abuse Policy*, 9.

75 UCC, *Record of Proceedings of the 36th General Council*, 413; UCC, *Sexual Abuse Policy*,13.

76 UCC, *Record of Proceedings of the 36th General Council*, 413, 418.

77 UCC, *Sexual Abuse Policy*, 9.

78 UCC, *Record of Proceedings of the 34th General Council*, 450.

79 UCC, *Sexual Abuse Policy*, 9.

80 UCC, *Record of Proceedings of the 34th General Council*, 450–51; UCC, *Record of Proceedings of the 36th General Council*, 415.

81 UCC, *Sexual Abuse Policy*, 9.

82 UCC, *Record of Proceedings of the 34th General Council*, 454.

83 Ibid.

84 Bob Campbell, Sexual Abuse Committee meeting, Minutes, June 26–28, 2003, 6.

85 General Council Sexual Abuse Committee to all involved in the administration of the policy, January 2001.

86 UCC, *Sexual Abuse Policy*, 21.

87 Ibid., 10.

88 Cynthia Gunn, United Church legal/judicial counsel, interview by the author, Toronto, Ontario, January 11, 2007.

89 Ibid. UCC, *Sexual Abuse Policy*, 22.

90 UCC, *Record of Proceedings of the 34th General Council*, 452.

91 Ibid., 131.

92 UCC, *Record of Proceedings of the 36th General Council*, 417.

93 UCC, *Record of Proceedings of the 37th General Council*, 2000, Petition 45 and Petition 44.

94 General Council Committee on Sexual Abuse Policy meeting, Minutes, November 13–15, 2001, 4.

95 UCC, *Sexual Abuse Policy*, 21–22.

96 Ibid., 3–4, 6–7.

97 Sub-executive of the General Council meeting, Minutes, April 25–28, 2003, 272 and 274.

98 Sexual Abuse Committee meeting, Minutes, June 26–28, 2003, 3.

99 UCC, *Sexual Abuse Policy*, 10, 18–19.

100 Ibid., 10–11.

101 UCC, *Record of Proceedings of the 34th General Council*, 132; UCC, *The Manual*, S. 72.

102 UCC, *Sexual Abuse Policy*, 6.

103 UCC, *Record of Proceedings of the 34th General Council*, 132; UCC, *Sexual Abuse Policy*, 6; UCC, *The Manual*, S. 72.

104 UCC, *Record of Proceedings of the 36th General Council*, 907.

105 UCC, *The Manual*, S. 363.

106 UCC, *Sexual Abuse Policy*, 7.

107 UCC, *Record of Proceedings of the 34th General Council*, 450; *The Manual*, S. 72 as amended by the 1992 General Council.

108 UCC, *Record of Proceedings of the 34th General Council*, 443.

109 UCC, *Record of Proceedings of the 37th General Council*, 1028.

110 John Asling, "Church Courts Can Investigate Sexual Abuse Allegations," August 19, 2000.

111 The Executive of Division of Ministry Personnel & Education, email to Sexual Abuse Policy Committee, February 8, 2001.

112 UCC, *Record of Proceedings of the 39th General Council*, 2006, 26.

113 UCC, *Sexual Abuse Policy*, 7.

114 Ibid.UCC, *Sexual Abuse Policy*, 5.

115 UCC, *The Manual*, S. 34.

116 UCC, *Record of Proceedings of the 34th General Council*, 443, 471.

117 Ibid., 131.

118 Ibid., 131–32.

119 bid., 130–31.

120 UCC, *Sexual Abuse Policy*, 10.

121 UCC, *Record of Proceedings of the 34th General Council*, 130; UCC, *Sexual Abuse Policy*, 10.

122 UCC, *Record of Proceedings of the 34th General Council*, 312.

123 Ibid., 130.

124 UCC, *Record of Proceedings of the 34th General Council*, 136; UCC, *The Manual*, S. 75 (m).

125 UCC, *Record of Proceedings of the 35th General Council*, 170.

126 *Sexual Abuse Policy*, Resource Packet, 2001, 54–56.

127 UCC, *Record of Proceedings of the 34th General Council*, 134; UCC, *The Manual*, S. 74(f).

128 UCC, *Record of Proceedings of the 34th General Council*, 136–37.

129 UCC, *The Manual*, S. 74(f).

130 UCC, *Record of Proceedings of the 34th General Council*, 313.

131 Ibid., UCC, *Record of Proceedings of the 34th General Council*, 457.

132 Ibid., UCC, *Record of Proceedings of the 34th General Council*, 457.

133 Ibid., UCC, *Record of Proceedings of the 34th General Council*, 458.

134 UCC, *Sexual Abuse Policy*, 11.

135 UCC, *Record of Proceedings of the 34th General Council*, 456–57; UCC, *Sexual Abuse Policy*, 11.

136 UCC, *Record of Proceedings of the 36th General Council*, 416.

137 Ibid., 420.

138 UCC, *Record of Proceedings of the 34th General Council*, 455.

139 UCC, *Sexual Abuse Policy*, 9, 13, 14.

140 UCC, *Record of Proceedings of the 37th General Council*, Petition 53 and see Petition 54, 1044–47.

141 General Council Committee on Sexual Abuse Policy Meeting, Minutes, November 13–15, 2001, 2–3.

142 UCC, *Faithful Footsteps: Screening Procedures for Positions of Trust and Authority in the United Church of Canada: A Handbook* (Toronto: United Church of Canada, 2000).

143 UCC, *Record of Proceedings of the 37th General Council*, 637; UCC, *Faithful Footsteps*, 4.

144 UCC, *Faithful Footsteps*, 4.

145 UCC, *Record of Proceedings of the 37th General Council*, 637.

146 Ibid., 638.

147 UCC, *Faithful Footsteps*, 1.

148 Ibid., 4.

149 Ibid., 1–2.

150 Ibid., 6.

151 Ibid., 7.

152 Ibid., 4.

153 Ibid., 9.

154   Ibid., 12–18.

155   October 1999.

156   UCC, *Camping Standards Manual* (Toronto: United Church of Canada, revised 2007), 5.

157   UCC, *Record of Proceedings of the 37th General Council*, 638.

158   Ibid., 638–40.

159   UCC, *Record of Proceedings of the 39th General Council*, 91, 743–44.

160   UCC, *Record of Proceedings of the 30th General Council*, 90.

Notes to Chapter 4

1   Special thanks to research assistant Ryan McNally for his work on this chapter. Through the online databases of the General Synod, he was able to access a record of official statements of the Anglican Church of Canada (ACC). Other sources consulted included the *Journal of Proceedings of the General Synod* meetings, located in the library of Huron University College, London, Ontario. The records of the Diocese of Huron Archives provided access to the *Journal of Proceedings of the Diocesan Synod*. The online archives of the *Anglican Journal*, the national publication of the ACC, provided a rich source of information on particular cases and events, and helped to establish the context in which events took place; this source was supplemented by directed searches in other electronic news databases. All of these sources are accessible to the public. Additionally, when contact was made with individuals, they were candid and helpful. Documentation regarding their approaches to child sexual abuse complaints was readily available from most Anglican dioceses. Most dioceses list their complete set of canons on their diocesan website, as well as applicable policies; the same is true of the national office of the General Synod.

2   General Synod of the Anglican Church of Canada (GS ACC), "About Us" (Toronto: General Synod of the Anglican Church of Canada, 2007); Statistics Canada, *Selected Religions, for Canada, Provinces, and Territories—20% Sample Data* (Ottawa: Statistics Canada, 2003), http://www12.statcan.gc.ca/english/census01/products/highlight/Religion/Page.cfm?Lang=E&Geo=PR&View=1a&Code=01&Table=1&StartRec=1&Sort=2&B1=Canada&B2=1.

3   GS ACC, "The Anglican Communion," Toronto, 2007, http://www.anglican.ca/search/faq/021.htm.

4   Edward Le Roy Long, *Patterns of Polity: Varieties of Church Government* (Cleveland: Pilgrim Press, 2001).

5   GS ACC, *Constitution*, Toronto, 2007, S. 8.

6   GS ACC, *Rules and Procedures*, Toronto, 2007, S. 18.

7   GS ACC, *Handbook of the General Synod of the Anglican Church of Canada*, 14th ed. (Toronto: General Synod of the Anglican Church of Canada, 2004), 1.

8   Ibid., 1.

9   Diocese of Nova Scotia and Prince Edward Island (D. NS and PEI), *The Role of Synod: The Democratic Model* (Halifax: Diocese of Nova Scotia and Prince Edward Island, n.d.).

10 Anglican Diocese of Huron–Anglican (D. Huron), *Constitution of the Incorporated Synod of the Diocese of Huron* (London: Anglican Diocese of Huron, 2006).

11 See D. NS and PEI, *The Role of Synod*.

12 Synod is composed of the bishop (as president of Synod), "all Coadjutor, Suffragan and Assistant Bishops," the licensed (and ordained) clergy of the diocese, the legal counsel of the diocese (of which there are three or more, entitled chancellor of the diocese, vice-chancellor, synod solicitor, and chancellor emeritus), as well as lay representatives and youth members "elected in accordance with the Constitution and Canons of Synod" (D. Huron, Constitution Diocese of Huron, 2006, S.1). The number of lay representatives

elected by each parish varies according to the number of members of the parish (D. Huron, *Constitution*, S.1). Additional members of Synod can include the presidents/ principals of ACC-related schools within the diocese, members of the order of deacons and the presidents of both the Diocesan Anglican Church Women and Diocesan Brotherhood of Anglican Churchman. It is not unrealistic for the number of voting members attending Synod to exceed five hundred people (D. Huron, *Constitution Diocese of Huron*).

13 D. NS and PEI, *The Role of Synod*.

14 D. Huron, *Constitution*, s. 43.

15 Ibid.

16 GS ACC, Organizational/Structural Definitions, Toronto, 2007.

17 D. NS and PEI, *Canon 30: Archdeaconries and Regional Deaneries* (Halifax: Diocese of Nova Scotia and Prince Edward Island, 2003); D. NS and PEI, *Canon 5: Archdeacons* (Halifax: Diocese of Nova Scotia and Prince Edward Island, 2003).

18 D. NS and PEI, *Canon 5*, S. 6.a.

19 Ibid.

20 Ibid., S. 6.b.

21 Ibid., S. 7.a.

22 Ibid., S. 7.b.

23 Ibid., S. 6.a.

24 Ibid., S. 6.b.

25 D. NS and PEI, *Canon 20: Regions and Regional Deans* (Halifax: Diocese of Nova Scotia and Prince Edward Island, 2003), S. 6.c.

26 Ibid., S. 7.a; and D. Huron, *Canon 31: Deanery Councils* (London: Diocese of Huron, 2005), S. 5.e.

27 D. Huron, *Canon 31: Deanery Councils* (London: Diocese of Huron, 2005), S.1.

28 Ibid. Each parish is governed by a combination of the vestry and the parish council. The vestry is "composed of all the baptized members of such congregation who have reached 16 years of age" and who have been "identifiably involved with [the] congregation with regular worship, fellowship and financial support" (*Canon 18: Vestries and Churchwardens*, London, 2003, S. 1). Vestry meetings are conducted at least "annually during the month of January," at which point reports are received and the members elect one of two churchwardens (the other is appointed by the incumbent clergyperson) who are responsible to provide leadership in the congregation (*Canon 18*). Each congregation also has a parish council composed of the clergyperson, churchwardens, lay representatives to Synod, and four to twelve members of the vestry (D. Huron, *Canon 19: Parish Council* (London: Diocese of Huron, 2003).

29 Ecclesiastical Province of Canada, 2007.

30 Phillip Carrington, *The Anglican Church in Canada* (Toronto: Collins, 1963).

31 D. Huron, *Constitution*.

32 GS ACC, *General Synod Task Force on Jurisdiction* (Toronto: General Synod of the Anglican Church of Canada, 2002), 7 and 10. Doctrine can be defined as "that body of agreed belief concerning the nature of God, the nature of humanity, the nature of God's redemption of humanity in Jesus Christ, and the nature of humanity's response to God's redemption" (GS ACC, *General Synod Task Force on Jurisdiction*, 7). Discipline is "the corporate witness offered by the Church in its way of life which expresses its common understanding of things which it believes as 'Doctrine.'" Both of these deal with "matters 'necessary to salvation'" (GS ACC, *GS Jurisdiction*, 8).

33 GS ACC, "A Self-Determining Structure," August 13, 2009, http://notes.anglican.ca/ sc2009/page/2.

34   Jane Davidson, "Anglican Diocesan Court to Try Priest for Immorality," *Anglican Journal* (June 2003): 16.

35   GS ACC, *Canon XVIII*, S. 7.

36   GS ACC, *Marriage and Related Matters: Civil Marriage* (Kingston: General Synod of the Anglican Church of Canada, 1962).

37   GS ACC, *Jurisdiction*.

38   Anglican Church of Canada, *Remarriage of Divorced Persons* (Toronto: Anglican Church of Canada, 1964).

39   General Synod, *Journal of Proceedings*, 23rd Session (Ottawa, 1967): 19.

40   GS ACC, *Journal of Proceedings* 23 (1967): 89.

41   Ibid., 90.

42   Ibid., 91.

43   Ibid., 91–92.

44   At the same General Synod, a motion was adopted regarding abortion requesting that the primate set up a study committee of "theologians, parish clergy, obstetricians, doctors engaged in family practice, lawyers and specialists in behaviour and medical sciences to prepare a statement on all aspects relating to abortion" and submit a brief to the Government of Canada; no specific mention was made of the inclusion of women on such a committee (GS ACC, *Journal of Proceedings* 23: 20–21).

45   GS ACC, *Journal of Proceedings* 23: 347.

46   GS ACC, *Journal of Proceedings* 27 (1975): Acts 64, 65, and 91.

47   See, for example, GS ACC Conscience Clause (1983): Act 32. GS ACC. "Conscience Clause." General Synod Session 30: 1983, Fredericton, NB. Act 32.

48   GS ACC, *Journal of Proceedings* 29: Act 22.

49   Anglican Church of Canada, *A Study Resource on Human Sexuality: Approaches to Sexuality and Christian Theology* (Toronto: Anglican Book Centre, 1985), 18.

50   GS ACC, *Journal of Proceedings* 30: 114.

51   House of Bishops, "Statement on Sexuality," 1983.

52   GS ACC, *Journal of Proceedings* 30: 114.

53   As part of the statement, the bishops affirmed that both males and females are created in God's image and share a "common responsibility to each other in their sexuality," which is a gift of God. The statement continued to make clear that only heterosexual married sexual expressions were acceptable since God intends for sexual unions to hold the possibility of "procreation" (House of Bishops, "Statement on Sexuality").

       Between the 1983 and 1986 meetings, the Pornography Taskforce prepared a report and was commended for its work (Act 61). The report urged the ACC to continue "educating the church at all levels about the destructive impact of pornography," with funding requested from the Program Committee; dioceses were also encouraged to support local work on pornography issues (GS ACC, *Journal of Proceedings* 31: 82–83). Likewise, the meeting acknowledged *The Report on Pornography and Prostitution in Canada* (Fraser Report) and urged the government to modify its legislation in light of the report's recommendations (GS ACC, *Journal of Proceedings* 31: 84).

54   GS ACC, *Journal of Proceedings* 30: 114.

55   See Gillian A. Walker, *Family Violence and the Women's Movement: The Conceptual Politics of Struggle* (Toronto: University of Toronto Press, 1990).

56   GS ACC, *Journal of Proceedings* 31: 43–44.

57   Taskforce on Violence against Women, *Violence against Women: Abuse in Society and Church and Proposals for Change* (Toronto: Anglican Book Centre, 1987), 57.

58   Ibid., 57–58.

59   Ibid., 18.

60 Ibid., 15–17.

61 Ibid., 33.

62 Ibid., 41, 43, 49.

63 Ibid., 36. Implicit in the woman's comments was the pastor's inability to comprehend that people within his parish could experience a marriage that did not match his idealized model. In response, the authors added that isolation of women is augmented when marriage preparation courses do not address the issue of violence, or in a "pastoral approach that minimises suffering, that individualises the problem, or that, passively or actively, upholds the abuser."

64 Taskforce, *Violence against Women*, 44–45.

65 Ibid., 14.

66 The task force gave the General Synod six recommendations. The first was that congregations should "devote the penitential season of Lent or Advent to a comprehensive study program in the areas of family violence, with an initial focus on wife assault." Second, it recommended that marriage and family life educators throughout the ACC "undertake a critical review of curriculum materials currently used in the church for marriage preparation, marriage enrichment, and parent courses" with a view to examining the messages being given by these materials. Third, there was a call for volunteers and staff at all levels to "evaluate the legislation and legal practices in their area" to ensure it reflected that wife battering was a crime and that perpetrators, and not victims, should be the subject of prosecution. ACC theological schools were asked to provide mandatory "education about family violence and skills training in dealing with the violent family." Bishops and diocesan staff were asked to provide training to clergy and to "recognize that wife assault is a problem in clergy families as it is in all other sectors of the population, and [to] develop strategies for responding to the special concerns and needs of battered clergy wives and abusive male clergy" (58–60); GS ACC *Journal of Proceedings* 31: 39.

67 Since the National Executive Council (NEC) was later renamed the Council of the General Synod (COGS), so both titles appear in ACC documents. The body will be referred to by the name it held at the time the specific action was taken; therefore, both names will be found in this chapter.

68 National Executive Committee of the Anglican Church of Canada, Resolution: Sexual Offences against Children and Youths, Toronto, 1985.

69 Ibid.

70 GS ACC, *Journal of Proceedings* 31.

71 GS ACC, *Journal of Proceedings* 32.

72 The Anglican Church of Canada, *A Study Resource on Human Sexuality: Approaches to Sexuality and Christian Theology* (Toronto: Anglican Church of Canada, 1985).

73 GS ACC, *Journal of Proceedings* 32: 118.

74 Anglican News Service, "Bishops Uphold Guidelines on Homosexual Ordination, Plan Further Study of Sexuality during the Next Year," Official Statements Database, Anglican Church of Canada, 1991, http://qumran.national.anglican.ca/ics-wpd/Textbases/officialweb.htm.

75 Sally Edmonds Preiner, *Stained Glass, Sweet Grass, Hosannas & Songs: A Snapshot of Anglican Issues and Visions in Canada* (Toronto: Anglican Book Centre, 2002), 12–13, 37.

76 Ibid., 42.

77 House of Bishops, *Discussion of Paedophilia Taskforce Report*, 1990.

78 Ibid.

79 Ibid.

80 GS ACC, *Journal of Proceedings* 33.

81 National Executive Council, "Sexual Assault and Harassment Policy," Resolution 63-11-92, November 1992, Official Statements of the Anglican Church of Canada Database, General Synod Library, http://www.anglican.ca/search/databases.htm.

82 Ibid.

83 National Executive, "Sexual Assault"; National Executive Council, "Officers of the General Synod—Revised Guidelines for the Implementation of the National Policy on Sexual Harassment and Sexual Assault Applicable to National Staff and National Volunteers," Resolution 41-11-93, 1993.

84 Anglican News Service, "Church Initiates First Review of Sexual Harassment and Assault Guidelines," 1997, http://qumran.national.anglican.ca/ics-wpd/Textbases/officialweb .htm.

85 Council of the General Synod of the Anglican Church of Canada, 1998, National Executive, "Officers of the General Synod."

86 Council of the General Synod of the Anglican Church of Canada, 1999; Council of the General Synod of the Anglican Church of Canada, 2001.

87 General Synod of the Anglican Church of Canada, Act 64, *Sexual Abuse Policy*, 2001.

88 House of Bishops, *Sexual Misconduct Policy*, 2002.

89 Ibid.

90 GS ACC, *GS Jurisdiction*.

91 Council of the General Synod of the Anglican Church of Canada (CGS), Resolution 06-11-04 *Sexual Abuse and Harassement Policy*, Toronto, 2004.

92 CGS, Resolution 27-11-05 and 28-11-05: *Handbook Concerns Committee Resolutions: Sexual Misconduct Policy*, Toronto, 2005.

93 CGS, *Sexual Misconduct Policy Applicable to National Staff and Volunteers*, 2005; CGS, *Sexual Misconduct Policy*, Toronto, 2005, 2.

94 CGS, *Sexual Misconduct Policy*, 3.

95 Ibid., 5

96 Ibid., 5–6.

97 Ibid., 5.

98 Ibid., 10.

99 Ibid.

100 Ibid., 6–7.

101 Ibid., 7.

102 Ibid., 8.

103 D. Huron, *Journal of Proceedings* 162: 5-0.

104 Ibid.

105 D. Huron, *Safe Church* (London: Diocese of Huron, 2005), 16.

106 D. Huron, *Journal of Proceedings* 158: 2–37.

107 Ibid., 2–37; D. Huron, *Journal of Proceedings* 159: 2–65; D. Huron, *Journal of Proceedings* 160: 2–55.

108 Rev. Susan Baldwin, email interview by R. McNally, London, Ontario, March 9, 2007.

109 D. Huron, *Journal of Proceedings* 162: 2–73.

110 D. Huron, *Journal of Proceedings* 161: 2–53; D. Huron, *Journal of Proceedings* 160: 2–55.

111 D. Huron, *Journal of Proceedings* 160: 2–55; D. Huron, *Journal of Proceedings* 161: 2–53.

112 D. Huron, *Journal of Proceedings* 162: 2–73.

113 D. Huron, *Safe Church*, 16.

114 In order to more fully provide for a positive environment, the Diocese of Huron has also enacted an *Anti-harassment and Anti-bullying Policy* to deal with complaints of harassment and bullying that are of a non-sexual nature or do not relate specifically to cases of child sexual abuse dealt with in the *Safe Church Policy*. (D. Huron, *Anti-harassment and*

Anti-bullying Policy (London: Diocese of Huron, 2005), 3. The policy explicitly "prohibits harassment or bullying by any member of the Diocese" and provides for complaints (submitted by someone other than a Church member, official, volunteer, etc., or a third party) "against a parishioner or employee who was involved in the course of her/his ministry or participation in Church sponsored organizations, activities and programs" (D. Huron, *Anti-harassment and Anti-bullying Policy*, 4). The policy outlines the process for initiating a complaint, and an informal, mediated, or formal process for handling complaints and seeking resolution (D. Huron, *Anti-harassment and Anti-bullying Policy*, 5–10).

115 Diocese of Kootenay (D. Kootenay), Diocesan Council, *Sexual Assault, Abuse, Exploitation, or Harassment*, Policy 07.06.10 (Kelowna: Diocese of Kootenay, March 1998); D. Huron, *Safe Church*, 17; D. Kootenay, *Sexual Assault*, Part A.

116 CGS, *Sexual Misconduct Policy*, 8.

117 Ibid., 8–9.

118 Ibid., 9.

119 D. Huron, *Safe Church*, 19.

120 Ibid., forms B and D.

121 Ibid., 17.

122 Ibid., 17–18.

123 Ibid., 18.

124 Ibid., 19.

125 Ibid., 17.

126 D. Kootenay, *Sexual Assault*, Part C.

127 Ibid., parts C and D.

128 D. Huron, *Safe Church*, 17.

129 Ibid.

130 Ibid., 16.

131 Ibid., 20–23.

132 CGS, *Sexual Misconduct Policy*, 11.

133 GS ACC, *Canon XVIII*, 2004, S.1.

134 Ibid., S.7.

135 Ibid., S.8.

136 Ibid., S.9.

137 Ibid., S.10.

138 Ibid., S.10.a.

139 Ibid., S.10.c.

140 Ibid., S.11.

141 Ibid., S.12.

142 GS ACC, *Canon XIX*, 2004, S.2.e

143 Ibid., S.2.f.

144 Ibid., S.2.

145 The initial jurisdiction for disciplinary action depends on the person being disciplined. In the case of a "bishop, priest or deacon subject to the jurisdiction of a bishop," it is that bishop who has initial jurisdiction; in the case of "a bishop subject to the jurisdiction of a metropolitan," it is that metropolitan who has initial jurisdiction (*Canon XVIII*, 2004, S. 2.a). The determination of whether or not an ecclesiastical offence has been committed can be made by the bishop or metropolitan or referred to the court of the bishop's diocese or the court of the metropolitan's ecclesiastical province (*Canon XVIII*, 2004, S. 2.b). Each diocesan or provincial synod enacts procedures to be used by the bishop or metropolitan (*Canon XVIII*, 2004, S. 2.c). Each "diocesan synod may provide for the

exercise of initial jurisdiction of the bishop" for lay people "who have been appointed, elected or commissioned to an office, appointment or responsibility in a parish of the diocese or the diocesan synod, for any ecclesiastical offence which they may commit in the diocese" (*Canon XVIII*, 2004, S. 2.d and S. 4.iii). Similar provisions are made for lay people who hold "an office appointment or responsibility in a provincial synod, or the General synod, for any ecclesiastical offence which they may commit in the diocese" (*Canon XVIII*, 2004, S. 4). If a priest or deacon subject to the jurisdiction of a bishop is alleged to have committed an ecclesiastical offence in a diocese different from the one in which the bishop of original jurisdiction governs, notice is to be given to the bishop with original jurisdiction so that they may consent to the offence being tried in the diocese in which it took place; if consent is not granted, proceedings must be commenced in the diocese of original jurisdiction (*Canon XVIII*, 2004, S. 16). Jurisdiction may be transferred from one diocese to another upon "application of a person charged with an offence ... to the president of the court having ecclesiastical jurisdiction over the person" and "where it appears to the president of the court to which the application is made, that such a transfer is necessary to ensure that the fundamental principles of natural justice are respected and where the court to which the transfer is to be made consents to the transfer" (GS ACC, *Canon XVIII*, S. 17, 3).

146 GS ACC, *Canon XVIII*, S. 3.a.
147 Ibid., S.3.c and d.
148 Ibid., S. 3.b.
149 Ibid., S. 14.
150 Ibid., S. 13.
151 Ibid., Part VI.
152 Ibid., Part VI; GS ACC, *Canon XX*, 2004, S. 2.
153 Kathy Blair, "Church on Hook for Abuse," *Anglican Journal* (October 1999): 1–2.
154 Kathy Blair, "Church, School Official Must Have Known of Rampant Evil, Judge Says," *Anglican Journal* (October 1999): 1–2.
155 Anglican News Service, "Cariboo Diocese Will Wind up Affairs in Next 12 months; Arbitration May Determine Who Owns Church Buildings," Official Statements Database, Anglican Church of Canada, 2000, http://qumran.national.anglican.ca/ics-wpd/Textbases/officialweb.htm.
156 Marianne Meed Ward, "Former Trainer of Servers Charged," *Anglican Journal* (December 1999): 18.
157 Ibid.
158 Jane Davidson, "Anglican Diocesan Court to Try Priest for Immorality," *Anglican Journal* (June 2003): 16.
159 Staff, "Church Court Clears Archdeacon of Charge of Immorality," *Anglican Journal* (September 2003): 13.
160 Steve Proctor, "One Priest Pleads Guilty, Another Still Faces Trial on Sex Charges," *Anglican Journal* (March 1999): 9.
161 Staff, "Crown May Drop Charges against Boyd" (May 2000), 7; Jane Davidson, "Life after the Sky Has Fallen," *Anglican Journal* (February 2001): 6.
162 Staff, "Boyd Charges Dropped," *Anglican Journal* (June 2000): 7.
163 Davidson, "Life after the Sky Has Fallen," 6.
164 Sarah Crosbie, "Disgraced Choirmaster Resurfaces at Ottawa Church," *Kingston Whig Standard*, May 15, 2004, A1.
165 Ibid.
166 Jeff Outhit, "Former Choirmaster a Free Man," *Kingston Whig Standard*, October 2, 1996, 9; Crosbie, "Disgraced Choirmaster."

167 "Anglicans Vow Zero Tolerance on Sex Abuse," *Toronto Star*, February 13, 1993, J15.

168 Mandatory reporting laws were more vague before the 1991 Ontario *Child and Family Services Act*, S. 72(1) (RSO 1990), Chapter 11. The Act came into force on December 31, 1991, the date on which the Revised Statutes of Ontario were enacted. Section 72(1) has been the subject of re-enactment in 1999 and revision in 2000. The Act existed prior to its inclusion in the RSO 1990.

169 Paulette Peirol and Michael Den Tandt, "Gallienne Admitted Abuse in '77, Cleric Says," *Kingston Whig Standard*, June 16, 1992, 1.

170 Staff, "Anglican Clergy Summoned to a Study Day on Abuse," *Toronto Star*, January 23, 1993, Sec. C, F 86.

171 Rev. W. Varley, email interview, 9 March 2007.

172 Crosbie, "Disgraced Choirmaster."

173 Ibid.

174 Under the advisement of the faith consortium, and working through Volunteer Canada, author Brenda Gallagher produced *Screening in Faith*, based upon the workbook *Safe Steps: A Volunteer Screening Process for Recreation and Sport*, which had been previously developed with the support of the Solicitor General Canada, Department of Justice, Health Canada, and the Department of Canadian Heritage (Gallagher, *Screening in Faith*); D. Huron, *Journal of Proceedings* 158: 2–79.

175 D. Huron, *Journal of Proceedings* 156: 3–2; reported along with the motion in the convening circular was the comment that "It is important to imagine how the church can keep this covenant with Christ without a clear commitment to create and maintain a safe environment, to protect those who are to be cared for and to prevent sexual, physical, and emotional misconduct from occurring in places of ministry" (Gallagher, *Screening in Faith*, 3–2).

176 D. Huron, *Journal of Proceedings* 157: 2–71.

177 D. Huron, *Safe Church*, 10, 13.

178 As reported in D. Huron, *Journal of Proceedings* 158: 2–7.

179 Ibid., 2–7. The following year (2003) the committee reported that a set of policy guidelines had been developed and adopted, and that Volunteer Canada was developing a risk audit tool that parishes might be able to use. Further, an EPO Synod Screening Conference had been held and resulted in the development of an Implementation Model Kit. It was also reported that 2003 would see the hosting of a workshop for youth leaders/ministers focused on the protection of youth and the development of a twenty-four-hour incident reporting line for the diocese (D. Huron, *Journal of Proceedings* 159: 2–103).

180 D. Huron, *Journal of Proceedings* 160: 2–55.

181 D. Huron, *Journal of Proceedings* 162: 2–73.

182 D. Huron, *Journal of Proceedings* 161: 2–53.

183 D. Huron, *Safe Church*, 13.

184 Ibid., 15.

185 Ibid., 17.

186 Ibid., 10.

187 Ibid., 1. To ensure adequate oversight of the screening procedures, "it is strongly recommended that each parish create the position of 'Parish Volunteer Manager,'" who, working with the clergyperson in charge, "should have primary responsibility for implementing and maintaining the Screening and Management Program" (D. Huron, *Safe Church*, 13).

188 Ibid., 13.

189 Ibid., 14.

190 Varley, interview.

191 Within its policy on sexual abuse, the Diocese of Kootenay provides a series of screening forms that can be used by parishes to examine prospective volunteers (*Sexual Assault*).

In the case of the Diocese of Toronto, screening includes a request for a letter from the family doctor as the diocese was told by the Big Brothers/Big Sisters organizations that "doctors are their most reliable reference checks." The diocese provides an introductory letter to the physician, explaining that "the person will be put in an unsupervised, very demanding job in a faith community in which he or she will be working with vulnerable individuals. Doctors are asked to comment on whether their patients can handle that"; the diocese does not ask for medical details but "whether the candidate can be trusted with children and vulnerable adults." Kathy Blair, "New Clergy Screened More Tightly," *The Anglican Journal* (October 1999): 1, 10.

192 General Synod, *Journal of Proceedings* 33: Act 119.

193 Since each diocese can implement its own policies and is not required to follow the national-level policy, most dioceses have now developed specific policies on sexual harassment and misconduct, and some have implemented screening policies for employees and volunteers, other dioceses remain without such policies (Blair, "New Clergy").

Notes to Chapter 5

1 Thanks go to Ryan McNally and Tim Crouch, who were research assistants for this chapter. The research was initiated by sending emails to members of Mennonite communities, including secretaries of conferences and people in positions that would likely require them to deal with abuse issues. For the most part, there were no responses. However, in 2011 there were some very helpful follow-up phone and email conversations. In order to source information, it was necessary to undertake document and Internet searches. Internet research led to a variety of educational and pastoral resources, which were subsequently ordered from the Mennonite Central Committee; the people responsible were very quick to respond and courier the said materials. Other research uncovered policies from the national and conference level of the Mennonite Church, as well as some historical resolutions. Two important documents are the *Volunteer Screening Policy and Procedures Manual*, and *Leadership and Accountability in Mennonite Church Canada*; both are documents promulgated at the national level. Secondary sources, including books and journal articles addressing abuse in Mennonite communities, were few. One such resource is Isaac Block's *Assault on God's Image*; it is the result of research into the prevalence of abuse in the Mennonite community in Manitoba.

2 Everett J. Thomas, ed., *A Mennonite Polity for Ministerial Leadership* (Newton, KS, and Winnipeg: Faith & Life Press, 1996), 5–6.

3 Ibid., 39.

4 Ibid., 30.

5 Ibid., 37.

6 Canadian Conference of Mennonite Brethren Churches (CCMB), "Our Story" in "Family Matters: Discovering the Mennonite Brethren" by Lynn Jost and Connie Faber (Kindred Productions, 2002), http://www.mbconf.ca/about/story.en.html; and Thomas, *A Mennonite Polity*, 32–39.

7 Mennonite Church Canada (MCCanada), "What Makes a Mennonite," http://www.mennonitechurch.ca/about/wmam/timeline.htm.

8 CCMB, "Our Story," 5.

9 Statistics Canada, *Keeping the Faith on the Farm*, 2001 Census of Agriculture, post-census analysis, 2003, http://www.statcan.ca/english/agcensus2001/first/socio/religion.htm.

10 Ibid., 18.

11 Mennonite Church Canada (MCCanada), "About Mennonite Church Canada," http://www.mennonitechurch.ca/about/.

12 James E. Horsch, ed., *Mennonite Directory* (Scottsdale, PA: Herald Press, 1999), 73–92.

13 MCCanada, "What Makes a Mennonite."

14 D. Nighswander, *Leadership and Accountability in Mennonite Church Canada*, rev. (Winnipeg: Mennonite Church Canada, 2007), 22 and S. III.8.a.

15 Nighswander, *Leadership*, S. III.8, III.9.1.

16 Helmut Harder, "Mennonite Church Canada," in *Global Anabaptist Mennonite Encyclopedia Online*, October 2001, http://www.gameo.org/encyclopedia/contents/M46607.html.

17 Nighswander, *Leadership*, S. V.18.a.

18 Ibid., S. VII.22–23.

19 Ibid., S. VI.21.1.

20 Ibid., S. VII.24–25.

21 Mennonite World Council, *General Council, Executive Committee, Commissions*, http://www.mwc-cmm.org/MWC/councils.html.

22 Mennonite Central Committee, "A Brief History of MCC," http://mcc.org/about/history.

23 Mennonite Central Committee, "Welcome," in the section "About Mennonite Central Committee," http://mcc.org/about/welcome.

24 Ross T. Bender, Wane North, Vern Preheim, Herbert J. Brandt, and R. Donald Shafer, "Polity," in *Global Anabaptist Mennonite Encyclopedia Online*, 1989, www.gameo.org/encyclopedia/contents/p658me.html.

25 J. Lawrence Burkholder, "Institutions, Church," in *Global Anabaptist Mennonite Encyclopedia Online*, 1989, http://www.gameo.org/encyclopedia/contents/i58me.html.

26 Bender et al., "Polity."

27 MCCanada, *By-Laws*, 2007, updated June 2007, http://www.mennonitechurch.ca/files/about/MCCanadaBylaws.pdf.

28 Nighswander, *Leadership*, 5.

29 Ibid., 14.

30 Thomas, *A Mennonite Polity*, 68.

31 *Confession of Faith in a Mennonite Perspective*, http://www.mennolink.org/doc/cof/, original published by (Scottsdale, PA: Harold Press, 1995); Everett Thomas, "Rules Help Discernment," in *DreamSeeker Magazine—Voices from the Soul* 6, no. 1 (Winter 2006), http://www.cascadiapublishinghouse.com/dsm/winter06/theome2.htm.

32 Nighswander, *Leadership*, 10–11.

33 Ibid., 13.

34 Ibid., 12.

35 Thomas, *A Mennonite Polity*, 60–61, 62.

36 Ibid., 50.

37 General Conference Mennonite Church, "Resolution on Human Sexuality," 1986, http://www.mennonitechurch.ca/about/ foundation/documents/1986-resolutiononhumansexuality.htm.

38 Ibid.

39 Mennonite Church, *A Call to Affirmation, Confession, and Covenant Regarding Human Sexuality* (West Lafayette, IN: 1987), http://www.mennonitechurch.ca/about/foundation/documents/1987-humansexuality.htm.

40 Mennonite Central Committee, *The Purple Packet: Domestic Violence Resources for Pastoring Persons—Wife Assault*, 1990.

41 Isaac Block, *Assault on God's Image* (Winnipeg: Windflower Communications, 1991), 80.

42 Ibid., 99.

43 Ibid., 82.

44 Ibid., 90.
45 Ibid., 97.
46 Mennonite Central Committee, *Crossing the Boundary: Sexual Abuse by Professionals*, 1991, 1–2.
47 Ibid., Reporting.
48 Mennonite Central Committee, *Broken Boundaries: Resources for Pastoring People—Child Sexual Abuse*, 1991.
49 Mennonite Church, "A Resolution on Male Violence against Women" (Philadelphia: Mennonite Church, 1993), http://www.mennonitechurch.ca/ about/foundation/ documents/1993-maleviolence.htm.
50 Thomas, *A Mennonite Polity*, 110.
51 Mennonite Historical Society of Alberta, "MHSA Archival Description Record," http:// www.mennonitehistory.org/archives/mennonite_church_alberta.html.
52 Mennonite Central Committee, *Crossing the Boundary*, cover letter.
53 Hugo Hildenrand, "Why Victims of Pastoral Sexual Abuse Stay Silent," in *Crossing the Boundary*.
54 Mennonite Central Committee, *Crossing the Boundary*, "Prevention."
55 Mennonite Central Committee, *Making Your Sanctuary Safe: Resources for Developing Congregational Abuse Prevention Policies*, 2001, introductory letter.
56 Ibid., "The Need for a Prevention Program."
57 Mennonite Central Committee, *Broken Boundaries*, "Practical Tips."
58 Mennonite Central Committee Ontario, "Restorative Justice," http://ontario.mcc.org/ restorative/smarrt/.
59 Mennonite Church Eastern Canada (MCEC), *A Plan to Protect Our Children, Youth & Leaders* (Kitchener: Mennonite Church Eastern Canada, 2003), 5.
60 Ibid.
61 Ibid.
62 Ibid.
63 Ibid., 6.
64 Ibid.
65 Thomas, *A Mennonite Polity*, 31.
66 Ibid.
67 Listowel Mennonite Church, *Safe Church Policy: A Plan to Protect Children, Youth, and Adults* (Listowel, ON: Listowel Mennonite Church, 2003), 6.
68 Ibid.
69 Mennonite Central Committee Ontario, "Restorative Justice," http://ontario.mcc.org/ restorative/.
70 MCC, *Making Your Sanctuary Safe* , "Basic Procedures for Safe Ministry."
71 Ibid., "Questions for Screening."
72 Ibid., "Organize a Safety Audit."
73 MCEC, *A Plan*, 1.
74 Ibid., 6.
75 Ibid., 3.
76 Ibid.
77 Listowel Mennoniste Church, *Safe Church Policy*, 1.
78 Ibid., 5.
79 Ibid., 3.
80 Kristen Schroeder, *Volunteer Screening Guide* (Winnipeg: Mennonite Church Canada, 2003).
81 Ibid., 1.

82 Ibid., 2–3.

83 Ibid., 3.

84 Ibid.

85 Ibid., 4.

86 Ibid., 6.

87 Ibid.

88 MCCanada, *Volunteer Screening Policy and Procedures Manual* (Winnipeg: Mennonite Church Canada, 2007).

89 Ibid.; Schroeder, *Volunteer Screening Guide*, 1.

90 MCCanada, *Volunteer Screening Policy and Procedures Manual* (2007), 5.

91 Ibid., 6.

92 Ibid., 7.

93 Ibid., 9.

94 Mennonite Central Committee, "Abuse: Response and Prevention," http://abuse.mcc .org/abuse/en/.

95 Mennonite Central Committee Ontario, "Policy 2.14: Children, Youth & Vulnerable Adults Protection Policy," http://ontario.mcc.org.

Notes to Chapter 6

1 Statistics Canada, "Population by Religion, by Province or Territory (Census 2001)," January 25, 2005, http://www40.statcan.gc.ca/l01/cst01/demo30a-eng.htm.

2 W. Murray Hogben, "Marriage and Divorce among Muslims in Canada," *Muslim Families in North America* (Edmonton: University of Alberta Press, 1991), 154.

3 Sharon Todd, "Veiling the 'Other,' Unveiling Our 'Selves': Reading Media Images of the Hijab Psychoanalytically to Move beyond Tolerance," *Canadian Journal of Education* 23, no. 4 (1999): 438–51.

4 Islamic Social Services Associations Inc. (ISSA) and Women in Islam Inc., *Women Friendly Mosques and Community Centers: Working Together to Reclaim Our Heritage* (Winnipeg: Islamic Social Services Association, 2005), 3.

5 Ahmad F. Yousif, "Family Values, Social Adjustment, and Problems of Identity: The Canadian Experience," *Journal Institute of Muslim Minority Affairs* 15, no. 1 and 2 (January and July 1994): 108–11.

6 The Campaign against Shari'a Court in Canada, "The International Campaign against Shari'a Court in Canada," http://www.nosharia.com/.

7 Mohamed Elmasry, president, Canadian Islamic Congress, interview by B. Adle, March 9, 2007.

8 Mohammed Elmasry, "Towards Smart Integration: The Choice of Canadian Muslims," October 19, 2005, http://www.canadianislamiccongress.com/ar/smart.php.

9 Elmasry, interview.

10 The Canadian Islamic Congress, "Facts about the CIC," http://www.canadianislamiccongress .com/cicfacts.php.

11 Mohamed Nimer, *The North American Muslim Resource Guide* (New York: Routledge, 2002), 105, www.routledge-ny.com/ref/namuslim/ServicesWomen.pdf.

12 The Canadian Council of Muslim Women, "About CCMW," http://www.ccmw.com/ about.ccmw.html.

13 Ibid.

14 Ibid.

15 Peaceful Families Project, "About Muslims & Domestic Violence—Peaceful Families Project," http://www.peacefulfamilies.org/aboutdv.html.

16 Shahini Siddiqui, interview by B. Adle, March 2, 2007.

17 Elmasry, interview.
18 Sarah Childress, "9/11's Hidden Toll," *Newsweek* (August 4, 2003), http://www.newsweek.com/id/152641.
19 Ibid.; Wahida Valiante, "Muslim Foster Homes: Community Responsibility," The Canadian Islamic Congress, June 4, 1999, http://www.canadianislamiccongress.com/ar/opeds.php?id=116.
20 Wahida Valiante, "Muslim Foster Homes."
21 Shahina Siddiqui and Samana Siddiqui, *Sexual Abuse: Prevention and Intervention: A Guide for Imams, Parents, and Muslim Counselors* (Winnipeg: Islamic Social Services Association, 2006), 11.
22 ISSA and Women in Islam Inc., *Women Friendly Mosques*, 16.
23 Ibid., 17.
24 Ibid., 9–12.
25 Bader Siddiqi, president, Ottawa Muslim Association, interview by B. Adle, March 16, 2007.
26 Elmasry, interview.
27 Shahina Siddiqui, president, Islamic Social Services Association of Canada, interview by B. Adle, March 5, 2007.
28 Elmasry, interview.
29 A.R. Gatrad and Aziza Sheikh, "Muslim Birth Customs," *Archives of Disease in Childhood— Fetal Neonatal Edition* 84 (January 2001): F6, http://proquest.umi.com.proxy.queensu.ca/pqdweb?index=17&did=67165856&SrchMode=3&sid=1&Fmt=4&VInst=PROD&VType=PQD&RQT=309&VName=PQD&TS=1244585867&clientId=14119&aid=1.
30 Siddiqui and Siddiqui, *Sexual Abuse: Prevention and Intervention*, 15–16.
31 Dr. Ahmad Al-Hashimi, Ihsan Muslim Heritage Society, interview by B. Adle, March 13, 2007.
32 Siddiqui and Siddiqui, *Sexual Abuse: Prevention and Intervention*, 8.
33 Ibid., 16.
34 The Canadian Council of Muslim Women, "About CCMW."
35 Mohammad Darr, vice chair, Cambridge Islamic Centre, interview by B. Adle, March 16, 2007.
36 Bader Siddiqi, president, Ottawa Muslim Association, interview by B. Adle, March 16, 2007.
37 Elmasry, interview.
38 Siddiqi, interview.
39 Shaema Samia, *Muslim Culture and Faith: A Guide for Social Service Providers* (Winnipeg: Islamic Social Services Association, 2002), 28.
40 Shahina Siddiqui, *Helping Victims of Domestic Abuse: A Guide for Imams and Community Leaders* (Winnipeg: Islamic Social Services Association, 2005), 1.
41 Ibid., 1.
42 Ibid., 2.
43 Siddiqui, *Sexual Abuse: Prevention and Intervention*, Preface.

Notes to Chapter 7

1 Special thanks go to Barbara Adle, who was the primary research assistant for this chapter. McNally and Crouch both contributed. Seventeen congregations were contacted in the course of research for this chapter; four responded and were helpful. Various individuals in other leadership positions were also interviewed and are referenced accordingly throughout this chapter.

2 Information in this chapter was gathered from: the Canadian Unitarian Council (CUC) and the Unitarian Universalist Association (UUA) staff, organizational websites, local congregations, and other secondary sources. Two different organizations, the CUC and the UUA, located in two countries—Canada and the United States—participated in this research. Inquiries were answered promptly and all materials requested, sometimes more, were provided without question. Each conversation revealed the importance given this matter within these organizations.

3 Unitarian Universalist Association of Congregations, "Process for Handling Complaints of Misconduct," April 4, 2008, http://www.uua.org/leaders/leaderslibrary/ethicscon gregational/20849.shtml.

4 Canadian Unitarian Council, "A Summary of the UUA-CUC Negotiation Meeting," http://www.cuc.ca/governance/archival/uua-cuc_mtg(010107).htm and Unitarian Universalist Association Articles XI Ministry and XII Religious Education Credentialing (UUA), http://www.uua.org/aboutus/bylaws/index.shtml.

5 Canadian Unitarian Council, "Principles and Sources" (Canadian Unitarian Council), http://www.cuc.ca/who_we_are/principles/principles_sources.htm.

6 Phillip Hewitt, *Unitarians in Canada*, 2nd ed. (Toronto: Canadian Unitarian Council, [1978] 1995), 20.

7 Statistics Canada, 2001 Census: Analysis Series: Religions in Canada, May 13, 2003, http://www12.statcan.gc.ca/english/census01/products/analytic/companion/rel/contents.cfm.

8 Conrad Wright, *Walking Together: Polity and Participation in Unitarian Universalist Churches* (Boston: Skinner House Books, 1989), 74.

9 CUC, "Vision Statement," http://www.cuc.ca//governance/council/vision_statement.htm.

10 Warren R. Ross, *The Premise and the Promise: The Story of the Unitarian Universalist Association* (Boston: Skinner House Books, 2001), 138.

11 Ibid., 138–39.

12 Ibid., 139–40.

13 Sylvia Bass West, email interview by B. Adle, March 2, 2007.

14 Unitarian Universalist Association of Congregations, "Process for Handling Complaints," Boston, 2008; and www.uua.org/cde/ethics/complaintprocess.

15 Ibid.

16 UUA, Policies of the Ministry Fellowship Council, 19.B.

17 UUA, Policies of the Ministry Fellowship Council, 19.B; Tracey Robinson-Harris, email interviews by B. Adle, February 26, 2007, and March 6, 2007.

18 Unitarian Universalist Association of Congregations, Policies of the Ministry Fellowship Committee, October 2009, http://www.uua.org/leaders/leaderslibrary/ministerialfellow ship/; UUA, Policies of the Ministry Fellowship Council, 19.C.

19 UUA, Policies of the Ministry Fellowship Council, 19.D.

20 Ibid.

21 Ibid., 19.E.

22 Ibid.

23 Ibid., 21.F.

24 Ibid., 19.E-F.

25 Ibid., 21.E.

26 Ibid., 20.A.

27 Ibid., 20.B.

28 UUA, "Process for Handling Complaints."

29 Tracey Robinson-Harris, email interview by B. Adle, March 21, 2007.

30 UUA, Policies of the Ministry Fellowship Council, 19.A.

31 Please note that older titles are used (e.g., "director of congregational services" instead of "consultant" in accordance with the April 2008 policy), as the policies of the MFC have not been updated, at the time of the writing of this book, since the release of the April 2008 misconduct policy (UUA, Policies of the Ministry Fellowship Council, 19.A).

32 UUA, "Process for Handling Complaints."

33 Tracey Robinson-Harris, interview.

34 UUA, Policies of the Ministry Fellowship Council, 22.

35 Ibid., 23.

36 Ibid., 20.C.

37 Ibid., 20.D, E, and G.

38 Ibid., 21.

39 As noted, before 2001 Canadian congregations were members in the UUA. All denominational records, policies, and procedures regarding member and clergy education are therefore housed in the UUA in Boston. When contacted, Robinson-Harris noted that Kay Montgomery, the UUA executive vice president, would need to be contacted to obtain archived information. Attempts to access this material were unsuccessful.

40 Brenda Gallagher, *Screening in Faith* (Ottawa: Volunteer Canada, 1999), iii.

41 CUC, "Safe Congregations/Screening in Faith," http://www.cuc.ca/safe/background.htm.

42 Ibid., "Recommendations."

43 Sylvia Bass West, "Volunteer Canada/Ontario Screening Initiative—Screening in Faith Report," 2002, www.cuc.ca/safe/PDF/SIF_annual_report_2002.pdf.

44 CUC, "CUC Youth Program Rules," www.cuc.ca/youth/CUC_Youth_Program_Rules_2007_DRAFT.pdf.

45 The policy also includes comment particular to the youths' sexual expressions and choices: "Sexuality is a healthy and important part of young people's lives. Youth programs are an opportunity for youth to express themselves in healthy ways. Exclusive relationships detract from the community. All members of the community must respect each other's physical boundaries. Inappropriate sexual behavior (i.e., sexual intercourse, oral sex, heavy petting or sexual harassment) is not permitted. Nudity in CUC youth con community is not permitted. The Conference Affairs Committee reserves the right to deem any behaviour inappropriate. Parents/guardians are invited to discuss this policy with youth" (CUC, "CUC Youth Program Rules," 3); CUC, Youth Program Rules, 1.

46 To ensure the safety of children the congregation developed the following principles:
   - Abusive, Harassing, Violent or Coercive Behavior will not be tolerated in our Congregation.
   - When unrelated children or adults are gathered, groups should consist of at least three individuals.
   - We recognize a special responsibility to safeguard children.
   - No individual who has been previously convicted of child or sexual abuse will be allowed to work with children or youth.
   - Volunteers and employees working with youth must attend a Worth and Dignity training.
   - Members or friends volunteering for jobs with identified risks will be required to go through an application process and sign relevant documents.
   - Registration forms designating caretaker(s) … will be completed for all children attending religious education programming.
   - There will be one adult present for every 5 children and every 7 youth at all congregationally sponsored functions.
   - Adult members or friends voluntarily working with children or youth must have been regularly attending Don Heights for a minimum of six months.

- Employees of volunteers who are transporting children are asked to sign a waiver indicating that they have a valid driver's license and at least $1,000,000 in liability insurance.
- Any adult person working with the children is required by Ontario's law to report to the local Children's Aid Society if they have reason to suspect any child may have been abused, whether at Don Height's of in the child's home.

Don Heights Unitarian Congregation, *Worth and Dignity Policy (Safe Church)* (Toronto: Don Heights Unitarian Congregation, 2007), 3.

47   Kingston Unitarian Fellowship, *Screening in Faith Policy* (Kingston: Kingston Unitarian Fellowship, May 9, 2005).

48   Of note is the *Child Abuse Prevention and Response Policy*. The procedures are: "If any complainant or other person reasonably believes that illegal actions have taken place, they shall contact the police.
- If the complainant wishes to pursue the matter within the Fellowship, the complainant is requested first to bring the concern to any one or more of the following contacts: the Minister, the Director of Religious Education, the President, or the Vice-President.
- If the complaint concerns the Minister, the complainant shall bring the matter to the Board, or the President, or the Committee on Ministry.... In addition, the President shall call on the Department of Ministry of the UUA for support and guidance.

The first person contacted by the complainant shall bring the matter to the Board.
- After being satisfied that the Board has all relevant information concerning the incident, the Board may take any of the following actions (or any other action they feel is appropriate):
- Immediately inform the police
- Restrict or ban communication between the parties involved during KUF-organized gatherings
- Withdraw the membership of the accused; or
- Dismiss the complaint

The Board shall, upon a majority vote at a legally constituted meeting, issued a decision stating the appropriate course of action to be taken, and the decision of theBoard shall be final."

49   Kingston Unitarian Fellowship, *Field Trip Policy*, August 2006.

50   Ibid.

Notes to Chapter 8

1   The Assembly of Quebec Bishops, *A Heritage of Violence: A Pastoral Reflection on Conjugal Violence* (Quebec: Assembly of Quebec Bishops, 1989).

2   The Anglican Church of Canada, *Violence against Women: Abuse in Society and Church and Proposals for Change* (The Taskforce Report to General Synod 1986 of the Anglican Church of Canada, 1987).

3   United Church of Canada, *Record of Proceedings of the 30th General Council*, 90.

4   Nancy Adamson, Linda Briskin, and Margaret McPhail, *Feminists Organizing for Change: The Contemporary Women's Movement in Canada* (Toronto: Oxford University Press, 1988).

5   The United Church had much earlier taken up this same cause in the 1930s.

6   The Canadian Association of Sexual Assault Centres (CASAC), "Evaluation 1979–1982, to the Department of Health and Welfare," December 1986, 13.

7 Toronto Rape Crisis Centre, *No Safe Place: Violence against Women and Children* (Toronto: Women's Press, 1985), 67.

8 This perceived numinous power and accompanying perception of the moral purity of religious leaders is a significant theme that is relevant to each the examined religious institutions. See, for example, Karen Lebacqz and Ronald P. Barton, *Sex in the Parish* (Louisville, KY: Westminster/John Knox Press, 1991). Unchecked, it leads to clericalism. Clericalism has manifested itself in an illusion of religious leaders being God-like and beyond reproach. This dynamic has made it extremely difficult for victims to speak out; they must be at fault, not the priest or religious leader. Not only do victims tend to internalize guilt and blame, many others in the Church have and sometimes continue to find it easier to blame the complainant and refuse to consider the possibility of their leader, who has represented both God and Church to them, sexually abusing a child. Harris provides an excellent, albeit disturbing, example of this dynamic in his retelling of the Mount Cashel abuses:

> The most eloquent insight into how men of the cloth had been able to perpetrate such monstrous crimes against their parishioners' children and get away with it for so long came from a woman who ... laid the blame for the tragedy on the traditional role of the priest, in Outport Newfoundland.... Expressing a feeling shared by many of Newfoundland's 205,000 Catholics, she told the meeting: If a child as born without an arm, people said it was because the mother said something against a priest. That was nonsense, but a priest with that kind of shield could get away with anything. (Harris, *Unholy Orders*, 19)

9 Some priests who were formerly Protestant clergy have been permitted to remain married if they were married when transferring into the Roman Catholic priesthood. Also, the Eastern Churches permit married priests.

10 Kathleen M. Sands, "Speaking out—Clergy Sexual Abuse: Where Are the Women?" *Journal of Feminist Studies in Religion* 19, no. 2 (Fall 2003): 80.

11 Thomas P. Doyle, "Roman Catholic Clericalism, Religious Duress, and Clergy Sexual Abuse," *Pastoral Psychology* 51, no. 3 (January 2003)," 197–99. Doyle described the parameters and outcomes of four studies, all of which demonstrate similar findings.

12 Ibid., 201.

Index

abortion, 5, 172n44

accountability: of Anglican Church of Canada (ACC), 95; mechanisms, 1–2; Mennonite Church efforts, 50, 104, 113–14, 119, 148; public, 16, 31; of Roman Catholic Church (RCC), 31–32, 40; United Church court of, 58, 61, 65–66; to victims, 30

adult-to-adult sexual abuse complaints, 27, 85

Advocacy Training Manual: Advocating for Survivors of Sexual Abuse by a Church Leader or Caregiver (Block), 109

Anglican Church of Canada (ACC): *Canon XVIII: Discipline*, 85, 90–91, 93, 99, 151; child sexual abuse case examples, 93–95; child sexual abuse policies (1960–80), 76–78; child sexual abuse policies (1981–91), 78–82; child sexual abuse policies (1992–2009), 82–85, 99, 145, 150; complicity in violence, 79–80, 98; critique of nuclear family, 78; ecclesiastical offences and penalties, 91–92, 99, 175n145; institutional structure and historical context, 73–76, 150; investigative procedures for complaints, 88–90, 151; marriage and remarriage policies, 76–77, 98, 173n63; membership total, 73; on pornography, 78–79, 172n53; procedures for addressing child sexual abuse complaints, 8, 85–88, 151; relations with First Nations peoples, 76; responses to child sexual abuse complaints, 90–93; risk assessments, 97; Safe Church Committee,

86–87; screening policies, 95–98, 152, 177n179, 177n187, 178n193; Sexual Abuse Response Team (SART), 86–87; on sexuality and homosexuality, 78, 82, 150; *Sexual Misconduct Policy*, 88, 99; Sexual Misconduct Response Team (SMRT), 87, 89–90; Taskforce on Violence Against Women, 79–84, 142; third-party complaints, 90; women's roles in, 77–78, 142, 150

anonymous complaints of sexual abuse, 23, 34, 63

apostolic succession, 147

archbishop: duty in investigating complaints, 18, 28, 32–33; role of, 11, 41

archdeaconries, 74–75

Archdiocese of Edmonton: *Guidelines for Dealing with Cases of Sexual Abuse*, 27–28, 33–34, 36

Archdiocese of Ottawa, 28, 32, 36

Archdiocese of St. John's, 16–17, 162n104

Archdiocese of Toronto, 22–23, 34–35, 159n1; *Strengthening the Caring Community: Parish Volunteer Screening Program*, 39

Assault on God's Image (Block), 106–7, 178n1

avoidant personality characteristics, 156–57n5

Badgely Report (1984), 6, 72, 126

bankruptcy, diocesan, 37, 76, 93

Barron, Brother John, 17

Bass West, Sylvia, 132, 138

birth control, 44, 142. *See also* contraception